D0070520

EX LIBRIS
NEW YORK INSTITUTE
OF TECHNOLOGY
NEW YORK INSTITUTE OF TECHNOLOGY
SCIENCE
TECHNOLOGY
HUMANITIES

BOOKS BY MICHAEL J. ARLEN

Living-Room War (1969)
Exiles (1970)
An American Verdict (1973)
Passage to Ararat (1975)
The View from Highway 1 (1976)

The View from Highway 1

Michael J. Arlen

The View from Highway 1

ESSAYS ON TELEVISION

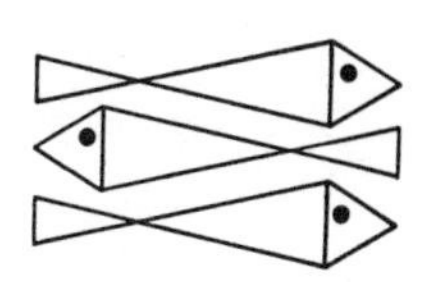

Farrar, Straus & Giroux

NEW YORK

Library of Congress catalog card number: 76-24900
Published simultaneously in Canada by
McGraw-Hill Ryerson Ltd., Toronto
Printed in the United States of America
Designed by Guy Fleming
First edition, 1976
All the essays in this book, with the exception of the introduction, appeared originally in The New Yorker *between September 1974 and December 1975*

For St.Clair McKelway

CONTENTS

The View from Highway 1

INTRODUCTION

Some Notes on Television Criticism

THERE ARE TWO CHIEF DIFFICULTIES IN WRITING television criticism. The first of these, and the most obvious, is that the content of American television is for the most part so meretricious and second-rate that it is nearly impossible to deal with on any other basis than that of the bare-bone, informational review in the daily newspaper. For example, a cops-and-robbers adventure, such as fills so much of the evening viewing schedule these days, is supposedly drama or at least melodrama, with many honorable antecedents in literature and film. But on television there is rarely even the dimmest substance to these stories. For thirty minutes or an hour, cartoon-like characters walk through their weekly paces: inevitably there is a criminal in such dramas, and nearly always a relentless hunt for him, which ends, naturally, in a gunfight, death, or his arrest. It is the simple stuff of pulp fiction, and in a sense who is to mind it? As who is to mind the pulp comedies, with their bantering, wisecracking stereotypes, or the pulp family dramas, with their treacly and artificial versions of American life, which populate much of the rest of the television schedule?

A critic in a democracy should obviously respect the nature of a democracy and hence its dynamic for expressing the tastes of the majority. Even so, regardless of the underlying and unanswered question here—as to whether television programming is produced in response to the unspoken demands of popular taste or is merely foisted onto the public by an elite of businessmen and producers—the fact of the matter remains that, for the time being, the bulk of American television production lacks sufficient substance (even as melodrama!) to warrant a sustained discussion on its own merits. This is not to deny that there are sometimes interesting and finely done programs on commercial, and especially on non-commercial or public, television. In the case of public television, however, this disorganized organization has been rather deliberately structured by the broadcasting and government authorities so as to be incapable financially, and sometimes politically, of furnishing the American public with programming of a quality competitive with the commercial networks, with the result that its better programs during the past few years have had to be mainly imported from England. And as to the occasionally superior production on commercial television (such as *Eleanor and Franklin*), the truth is that these special programs stand out not because talent is rare but because the bulk of programming is so deliberately banal. It is not a question, then, of a critic dutifully seeking out the scarce wildflowers in a meadow; it is a matter of his wandering about in a garden which the gardener himself has painstakingly planted with weeds.

It is this factor of deliberate intent which brings one to the second, and perhaps less obvious, critical obstacle. For not only do one's eyes and ears tell one that a certain program is meretricious and second-rate, but it is clear, on a different level, that the program was deliberately fashioned so as to make it inevitable, even desirable, that it should turn out that way. Doubtless, the program's creators would prefer to have their purpose described as the making of something popular—this, after all, being a word that can be applied to either the New Testament or a dime-store table lamp, and thus can mean nearly anything one wishes it to mean. Still, as the semi-sciences of sociology and marketing psychology continue to be increasingly employed by businessmen in their hunt for the public's fancy, it has come to be accepted, almost as one of the conventions of the present era, that virtually nothing created for the public is created either intuitively or innocently. In other words, what was once a bad joke in the hoary period of the Hollywood studio bosses—namely, the subversion of supposedly innocent talent by the profit-obsessed whim of nickelodeon millionaires—has become an even worse joke in the era of American commercial television. For, while the TV industry is often still treated with a romance left over from the Hollywood days, as if the paraphernalia of stars, starlets, writers, and directors had been transplanted in essence as well as in person from the era of the big studios, the truth seems to be that hardly anyone in commercial television is innocent any more. Today, the writers, directors, stars, starlets, and newsmen of the television industry know exactly what they are doing.

Thus, a rather new problem has arisen for the television critic, as well as for those members of the audience seeking a perspective, or organizing focus, upon what they watch. For example, when a critic of a traditional art—say, a music critic—approaches a performance of Verdi's *Otello*, he not only has a substantial and formal work to deal with but also the generally artistic ambitions of the singers, the conductor, and the orchestra. But what can a critic do in the face of a work which has almost no substance or dimension (as in most television productions, where, for instance, the acting possibilities are so narrow as to be scarcely worth judging in those terms), and where, furthermore, it is generally understood that the work's creators and participants have no ambitions for it beyond the simplest commerce? In all too many cases, it seems to me, the tendency of television criticism has been to run itself aground on the shoals of popular culture. By this I mean that in recent years something amounting to an orthodoxy of criticism (and critical journalism) on the subject of popular culture has developed, centered originally on the "classic" period of the Hollywood film and the Broadway musical, which has sought to embrace or at least find merit in individual works, regardless of their preponderant qualities of kitsch or glibness (regardless even of their occasional artistic or professional virtues), on the strength of those more subjectively appreciated qualities of romance, ebullience, or even innocence which have appeared to animate the work as well as the performance. Around Hollywood movies, for instance, a whole mythology has grown up, abetted once by studio publicity, but also based, as it turned out, on more lasting parables of good and evil, of triumph, temptation, of Cinderellas raised up from Schwab's drugstore, of princesses locked away in studio contracts. When movie critics now talk of their love of movies, it is surely not only of the arts of direction and cinematography that they speak but of some, perhaps childhood, involvement in the texture of this mythology—this larger-than-life play-acting of the American dream of innocence, with all its temptations and rewards. But how to transplant this dream, or these parables, to television? It seems to me that it cannot be done, at least not with serious justification. Even so, a whole apparatus exists, even larger than before, combining the techniques of public relations and entertainment journalism, but the mythology at the center of this entertainment world has moved or vanished, and all that remains of any consequence is the apparatus: not only the techniques of manufacturing celebrity, but the newer techniques for examining, and somehow fondling, those previous techniques. This current embrace of television as popular culture isn't by any means always adulatory. Indeed, most current writing about television seems to be characterized by an assertively cynical savviness. Where once the journalist Lillian Ross caused a sensation by revealing the commonplace scheming and manipulation that was a large part of the making of even a "quality" movie such as *The Red Badge of Courage*, lately it has become almost a staple of Sunday newspaper magazines (and of much other journalism about television) to describe the possibly even more cynical and manipulative workings that regularly take place behind the scenes of a popular television show. Still, it strikes me that this determined savviness and determined concentration on the behind-the-scenes workings of the industry is merely another aspect of an intrinsically sentimental and even passive view of commercial television. In other words, the critical perspective is often cynical or what is called "tough-minded," but for the most part it seems to be part of a general embrace of the television industry by critics and audience alike, who while sternly describing behind-the-scenes manipulations also pay dutiful and sometimes scholarly heed to "the industry" 's grandly announced doctrines and imperatives, and tend to treat its personalities and productions as if they were linked—by some invisible cord of popular culture—to an earlier, more spontaneous era of American show business.

My own approaches to television, then, represent one writer's attempts to get around what seem to be the chief obstacles in the way of writing usefully about contemporary television: that is, how to take the overall subject seriously, when the content of individual programs or performances belies seriousness? How to write about American television as part of American life, without being so practical or professional that one never sees beyond the imperatives of the television industry? This last matter has been the most troublesome, and I note—with no perverse satisfaction at all—that the most frequent comment my essays (especially on the subject of news) have received from people within the television industry has been that they are "unrealistic." I think I understand the comment, though I also think that it is wrong and in a way indicates the nature of the problem that faces not merely critics but viewers. At the source of the disagreement, if one might call it that, is the supposition—advanced generally by the television industry—that commercial television somehow is a willing, or at least a neutral, servant of the public. Thus, the world view or life view expressed by television is bound to be "realistic," according to conventional notions of reality, or else—as runs an argument which was advanced for many years, until the consumer revolution, by American manufacturers—the public would not accept it; and any challenges to these expressions of so-called conventional reality are thereby "unrealistic."

It seems to me that there are two key flaws to this supposition. The deepest of these has to do with the fact that surely one of the most visible lessons taught by the twentieth century has been the existence, not so much of a number of different realities, but of a number of different lenses with which to see the same reality. Consider: America is primarily an industrial and business-oriented nation, and businessmen are said to be mainly concerned with matters of profit, trade, financial stability, and so forth; such concerns, one might say, represent the conventional reality of a major segment of the country. For roughly the past ten years, however—a period dominated by the Vietnam war—the lenses through which so many Americans scanned the landscape of their nation and the world proved to be so shortsighted and out of focus that tens of thousands of American lives were lost in Asia, apparently to no purpose, and a poisonous and highly unstable division was allowed to appear in American life, such as had not been seen since the Civil War; and on top of that, as a result of the inflationary armament expenditures under two Presidents, the once-vaunted American economy was seriously weakened and was propelled into a decline from which it is only now allegedly beginning to emerge, albeit with immense intervening loss of jobs, loss of profits, and loss of the domestic, social legislation which might have made the underpinnings of a mercantile nation more secure.

Television was only one of the lenses through which Americans were offered a view of this supposed "reality" of Vietnam, but I think many people are agreed that, in its commissions and omissions, it was a crucial view. In short, the television cameras helped America march into Vietnam in the middle 1960's, and attended each evening, year after year, while America marched farther in, and farther in, and *farther* in . . . And then suddenly, or so it appeared, with the national spirit in shambles, and the national economy already beginning to collapse, and with the war nowhere nearer to being won than it had ever been, television—aligning itself with, and also authoritatively expressing, a new shift in conventional reality—now told its public that the war was wasteful and ill-advised (save, temporarily, for the prisoner-of-war issue, which was soon forgotten), and, by implication, that it had been of no importance. With one or two minor exceptions, at no time during the period of the major American involvement in Vietnam did the television networks employ their vast financial resources in an honest attempt to discover the actual reality of the Vietnam situation. Even in the fading reign of an American President, Lyndon B. Johnson (whose own political insecurity was such that he virtually resigned from office—at least from a second term—as the result of antiwar protest), at no time did the networks appear willing to encourage even their own correspondents in pursuing an independent, and perhaps "unrealistic," course in charting the strange and deadly geography of the war. In such a fashion, during a crucial, communications-dominated period of American history, was "reality" presented to the American public.

One difficulty, then, that I have had in accepting television's view of its performance is not that it serves a mass audience but that it serves this audience so badly. To whose benefit, after all, was the reporterlike promotion and acquiescence in a lengthy war which gained no objective and which seriously undermined (among other things) even the mercantile basis of a mercantile nation? When, in 1967–8, the networks glamorized the air-bombing of North Vietnam while noticeably refraining from following up reports (as well as stories published in reliable journals) of the wasteful and pointless destruction of South Vietnamese land and life that was then taking place as a result of American military policy, in what way could such a glimpse of the war be said to have been viewed through a "realistic" lens, and who gained by it? Surely not the mass audience (many among whom lost their sons and, later, their jobs), which the commercial television establishment has been in the habit of exploiting by professing to regard the public's silent acceptance of triviality and trivialization as if this were the same thing as an enthusiasm or appetite for the second-rate, and, indeed, by constantly asserting the very notion that a homogeneous, monolithic mass of the public somewhere exists, when it has become abundantly clear that, despite the pressures of national advertising, the populace continues to be composed of innumerable regional, political, and ethnic groupings whose definition is at least as vivid as that of any abstract "mass."

For the second flaw in the argument on behalf of American television's intrinsically "real" or benign basis in American life has to do with the television industry's own shortsighted and delusive relationship with the public. Here the allegation persists that commercial television exists as a kind of neutral provider of "what the public wants," whether it be entertainment, sports, news, or advertising: a sturdily profit-minded storekeeper who would as gladly furnish marmalade as motorcars, who would as soon display a Dürer woodcut, or a bowl of Jell-O, or a comedy series about a talking horse, depending only on the public's preference—a preference increasingly determined by the taking of polls and "samplings." It seems to me that there are several rejoinders that can be made to such an important assertion, though admittedly none of them is likely to be entirely satisfactory in an age which shies from making intuitive judgments, even on deeply felt issues, unless accompanied or transformed by scientific-like evidence.

Even so, speaking of science, it seems to run markedly counter to one of the principal laws of modern physics (to say nothing of plain reason) to insist that an institution is, so to speak, what it says it is. Since the formulation of Einstein's Special Theory of Relativity, the world has had to accept the notion that the position of any object is relative to the position of the observer. In this case, one might say that the American television industry is the "object," and that the position it claims for itself is that of a neutral provider of entertainment, information, and advertising. And, clearly, this simply cannot generally or necessarily be so. That is, for each viewer there is bound to be a different, and sometimes a very different, relationship with television, and more importantly: in a majority of instances the position or role of television has increasingly become that of an authority. In recent years, to be sure, there have been attempts by various observers to play down television's authoritarian role, with one writer, in a popular disclaimer, characterizing television as being merely "another utility, like the telephone." Aside from the fact that utilities are not notably alike or neutral even in *their* roles, this cozy, matter-of-fact view of television seems disingenuous. Statistical-minded journalists, I know, have shown that despite the expenditure of *x* amount of money for *y* minutes of air time, a certain candidate has still not been elected to public office, but to argue from this that television is non-authoritarian in its influence seems to me to be countering one simplistic view with another. Television, to take one example, seems indubitably authoritarian in the position it has assumed in this country (as in most) of delegating *to itself* the majority as well as the minority expressions of politics, culture, or even sensibility in the nation. The television set transmits *its* version of our Yeas and *its* version of their rebuttal: our Nays. It seems fair to say that while some writers in the past have overstated the demonological implications of television's role, this most definitely does not rule out the larger fact that television *does* have a role and that it is virtually impossible for this role to be matter-of-fact or neutral.

But whenever a critic, armed not only with the evidence of his eyes and ears but with a passing, school-text acquaintance with the laws of nature, points out that television, despite its pronouncements as to its own fixed position, is certain to be in a variable and dynamic (rather than passive) relationship with its viewers, what usually happens is that a member of the television elite announces that, though a certain dynamism may well exist, this dynamism is rigorously shaped and even controlled by the viewer himself. Thus, television managers, it is said, far from being arbitrary or self-serving autocrats, disseminate their broadcast messages at the mercy of the polls, and consequently of the public.

This is a trickier terrain for a critic to maintain his footing upon, for the recent generation, while perhaps being less scientifically creative than its immediate predecessors, has nonetheless advanced the new technics of measurement to their greatest heights. We have measured the speed of the electron and the distance between ourselves and Betelgeuse; why should it be so implausible that one might measure the preference of a man for eggs or apples? Common sense is usually a help in these matters, and common sense here at least tells one that, given the complexity of the human brain, one cannot merely ask someone what he or she wants, and then give it to them, and then, having given it to them, count on having done very much by the overall possibilities. This is perhaps a corollary of what might be called the *Moby Dick* theory: namely, if a reader cannot, in advance, conceive of *Moby Dick* on his own, how should he ask the culture somehow to provide such a work? It also strikes me that maybe the distant voice of another great physicist, Werner Heisenberg, has something to communicate in this regard, though admittedly less by the intended application of his equations than through a more philosophic inference that might be drawn from some of them. For it was Heisenberg who in 1927 formulated the influential Uncertainty Principle, which has to do not so much with states of mind as with the behavior of subatomic particles and the uncertainty—even employing the best measuring devices imaginable—with which they can be effectively measured. In essence, the Uncertainty Principle states that it is impossible to "specify or determine simultaneously" both the position and the velocity of a particle with full accuracy, and from this it goes on to declare that even the act of measuring these tiny elements of the universe inevitably alters their disposition and behavior: that is, one cannot ever ascertain their exact position because the very act of observation or examination invariably will change the pattern. What is true for subatomic particles admittedly may not be precisely true for humans, though often it seems that there is a general consistency in nature which envelops some unlikely components. One of the distant messages of Werner Heisenberg, then (or so it seems to me), is one of *modesty:* the need for a certain reserve or caution in asserting the exactitude and meaning of certain measurements—for example, of units as volatile and complicated as exist within the minds of men and women. As perhaps too glib or early a confirmation of this conjecture, I noticed, in the course of the much-troubled and much-measured 1975–6 television season, a report by *The New York Times*'s television reporter Les Brown which commented not merely on a sudden, unexpected drop in the public's viewing hours but also on a new disparity which seemed to be appearing between the responses the public was making to the attempts to measure what it liked to watch or wished to watch—and what, in fact, it actually did watch, or not watch, in the relative privacy of its homes.

Even so, for all the marshaling this way or that way of supposedly factual argument, in the end the point seems to be that ours is predominantly a moral society—whether conforming to the physical laws of Copernicus, Newton, or Einstein, and whether disagreeing among ourselves, or with other societies, as to the precise nature of desirable morality—and that, at present, the tension of American television with—or, one might say, against—American society is primarily a moral tension: a conflict of competing moral views of life and of its possibilities. On the one hand, armed with vast, concentrated resources of power and organization, and clutching official-looking certificates insisting that it is really the *servant* of the people, stands the television industry, motivated and shaped by the well-ordered and articulated morality of business, with its short-term, close-focused, tidy dynamism of annual sales and growth and profits. On the other hand stands, or rather sprawls, the public—that untidy multitude that lurks behind the "mass"—with scant organization, a most diffuse and unrealized power, and not so much armed with, as often merely occupied by, a far vaguer, longer-term morality of human existence: that most bewildered, and perhaps most noble, dream of living through one's life as if it mattered. The critic, I think, must choose his own place on this new terrain, and must learn to speak of television as if it were part not only of a world of facts and measurements but of a larger, changing world of untold possibilities—not the least of which would be for it to truly serve its audience. In other words, he should speak of television as if it mattered.

Good Morning

THE TELEVISION SCREEN SHOWED AN ORANGE SUN rising slowly above an expanse of serene and empty farmland. There was a scene of horses frisking about a dewy paddock. A freight train rushed silently across a desert.

"I can't find my shirt anywhere," said Father.

"Here's your orange juice," said Mother.

"Good morning, I'm Bill Beutel," said Bill Beutel, his jacket flickering in alternating shades of green and yellow. "The Westminster Kennel Club Show is opening in New York, and in a few moments we're going to be talking to you about that."

"Don't you want your orange juice?" Mother said.

Father took the glass of orange juice and held it in his hand, and then put it down on the kitchen counter.

"I saw it in the closet only last night," he said. "Joey, you leave the set alone. The color's automatic."

"Joey, go get your juice," said Mother.

Stephanie Edwards said, "I'm really looking forward to hearing about that dog show, Bill, but right now we're going to have a report on the unemployment picture that's been causing such widespread distress across the nation."

"Mom, did you see my homework anywhere?" said Clarice. "Hi, Dad. That looks real cool without a shirt."

Peter Jennings, in Washington, said, "President Ford's top economist, Alan Greenspan, testified yesterday on Capitol Hill that the country will just have to reconcile itself to 8 percent unemployment through 1976." Alan Greenspan said, "As I evaluate the current trade-off between stimulus and unemployment, I do not give great credence to the idea that a significant reduction will be caused by a stimulus greater than that proposed by the President."

"It was the white shirt," Father said. "The one with the shoe polish on the cuff. Is that coffee ready?"

"I'll get the coffee, Dad," said Clarice.

"Clarice, you do the toast," said Mother.

"Mother, I have all this *homework*. I have a quiz in social studies."

Bill Beutel said, "Johnny Miller's 69 keeps him out front in the Bob Hope Desert Classic. As of this moment, it looks as if the women are going to boycott Wimbledon."

Father switched channels. Frank Blair said, "Yesterday, in Cambodia, a direct hit was scored upon this school in Phnom Penh."

Father said, "I guess I'll go look for it myself."

Frank Blair said, "Repercussions from yesterday's rioting in Lima, Peru, are still being felt today in that strife-torn capital." There were scenes of tanks driving down a city street.

"Clarice, remember the left side of the toaster doesn't work," said Mother.

"Mother, I *know*," said Clarice.

Frank Blair said, "North Dakota has an advisory for snow. Pacific Ocean storms are moving toward the Pacific Coast."

The telephone rang. Father reappeared, holding his shoes and a towel. He picked up the phone. "No, there isn't any Lisa here," he said, and started to put the phone back. "Oh, Dad, is that *Lisa?*" Clarice screamed. Father handed her the phone.

On the television screen, soldiers were now walking slowly down a country road. "Patrols fan out from the city, looking for insurgents," said a voice.

Mother said, "Joey, you finish the toast."

Joey said, "How come I have to do the toast when I don't eat toast?"

"Do you think it might be in the laundry?" Father said. "It might have fallen to the floor of the closet, and somebody might have put it in the laundry." Father passed by Clarice on his way out of the kitchen. "Don't talk all day on the phone, Clarice," he said. Clarice rolled her eyes at the ceiling.

Frank Blair said, "Scattered fighting continued until well toward evening." There were scenes of more tanks speeding three abreast down a road.

"Here's your coffee," Mother said. "Now, where did he go?"

Frank Blair said, "Armored cars and Russian-made tanks broke up the disorder. A curfew and a state of national emergency have been proclaimed."

There was the sound of a crash from the back of the house.

"Eggs are ready, everyone!" Mother said. On the television screen, two tanks were firing into a brick wall. "Fix the set. That's too loud, Joey," she said. "Everyone! The eggs are getting cold."

Father came back into the kitchen, with a blue shirt hanging partly out of his trousers, and clutching one of his fingers, from which a small drop of blood appeared. "Goddamn towel rack," he said.

"Here are your eggs," Mother said. "I thought you were going to get it fixed."

"I think I may have hurt myself," Father said.

On the television set, Fred Flintstone was rolling a stone wheel down a long hill. Father looked at the stone as it sped down the hill. At the bottom of the hill, there was a dinosaur sleeping. Father watched as the wheel rolled down the hill and then along the back of the dinosaur until it hit him on the head. "Who turned this on?" Father asked.

"Mom asked me to," said Joey.

"I did no such thing, Joey," said Mother. "Eat your eggs before they're cold. Clarice, come eat your eggs!"

Father switched channels. Stephanie Edwards said, "Nearly the entire central part of the country is in the grip of a cold-air mass. In Oklahoma City, the high today will be thirty-seven, the low around twenty."

"Did you know that thirty-two degrees is freezing, Mom?" said Joey.

"I don't like it when it gets that cold," said Mother.

"That was Oklahoma City," Father said. "Oklahoma City, Oklahoma."

"Clarice, you get off the phone this instant," Mother said.

Bill Beutel said, "In a little while, we're going to be talking about that Westminster Kennel Club Show, but right now we're going to Washington to visit with sociologist Donald Warren, who has been in the nation's capital all week examining the way that unemployed workers handle stress." Peter Jennings, in Washington, said, "Professor Warren, I understand that you're here in the nation's capital trying to find out more about how the unemployed react in times of stress. Is that correct?" Professor Warren said, "Yes, that's fundamentally correct, Peter. We've been following people through a series of crises, and these have been difficult times."

Mother said, "I ought to check at Garfields and see if they got in any of those new bird feeders yet. How come you're eating with your hand all bent like that?"

"Can't you see my finger is bleeding?" said Father.

"You're supposed to hold it above your head, Dad," said Joey. "If you hold it above your head, then gravity stops the blood from spurting up through your arm and sloshing all over everything."

"That's the most *disgusting* thing I ever heard," said Clarice, sitting down at the table. Clarice spread butter over a piece of toast and began to eat it.

"The fact is our formal institutions lie to us. They do not and are not able to give us the true picture of the crime rates and issues which confront people," said Professor Warren.

Clarice got to her feet. "Mom, I have to run."

"Eat your eggs, Clarice," said Joey.

"Where do you have to run to, young lady?" said Father. He reached forward and changed the channel again. Jim Hartz said, "In a moment, we'll be talking to a United Nations official who says that five hundred million people in the world aren't getting enough to eat. Here is Mr. Eric Ojala, head of the United Nations food program. Mr. Ojala, I understand that the United Nations has been developing an early-warning system for the world food situation."

The telephone rang. Father answered it. "Lisa?" he said. "I thought you just called."

"Oh, *Dad*," Clarice said, taking the phone.

The doorbell rang. Mr. Ojala said, "We receive reports nowadays from all member countries."

A door slammed, and a boy's voice bellowed, "Joey!"

"Why, good morning, Gordon," Mother said.

Mr. Ojala said, "Although this system is still in its early stages, nonetheless it gives us time to anticipate where certain crops may fail." Jim Hartz said, "Mr. Ojala, do these reports have to do with crops as well as weather?"

Father suddenly got to his feet. "Have you seen the car-insurance papers?" he said.

"I can't imagine where," said Mother. "I thought you always kept them in the envelope with the stereo warranty."

Mr. Ojala said, "It's true that fertilizer has been in short supply all during the year, but I don't believe it is fair to blame this shortage on the petroleum industry."

Father came back in. "I can't find the stereo warranty, either," he said.

"Are we getting a new stereo?" asked Clarice, still on the phone.

"Don't bother your father," said Mother.

Joey changed the channel.

"You'll be late for the bus," said Mother. Clarice hung up the phone. "Who put this *disgusting* sticker on my notebook?" she screamed.

Bill Beutel said, "Now we're going to see three very unusual species of the canine family. This aristocratic pooch, I think, is called a Pharaoh hound, and I gather they're supposed to smile when they're happy, and they're supposed to blush."

Clarice said, "Joey, someday I'm going to kill you. Honestly, I am going to *kill* you. Mother, I'm going to Modern Dance this afternoon with Lisa."

Father reappeared, wearing an overcoat and holding a white shirt. "I found the white shirt," he said.

"Dad, you've got shaving cream on your ear," said Clarice.

Bill Beutel said, "Miss Laventhall, would you say he is blushing now?" Miss Laventhall said, "Oh, definitely. He is definitely blushing."

"I wouldn't feel safe with a dog like that," said Mother.

"I'll call you from the office," said Father.

"Can Lisa come overnight Thursday?" asked Clarice.

"Now, this is an extremely rare breed of Chinese dog. Two thousand years ago in China, it was the pet of the aristocratic set," said Bill Beutel.

"Don't forget to stop by Windsor Supply on your way home," said Mother.

"How come Clarice always has overnights?" said Joey.

"Can I have some ice cream?" asked Gordon.

"You run along now, boys," said Mother.

There was the sound of the storm door slamming, then reopening, then slamming. Mother changed the channel on the television set and started collecting the dishes. The door opened again. "Somebody left roller skates in the car," Father said. The door closed again. A car engine started, missed, started, missed, then started. Mother stood before the sink, rinsing dishes. On the set behind her, Barbara Walters said to Charles Colson, "Tell us about that prison experience, will you. Tell us about the first night." Charles Colson said, "Well, I think, Barbara, from my standpoint, it was just one of the most revealing experiences of my life." Mother put the dishes one by one into the dishwasher and turned the switch. Outside the window, two robins padded on the snow. The rumble of the dishwasher filled the room. Mother sprayed the skillet with a jet of hot water. Charles Colson said, "There was certain information of that nature which was passed to us in the White House in 1972." The refrigerator clicked on. The dishwasher churned. The telephone began to ring. "Hi, Beth," Mother said. "Wait a minute while I turn the TV down. We were just listening to the morning news."

Spokespeople

WE'RE WELL INTO FALL NOW. PEOPLE IN OVERcoats on the streets. Men selling roasted chestnuts. The remains of pumpkins on the insides of windows. There's a cold front moving into the Great Lakes area, the man on the *Today* show said. Snow flurries in the Mountain States. The skies here are clear and cold. Two men I know have lost their jobs this week—have been "let go." Also a great many other men, whom I don't know. The other day, driving back through an unfamiliar part of town, I passed by a truck-company depot—the employment office, as it turned out. Men were standing on the sidewalk, leaning against a Cyclone fence. Some wore windbreakers and clasped their arms in front of them. I remembered a line in one of John Steinbeck's books: "There's a certain way men have of standing about when they're out of work."

I watched the news at home that evening. There was nothing special about this particular night, which is to say there was no national crisis to attract my attention or to require my being further informed about. It was just an evening—an evening following a day. Perhaps I was thinking about the men I had driven by, although it's hard to say. News is news, isn't it? We witness the world through television. Though sometimes I have the feeling that events of the utmost importance take place, untelevised, beneath one's nose, or at least on sidewalks as one's car glides by.

The news I chose was on CBS–a fairly random choice. The program went like this: First, there was a report, originating in Washington, that showed President Ford's visit to Mexico. There were scenes of official greeting at the border and of handshakes with the Mexican President. Mr. Ford's visit was described by the CBS correspondent as his "first step onto foreign soil as President." There were views of both Presidents speaking. President Ford talked of "a working partnership" and of the "new dialogue into which we have entered with all nations of Latin America." He said, "Let us today consider how we can cooperate in solving common problems."

Then, also originating in Washington, there was a tape edited from an upcoming CBS interview between correspondent Dan Rather and the Cuban Prime Minister, Fidel Castro. What one mainly saw was Castro's face, his lips moving, his own voice unheard as an interpreter spoke for him–a speech, or perhaps the long answer to a question about future Cuban-American relations. "At least, he does not have the personal involvement that Nixon had," said Mr. Castro.

Then, still from Washington, there were views of the Watergate coverup trial, currently in session–an artist's drawings of the familiar faces of John Dean, Judge Sirica, and John Mitchell, and of the jury listening with earphones to the White House tapes. Correspondent Fred Graham provided a brief commentary and quoted that part of the tapes which begins, "I want you to stonewall it."

There followed another Washington story, on another court case—the one that involved Mr. Nixon's attempts to get his tapes back. An artist's drawing showed Judge Charles Richey issuing a temporary restraining order against the government.

In New York, Walter Cronkite then said that the Supreme Court had refused to hear an anti-abortion case.

From London, there came a picture of Albert Pierrepoint, "Britain's chief executioner for twenty-six years," with a short comment by Walter Cronkite that Pierrepoint, after retiring, had come to the conclusion that the several hundred executions he'd performed had "achieved nothing except revenge."

Walter Cronkite read an item about the Greek colonels' being sent into exile.

From Portland, Oregon, there was a taped story about a threat (from an anonymous dynamiter) to blow up certain facilities of an Oregon power company. There were shots of a tall transmission tower. Also a statement by a power-company official on the company's refusal to submit to blackmail.

From Cleveland, there was a report on the eight National Guardsmen who were just going on trial for the killings at Kent State. The tape showed eight men in civilian clothes walking down a sidewalk toward the court building, where they were stopped by the CBS correspondent. "Are you scared?" he asked. "Of course," one of the men replied soberly. "This is a big experience . . . I lost my job last weekend." "Why was that?" the correspondent persisted. "Because of this," the Guardsman replied, pointing to the correspondent and the camera crew.

Walter Cronkite announced that air fares to Europe were about to go up by 10 percent. Also that the Dow-Jones industrial average had risen that day by 14.94 points.

There was an ad showing a pretty teacher seated in a sunny and immaculate classroom and talking about her problem with psoriasis. Also a tire-company ad showing dozens of gleaming new cars speeding by, with closeups of tires bouncing over obstacles on the road.

There was a longish taped report on the Colorado Senate race between Gary Hart and incumbent Senator Peter Dominick. Each man was shown making a short speech. There were scenes of Hart campaigning before young Coloradoans and of Senator Dominick riding in a car.

There was a report from Mexico on illegal Mexican immigration into the United States. A spokesman from the Immigration Department said that illegal immigration was on the rise. There were scenes of a village near Guadalajara. A spokesman for an American farm association said that the Mexican immigrants did the sort of work that Americans didn't want to do.

Eric Sevareid appeared from Washington with an analysis of recent Russian policy on Jewish emigration. He said, "The Russians have conceded, so Kissinger conceded; and Jackson is proved right."

In New York, Walter Cronkite concluded, "And that's the way it is, Monday, October 21 . . ."

It had been a fairly typical day, and there was the news: the evening news. Big News. Was the news too glib or superficial? Was it possible to deal usefully with Kent State or Russian policy in a couple of minutes? It's hard to tell. There are arguments on both sides. Apparently, it is a question of procedure. The networks always say they have these *time imperatives*. They say they absolutely have to chop up the news *in a certain way*. Probably—just like anyone who keeps saying, "I absolutely have to do it *this* way"—they're right as well as wrong. But the question I'd like to ask is this: *Whom* were these newsmen talking to? What world were they describing back to *which* kind of people?

Consider: There were at least eight High Government stories, which is to say surface accounts of events taking place in the top reaches of national or international bureaucracies—often in Washington or in foreign capitals, often defined by important persons talking in government idiom to other important persons.

Consider: Our President shook hands with the Mexican President and discoursed on international cooperation. We were given glimpses of two important government court cases in Washington. There was an item about the former Greek regime; about a Supreme Court ruling; about the strategy behind the Russians' Jewish-emigration policy. Even when the High Government figure on the screen was Fidel Castro—he formerly of the baseball cap and the Hotel Theresa chickens and the Great Experiment—one heard him speaking only the stolid language of international relations.

When Walter Cronkite said that transatlantic air fares were going up, whom was *he* speaking to? Most people in this country have never flown in a plane anywhere, let alone to Europe. When Mr. Cronkite reported the Dow-Jones average for the day (as CBS and ABC do each evening), with the implication that this was the definitive measure of the nation's business condition, which audience was he addressing? A nation of stockholders? Or of men leaning against a fence?

Who cared about Albert Pierrepoint, the retired British executioner? One doesn't mean to suggest that nobody cared. But *who* cared?

The Kent State affair and the Oregon-power-company threat were both stories that contained potential human material, such as might be communicated to a wide audience. But in each case the story was presented on the news as a glimpse through a remote, high-level, semi-official eye. With the Kent State trial, the "story" was really no more than the television correspondent's perfunctory view of the defendants, and his awkward questioning. In the Oregon-power-company matter, the report was confined mainly to statements by officials. The account of the Colorado Senate race showed two important persons running for an important government office, and quickly sketched in the issues the way one important journalist might describe them to another.

It seemed to me that the only "popular" account on the news that evening—that is, the only story that appeared to be about ordinary people, that showed ordinary people and was drawn from the common experiences of humankind—was those passing scenes of Mexican village life and Mexican field hands, which had been caught and relayed by the camera in intervals between the discourses of immigration officials, CBS correspondents, and farm-association spokesmen.

Perhaps the true "mass audience" for network news now consists of stockholders, television correspondents, high government officials, and Mexicans. One makes a joke.

But it is not a joke. Criticisms of television news have multiplied in recent years, as network news operations have grown in size and recognized importance. Intellectuals have criticized Big News for being too deferential to Administrations in power (which it is, although that's partly understandable, considering the broadcasters' legal and semi-legal responsibilities to government agencies); for being too slick and superficial in its presentation (which it also is, although that's partly understandable, too, given the networks' self-inflicted scheduling imperatives); and, in general, for giving the mass audience what it wants rather than what it ought to have—which, one gathers, is whatever intellectuals want.

At the same time, a far larger number of critics, but less articulate ones (who perhaps first announced themselves at the Republican National Convention in 1964, by booing the press at General Eisenhower's request), have been criticizing the "news media," and especially network-television news, for being leftist and Eastern and for disseminating the views of an "elite." Indeed, I read only recently that an organization with one of those solid, governmental-sounding titles—the Institute for American Strategy—had accused none other than CBS News of "partial and slanted reporting." As it happens, I also remember reading that one of the directors of this private fact-finding group was none other than former Representative Walter H. Judd, who nominated Richard Nixon for President in 1960, and who campaigned so tirelessly some years ago to try to prevent public television from showing Felix Greene's fine documentary of North Vietnam at war. Clearly, partiality is in plentiful supply on all fronts these days.

Even so, criticisms of network news for being leftist or Eastern don't seem to lead very far, especially considering the irredeemable political orthodoxy of most network newsmen, and the mainly non-Eastern regions of the country so many of them grew up in, and the often witless lengths they go to in order to provide "balance" and "objectivity." But there is some truth to these charges of "elitism." That is, there is some truth embedded in the charges. The question is: What kind of "elitism"? What type of slant or partiality?

It seems that all too often the partiality has been toward a new officialdom: the world of "newsmakers" and official spokesmen. As an example, in the years of crisis of the Nixon Presidency, whenever there was a news query concerning the Republican Party, how many times did the cameras and reporters of network news place themselves before the person of Senator Hugh Scott—the Republican Senator from Pennsylvania and a party spokesman—and ask *him* their questions; and dutifully record his answers? Had Nixon and Scott been Democrats, the television news-gatherers would certainly have acted the same way, for television news' partiality is preponderantly toward the official statement: the important, or self-important, presence. In fact, notwithstanding the concerns of the Silent Majority, and of Walter Judd and the Institute for American Strategy (whose other directors include Clare Booth Luce and George R. Hearst, Jr., publisher of the Los Angeles *Herald-Examiner*), it is a singular kind of bias that has developed on the public airwaves. It represents an elitism, really, neither of the right nor of the left; neither of the East nor of the West, nor of the Midwest nor of the South. (For instance, as has been amply shown in the past few years, when High Government moves to Key Biscayne or Vail or China or Mexico, Big News moves with it.) Indeed, elitism surely isn't the best description of what exists, although we are probably stuck with the term for a while. The trouble with network news isn't mainly its politics, or its slant, or its show-business quality. The trouble is that it has become a bureaucracy news: an impersonal, high-level news; an establishment news, where the establishment is no longer liberal or conservative, Democrat or Republican, Guelf or Ghibelline, but has become an establishment of newsmakers. The slant or partiality is toward "the official version." In short, we have an *important*, bureaucratic-class news, composed in an era of *important*, bureaucratic-class government, transmitted every evening to the nation—with a few visual touches (that tall transmission tower) thrown in, and expert editing, so as to make it seem more popularly appealing.

The census informs us of how many millions of people inhabit our nation. Television, we are told, is a "mass medium" and attracts a "mass audience." But what is this "mass" that our national news addresses each night—this news of handshaking dignitaries, of Washington, of spokesmen, of stock-exchange averages? Admittedly, the current theory (as it is conceived in Washington) is that local news programs should communicate to the "grass roots." But the difficulty with that notion is that in most areas of the country local news borrows the same official pretenses as network news, the same deference to bureaucratic importance, the same tendency to define the world through spokesmen, meetings, and official statements—only with not enough money and expertise to do it skillfully.

New York City, which is luckier than most American cities in this respect, publishes the *Times* and also the *Daily News*—which reaches more than twice the *Times*'s audience. And so here's another question: Where is television's *Daily News?*

Did someone ask where is television's *Times?* It's on CBS and NBC and ABC, and even PBS, each evening—maybe a skimpier version, with less space, less texture, less intelligent reporting, but with the same kind of stories, the same world view. Besides, intellectuals aren't so badly off when it comes to finding news; they can usually find the news somewhere. But *who* communicates to the rest of the country? That is, who makes sense of the reality of the nation to the men and women who live in it—this so-called mass of men and women, which consists of such innumerable groups, subgroups, and individuals, and is the reverse of "mass"? Perhaps that's why so many people watch the sports programs and feel a rapport with the announcers—hang those signs and messages from stadium balconies. At least, the sports announcers speak to them.

Now a fall wind stirs the street outside. Bare branches shake in the wind. A man walks by, bent over, leaning forward. Maybe it's that cold front moving in from the Great Lakes, or a snow breeze whispering in from Montana.

I wonder if the men standing outside the Cyclone fence will find work soon.

It's strange enough to be cut off from them—faces glimpsed from a car window, driving through the Communications Era. But what larger world is it that *they're* connected to? What pool or pond of the "mass media" reflects a recognizable image back to men and women whose lives and concerns exist beneath the level of official statements?

"It should be no surprise," said Walter Cronkite, "but air fares between the United States and Europe are going up."

What spokesmen speak to all the stay-at-homes?

The Interview

A FEW WEEKS AGO, VIEWERS OF NEW YORK'S WCBS regular Saturday-evening news broadcast were shown a fairly long film report of a fire in a Harlem tenement, which early that morning had killed a six-month-old Puerto Rican baby and had destroyed a good part of the building. It was a depressing and grief-stricken scene. The dead child's parents, who had been out at the time of the fire, were very young and very distraught. The child's baby sitter was also on hand: a frightened, tearstained, Puerto Rican girl of sixteen, who unfortunately had left the apartment for a few key minutes in order to buy some diapers for the baby. "This is a story of human lives and tragedy," intoned the WCBS reporter, Lucille Rich. A microphone was thrust at the young babysitter, who muttered wretchedly, "I went to take out the baby and I get to the kitchen, but I can't see nothing, so I can't take out the baby . . ." Then the baby's mother was produced, or, rather, discovered, sitting stunned in her sister's apartment in the same building. A microphone was thrust at the eighteen-year-old mother and she was asked, "Do you feel any animosity toward the young babysitter?" The young girl, barely in control of her feelings, stumbled through an awkward reply: "Well, I don't know, I don't know how to say it. I don't feel it right now. In a way, I don't know if . . ." At the end, she simply said, "It doesn't matter, right?" Finally, Miss Rich went to interview the family that lived on the floor below, whose small apartment had also been ruined. "And now that you see all this mess, with your apartment ruined, how does that make you *feel?*" the reporter asked a woman in the family. "Bad," said the woman. Miss Rich then summed up the experience for the benefit of the audience: "In the midst of grief and pain, one looks for answers, but answers to the whys and ifs and onlys don't come easily. Maybe time is there to help heal the hurt . . . Lucille Rich, Channel 2 News."

When I called WCBS a few days later to ask for a transcript of what had seemed like an astonishingly jarring set of interviews, the news director expressed regret at the quality of media intrusion that had been visited upon those distraught people in the fire-torn tenement. "It should never have happened," he said, which seemed a decent attitude for a news director to take, even though one knows that should an airliner crash tomorrow near a Trappist monastery not even the brothers' celebrated vows of silence would protect them from the bombardment of inane and often unanswerable questions which is by now an accepted convention of television's crisis-oriented news coverage. Even so, it was not merely the issue of invasion of privacy which made me prick up my ears at the WCBS Harlem-fire story, for that is both a larger issue and one which is as deep and tangled as the country's psychology itself. Rather, it was the story as an *interview;* for this was an unusually bad series of interviews and it made me wonder, generally, about the role of interviewing on television.

To take an obvious example (which occurred twice in Miss Rich's questions): Why is it that, time after time, almost as if it were an inevitable—a magical—question, TV reporters at crucial moments must extend their microphones toward a subject and ask, "How do you feel?" Whether the interviewee is an astronaut returned from walking on the moon or a politician who has won or lost an election or someone in the middle of a personal tragedy, the question, or one of its equivalents, is so frequently asked by television reporters as to have become a commonplace. "Well, Luis, how does it feel?" a microphone-thruster asked the Red Sox pitcher after a recent World Series victory. Another reporter went further: "I bet victory can't feel much better than that now, can it?" Or "Tell me what you felt when you saw your new face," as a local-news reporter asked a patient in a story on plastic surgery.

It seems to me that there are two ways of looking at these TV reporters' questions. On a certain level, they are simply childish and inept, though I think the ineptitude often lies not so much in the triviality of the question as in the unaware hostility behind it. Only in movies, for instance (and not the classier sort of movies, either), does a man who asks his wife, "How do you feel?" or "What's the matter?" ever receive a satisfactory answer. In real life, the hostility behind the question is usually picked up by the other person, who then counters, "Fine" or "Why, nothing." In the case of television interviews, of course, the reporter and his subject generally have no previous association, and also the subject is trying his best to be helpful.

Thus, *some* kind of reply is finally produced. For instance, in a locker-room interview after the last of this fall's World Series games, the camera picked up the weary figure of pitcher Bill Lee, who was seated alone on a bench. The reporter put a microphone under Lee's lowered chin. "Does it hurt to smile?" he asked, in that mixture of bogus concern and smiling disconnection which may well be the future language of World Government. Unable to move away, Lee slowly replied, "No, I can smile all the time." On another local news report, about a Phoenix House project for helping backward poor children, a reporter put a microphone in front of a young, nervous, and possibly retarded black boy. "Do you like it here?" she asked. "Yes, something about it," the boy replied uneasily. Aside from their insensitivity, these simplistic leading questions are patently non-evocative, in that they don't lead you anywhere. "Do you like it here?" addressed to a troubled, backward kid in a self-conscious "media" situation is basically little more than a careless act of aggression, exploiting the boy's awkward personal voice for the benefit of the reporter's own view of the story—besides being the kind of question that would leave any but the deftest of talkers high and dry after little more than a yes or no.

The ineptitude of TV reporters' questions, then, is a fact to be reckoned with on all too many television news interviews, especially on the local level. There are a number of surface reasons for this state of affairs. For one, few stations, or even networks, appear willing to spend their riches on hiring as reporters men and women who are specifically knowledgeable about specific areas of national life, with the result that there is a constant demand for "instant expertise" from the general reporters; consequently, a lot of dumb questions get asked, and a lot of useful questions don't get asked. However, this small-town-newspaper approach to handling modern news flow is only part of the problem. At the back of whatever ails the TV interview seems to be a needlessly confused and conservative approach to what a TV interview can be or can't be. In a sense, a TV interview can be just about anything, in that, in the right circumstances, people might attentively heed a Venusian visitor replying in equations, or even a New York mayor speaking forthrightly in dollars and cents. But, practically speaking, a TV interview is not there to provide the same "information" as a print interview with pictures added. The audience knows this. The reporters know this. Certainly, when a TV reporter goes into a World Series locker room, he knows that he has not been sent there to find out the score or to get a pitch-by-pitch account of the fifth inning. He knows he is there to capture a moment, to show the "feel" of something. Likewise, at the campaign headquarters of a winning candidate, viewers (and the reporter) seek a human display—again, the "feel" of something—not a review of the issues or an account of how the precincts voted in the suburbs.

So what goes wrong? Two things, I think. The reporter often distrusts himself, meaning that he is often supposed to evoke feeling about an event that he has no feeling for himself—or about which he feels hostile, perhaps, or scared, or tired, or bored—and so, rather than let the real subjects (politicians or baseball players or whatever) go about their own activities, with him following *them*, and perhaps connecting finally to genuine feeling, what he does time after time is insistently impose his own authority. Though classic questioners—chiefly spies and psychiatrists—know that only the reverse is likely to produce anything of value, the TV interrogator asserts *his* preconceptions, even offers *his* answers, in a lengthy question that he unrolls into his microphone and then allows the interviewee to sign. "After the years of oppression and danger in your homeland, and after the incredible danger and difficulty of your escape, which carried you to England ten years ago—well, perhaps you can tell us about the kind of hospitality you've met with here?" I heard a network interviewer ask a perplexed but amiable Soviet scientist a while ago.

The other thing wrong with TV news interviews, I think, is that the form they take often seems dictated by a lack of confidence that television newsmen appear to feel in the special *visualness* of their own profession. It would be strange if this feeling of uncertainty were not there to some degree, for television news has been a fairly recent development in journalism's long history. Television newsmen have often been looked on—and looked down on—as being the "glamour boys": long on good looks, announcerish voices, and high salaries, and short on "newsman's savvy." Unfortunately, this point of view has had a certain plausibility to recommend it, not really because TV newsmen are genetically more inept or shallow than print newsmen but because the demands of even most major TV news organizations on their reporters in terms of originating stories, developing contacts, accumulating background interviews, doing legwork, and all the other rituals of the print reporter's trade have been comparatively insubstantial. When a national crisis occurs and the engines of TV news are geared to produce radiant and ghastly streams of "actuality" for days on end, then even hard-boiled print journalists acknowledge that TV newsmen have a place of their own. But most of the time, as one watches the evening news, this "place" becomes less easy to define. I suspect that this is true for the TV newsmen themselves. They are supposed to be children of the Grand Old News-Gathering Profession—but they are rich stepchildren, with flashy clothes, new toys, and hopeful and insincere smiles, and naturally they have their share of professional insecurities. Insistently, the television people call their continent-hopping crisis-reporters "correspondents." Venerable anchormen have been known to refer to themselves on the air as "this reporter." Harmless gestures. The point of the business is supposed to be "hard news"—at least, so says the news establishment. This is what print journalism is about. This is what TV journalism is about—and, conscious of the raised eyebrows of the unflashy Old News-Gatherers in the print sector, the TV journalists keep trying to go them one better. Can the *News* get a tugboat sinking into tomorrow morning's paper? TV news will show it two hours after it happened. Does the *Times* report a subway fire? TV news had it the evening before. And when the TV reporter arrives by radio car at his fire, you can be sure he is going to act like a proper newsman at a hard-news event and ask "hard"—in the hard-news sense of the word—questions. Actually, on most such stories, he is going to confuse himself and blur the moment, because part of him is assertively asking hard newsman's questions, in a hard newsman's manner, while the other part of him—the TV-oriented reporter—is vaguely looking for the "feel" of the event.

Ironically, a better intuitive grasp of the form of television interviewing can be found in an unlikely area: that of the talk shows. On these strange programs, with their grinning hosts and ingratiating show-business guests, two important TV interviewing principles can be found. One is that it is the interview subject who is supposed to do most of the work; the other is that the conduit for conversation is usually a quite "soft" and aimless question. For instance, on a Merv Griffin show the other evening, for no apparent reason at all, Griffin turned to his various guests with such random gambits as "What was the first job you ever had?" or "You've never lacked for beautiful women around, have you?" or "Are you working now when you feel like it?" or "How come you're looking so happy and successful?" I call these soft questions because they aren't trying to elicit any preconceived reply. "Do you feel any animosity . . . ?" directed at the young mother in the Harlem-fire story has a preconception built into it that the woman does feel animosity, which she will now produce, or somehow handle (in the manner of a theatrical exercise) for the benefit of the television audience. It is a manipulative question. But when Merv Griffin asks Lucille Ball, "Are you working now when you feel like it?" he doesn't have anything in mind. The question has a remote, vague meaning, but no present meaning. Griffin is merely making celebrity small talk, nudging the show along on its prescribed track. Now and then, of course, an unexpected (or unprescribed) revelation of personality occurs on these programs, but the chances of this are slim, and are carefully hedged by making sure that most of the guests are tried-and-true TV performers. When a potentially interesting performer such as Lola Falana appeared on *The Tonight Show* recently, there was little attempt by Johnny Carson at interviewing her, or even at holding what might be called a conversation. As a professional talk-show guest, she was supposed to make her appearance, chat up the host, do her number, and generally provide her own small talk—much of which, as is customary, was directed at further chatting-up the host. "I'm so glad you were born," she said to Carson at one point.

Still, for all their silliness, these talk-show interviewers are onto something, in that they know that the audience is very minimally interested in traditional news-interview information. This is not to say that there is no place on television for hard-news interviews, but the place where such fact-oriented journalism occurs (as on the Sunday *Meet the Press* and *Issues and Answers*) is on the whole a small one. The talk-show hosts also know that their large audiences are only slightly interested in the information rewards of consecutive conversation but are agreeable to the semblance or rhythms of conversation—and that this is rarely produced by the asking of hard or leading questions. The chief trouble with these shows, really, is that they are so bored and so trapped in show business: an endless parade of celebs and semi-celebs, prattling away about their agents, or Mexican vacations, or new projects—sometimes joined by, say, a glamorous heart surgeon who has written a new book, and who in a matter of moments is grinning inanely at the host and talking about his Mexican vacation like the rest.

Close to the atmosphere of a talk show in its format, but nonetheless a program that has been capable of many fairly solid interviews, is the *Today* show. Across the years, this program has achieved a considerable level of distinction—without its individual parts' necessarily being distinguished—because it somehow expresses a quality of being willing to bet on itself. It does things because it does them—and in the TV world of constant over-the-shoulder glances that is something of a rarity. Jim Hartz, for instance, is not a Great Interviewer in any theatrical sense. He doesn't ask the hard question that print newsmen suggest should continually be asked. But he is a good television interviewer, in that he expresses a quality of civil regard for his guests, and though his questions sometimes contain too much of the expected answer, he manages to give his interview subject (and the viewer) room to breathe. This matter of the "regard" of the interviewer is not so unimportant, by the way, having no real parallel in print interviewing (where the interview subject can slam the door on an unpleasant or tricky interviewer), but being in fact a quality that can either effectively create a bond between the subject, the interviewer, and the audience or—when it is absent, as it often is—create that semi-sadistic, static effect of the interviewer's "playing off" on his subject while seeming to smile at him. Barbara Walters has also become a consistently good interviewer, having subdued her most noticeable flaw—interrupting guests mid-sentence—and somehow having channeled perhaps the same tendency so as to produce an atmosphere of modest unpredictability. In any event, the *Today* show interviews are certainly a large part of the reason for the great success of the program, and it is interesting that they seem to combine the qualities of "hardness" and "softness" found on the regular news programs and the talk shows. The *Today* show, however, remains something of a special case, for the real basis of its appeal lies in its having taken hold of what might be called the morning-newspaper experience and remythologizing it into a television format. It is the habit of "touching" a basic early-morning stability that seems to still bring and hold the audience.

A different but equally special case, in terms of interviewing, has been the work of Mike Wallace. For some years now, Wallace has cast himself as the abrasive investigative reporter, ferreting out facts, and willing to bully his subject in order to get them. Wallace is the antithesis of the talk-show host, or appears to be so. Wallace is the hard-news investigator who asks the hard question. In fact, Wallace is probably more theatrical than any other working newsman, and though he is a capable reporter (who has handled a number of untheatrical interviews), the role he seems to favor is borrowed largely from courtroom drama. He is the fiery prosecutor—the righteous and wrathful D.A. determined to rid Gotham City of its undesirables. At times, this can be very effective in dealing with the big-shot interviewee who is determined to appropriate the platform of the interview for his own benefit—a common failing of the TV interview, and a situation to be found almost every night on the news. A few weeks ago, for example, a reporter from Channel 7—supposedly interviewing the mayor of Elizabeth, New Jersey, about a teachers' strike—was put in the role of a dutiful student, with microphone outstretched, while the mayor proceeded to deliver unchallenged what sounded like a much-rehearsed speech. And, on a more disastrous level, there was the occasion, during the ugly hurly-burly of the 1968 Democratic Convention, in Chicago, when CBS sent Walter Cronkite to interview Mayor Richard Daley, whose police had clearly perpetrated much of the ugliness. Cronkite was so determinedly centrist in this interview as to be passive, almost apologetic, with the result that the roughneck mayor had the opportunity to define the event and the rioting pretty much on his own terms. Mike Wallace, one imagines, would have been a better choice for the assignment—except that Daley almost certainly wouldn't have agreed to see Wallace. Wallace's interviews provide a point of view, which is an asset of sorts, but since this point of view is mainly theatrical, it tends to focus the interviews on Wallace's personality. Also, they only work when Wallace's subjects can be persuaded or bullied into playing his game. When Wallace runs into someone with an equally strong ego and sense of theater, as in his interview with H. R. Haldeman some months ago, the result is a standoff, or worse. Haldeman, simply straight-armed most of Wallace's edgy, leading questions, playing them back on their own theatrical quality, and appearing to know that—unlike in the Perry Mason dramas—there was no judge sitting behind him to say, "Witness must answer the question!"

What all this adds up to, I think, is that, though there are individual examples of good interviewing on television, especially in the entertainment and cultural fields, TV news interviewing appears to be in some kind of limbo. Its often inexpert reporters are looking for the "feel" of things, which in many situations is a good way to begin, but they start asking those hard questions in order to get it. Or when they're not asking hard questions, they're letting those politicians or endless spokespeople make speeches into their microphones. Or they're trying so strenuously to control the event—to be proper hard-news authority figures—that the event and the people in it all end up awkwardly choreographed into some lifeless and ritualistic dance.

The waste of it is that TV has the capacity to provide a unique kind of "information" about its subjects—not the kind of information one looks for in a newspaper or magazine. Think of the advances in film or visual language over the past thirty years. Think of the ways that people have found to tell stories, play dialogue, set scenes, handle motion—and think of the incredibly expanded vocabulary of the modern film audience. Think of what in the way of new visual language people are given, and expect, in TV advertising. But TV news remains the Old Religion. Nothing must change, though there is much whiz-bang talk about new gimmicks—new instant replays, new minicams—with which to conduct a Front Page operation on a faster Front Page basis. There is something endearing about the conservatism and devotion with which the TV news priesthood cloaks its worship of the News—this sacred and venerable object that can only be presented to the public in *such* a manner, with roughly *so* many stories, and done either *this* way or *that* way, though clearly, by all accounts, this selfsame venerable object is often tossed about by the priesthood in the manner of the Dormouse at the March Hare's Tea Party.

I suspect that nothing much will ever change TV news, this side of a decline of the West, or a melting of the polar ice caps, or whatever it is that could require a basic restructuring of network broadcasting. But one way to improve it would be to start cutting those ties to the Old News-Gatherers of the print medium. In this matter of interviews: Why so many interviews to begin with? If you have a scene playing, as in a World Series locker room, let it play. Listen to conversations, or start one, and let it move, and see what happens. Tell the boss back in the control module or action central that you're not a ship's reporter, you're in a movie, with any luck—unless you blow it by grabbing some poor infielder, and throwing a microphone at him, and asking him how he *feels*. TV reporters now seem to include interviews because that's what a news story does—it has interviews. But why, if the interviews are going to come out strained and artificial? What is the "information" in glassy-eyed people mouthing helpless insincerities? And what's the advantage of breaking up a terrific small movie with a lot of control-and-authority numbers by the reporter? And, on the occasions when it's necessary to actually interview a specific person, surely in this era of psychiatry there must be some way of devising questions that do not either hang heavy with hostility or simply stop the interviewee dead, or both?

In this last matter, I've noticed that TV news' heroic Edward R. Murrow was wrestling with such dilemmas in his final years at CBS, when he combined his regular news reporting and analysis work with the softer format of *See It Now* and *Person to Person*. *See It Now* was definitely the better of the two shows. Murrow had the great interviewing skill as well as the nerve for collaring as elusive and complex a subject as Dr. J. Robert Oppenheimer and creating a classic television interview—all Oppenheimer. On *Person to Person*, though, where Murrow was clearly one of the early brave pioneers in the unasked-for enterprise of bringing the print feature story to television, even the Master clearly showed signs of succumbing to interviewer's dengue. Herewith a sample of questions asked by Edward R. Murrow of the then Cuban Commander in Chief Fidel Castro, in February 1959:

> Fidel Castro, I'm told you've just seen your mother. That must have been a great reunion. What did she have to say to you? . . .
>
> Well, Fidel Castro, when do you think you'll be with us again? Will that be with the beard . . . or without it? . . .
>
> Youth is a wonderful period. Sometimes I'm afraid we remember that too late . . .
>
> Thank you very much, Fidel Castro, for letting us come to see you in your hotel in Havana.

However, even this seems to be at a loftier level than the dialogue of another great interviewer, Ed Sullivan, who was also in Havana, interviewing Castro, during the month of February 1959.

"I heard you were Cawm-oo-neest," said Mr. Sullivan. "Were you Cawm-oo-neest?"

"No," Castro started to say, but Mr. Sullivan interrupted. "I saw scapulars around your men's necks," he said. "You're not Cawm-oo-neest. You're *Catholic*, Fidel!"

With such examples from the Golden Age, our modern interviewers have little place to go but up.

The Media Dramas of Norman Lear

I HAVE BEEN TRYING TO FIGURE OUT WHAT IS SO FASCINATING about the comedies of Norman Lear. Right now, six of Mr. Lear's shows are being broadcast every week to a prime-time audience: *All in the Family*, *Maude*, *Good Times*, *The Jeffersons*, *Sanford and Son*, and HOT L BALTIMORE. The first five programs named are currently among the dozen most popular programs in the nation, while the sixth, and newest, HOT L BALTIMORE (the title refers to the Hotel Baltimore, a riffraffy version of *Grand Hotel*), after just six weeks, has received a warm reception, despite a degree of wariness on the part of network-affiliate stations, several of which appear to think that in populating his run-down inn so freely with prostitutes, homosexuals, and other social misfits Mr. Lear may have been pushing his gift for jokey topicality farther than the mass audience will bear. Even so, it's probably a good bet that roughly a hundred and twenty million Americans watch Norman Lear comedies each week—which adds up to a total of roughly five billion viewers every year. Perhaps what is most fascinating about Mr. Lear's œuvre is the dimensions of its success, for he seems to be one of those ordinary but uncommon figures who come along every so often in our mass-entertainment culture and manage to achieve—more or less single-handed and with the appearance of naturalness—what tens of thousands of business geniuses and consumer theoreticians spend half the energies of the Republic vainly striving after; namely, a "feel" for what the public wants before it knows it wants it, and the ability to deliver it.

What is *not* so fascinating about Lear programs is easier to determine. Surprisingly, they are not very funny, for the most part, which is to say that the level of acting—at least, the stage presence of the actors—is generally of a higher order than the humor in each show: the jokes and joke situations. The humor isn't bad, but a surprising amount of it seems contrived and second-rate. "In my building, the roaches are so big that the crunch drowns out the television." And "Deep down, you know, he respects you." "Yes, but I don't want to dive that deep." On the whole, there are few unusual comedy routines in Lear comedies, and there has been virtually no introduction or creation of striking new comedy characters, with the possible exception of Archie Bunker, in *All in the Family*, who was transplanted from the successful BBC series *Till Death Do Us Part*, and, in any case, derives from a mass-entertainment cartoon that stretches back from William Bendix and Wallace Beery to Sancho Panza and Shakespeare's Pistol. And even Bunker, who has most of the best lines in his show, is given an overabundance of easy malapropisms:

"Salivation Army," "Let him who is without sin be the rolling stone," " 'Pilferers will be prosecuted' means 'Queers stay out of the men's room.' " In fact, much of the feeling of comedy in these Norman Lear programs seems to stem neither from the jokes, nor even from the situations, but from a mainly acoustical atmosphere of hilarity woven into the dialogue by means of the sounds of audience laughter which accompany each program. This laughter, it should be noted, is not the so-called "canned laughter" with which broadcast comedians traditionally augmented their routines. The Lear dramas, as self-proclaimed, are recorded before a "live audience," and so the laughter one hears is at least the sound of real people watching the same program that the home audience watches, albeit some days apart. Even so, while this represents a small advance in the production integrity of mass-entertainment comedy, the presence of this taped laughter as a formal part of a taped show—laughter emanating from the television set, from the same apparent source as the dialogue—is bound to have a defining effect on the viewer. Consider, for example, how one's perceptions of a movie or play can vary according to the responsiveness of the audience; how the presence of certain kinds of insistent audience laughter (such as the "bad laughs" which in many instances accompanied the movie *One Flew Over the Cuckoo's Nest*) can have almost a controlling effect on the rest of the people watching. Moreover, though the laughter which sets the tone for a program such as *All in the Family* derives from a real audience rather than from an old-fashioned "laugh machine," there are now new machines—indeed, a whole new science of acoustics and audio engineering—which make it possible for the laughter to rise and fall and throb ever more subtly and "realistically" behind the dialogue, but in the integrated manner of a rock band's second guitar. Thus, the audience is real, although the producers control its composition as well as the engineering of the sound, with the result that the humor of these most successful American television comedies is seldom witnessed by the viewer unattended by the whoops and giggles, the chuckles and vocal nudges, of this latest electronic institutionalizing of the old theatrical claque.

Also, whereas the level of comedy in the majority of the Norman Lear series is no more (and no less) than routinely professional, with its dependence on gags and grimaces, what often seems more evident than humor is the constant and steady presence of anger. All too frequently, while the persona of the studio audience booms out its merriment in the fashion of a lunatic Greek chorus, the on-screen characters appear to be caught up in a quite separate, verbal ballet of insult and vituperation. Again, Archie Bunker stands as the prototype of the Lear angry-man character. When Bunker first appeared on American screens in 1971, representing the politically and socially threatened silent-majority blue-collar worker, his outbursts on politics and race were taken as quaintly liberating and timely. They also had a specific quality and direction to them: blacks moving into the neighborhood, or being hired at a nearby factory. For some time now, though, Bunker's anger has become random—a random musical note that is methodically sounded by the script as it travels through each half hour. It is an accepted form of stage business. In a recent episode of *All in the Family*, for example, within a space of about fifteen minutes Bunker snarled and mugged such lines as "What's the stink in the oven? What kinda animal you cookin' in there?" (It's a fish.) "So, Irene is a Catholic. That means I gotta pay for *her* mistakes?" (Irene leaves.) "Whadda I care if she leaves. She's not my guest, she's your guest." "C'mon, throw the fish on the table!" "Don't stay in there—c'm here! Move it!" "Listen to this, Commie pinko!" "Let me remind you of something, Meathead!" "Yeah, Dingbat, I'm talkin' to you in English!" "Get in, get in. Just put your keyster in the chair and shut your mouth." If Bunker's anger has settled in as a conventional shtick—like Groucho Marx's walk or Jack Benny's stinginess—it has also been picked up and incorporated into all the other Norman Lear shows, and, for the most part, with the same quality of randomness. On *Sanford and Son*, which was transplanted from *Steptoe and Son*, another BBC series (about two Cockney junk dealers), Fred Sanford is an irascible and bullying black man—often with only the sound track and the vaudeville mugging to tell one that the show is a comedy. In a recent episode, Sanford was waiting for the arrival of his younger sister and her new "mystery" husband. First, he wanted his truck. "Where's our truck?" he asked angrily. "Julio borrowed it," said his son, referring to a Puerto Rican neighbor. Sanford grimaced broadly and slammed his fist on a table. "Now, you gone got *Puerto Rican* all over our truck!" The taped audience erupted in laughter, the joke presumably being that it *was* a joke. Then the married sister appeared with her new husband—a white man. The audience giggled apprehensively but delightedly as the husband—a soft, droll figure—sidled warily into the room, unseen by Sanford. Time passed and Sanford still didn't notice him. Then he mistook the man for a taxi driver. Then, finally introduced to and embraced by the new brother-in-law, he went into an elaborate and energetic sequence of grimaces and double takes, crashing about the room in a fury that was again comic mainly in the laughter of the unseen audience. "How come you're lookin' that way?" Sanford's sister said to him, feeding the line. "I just got hugged and kissed by a Snow-Whitey," replied Sanford. Afterward, he called the white husband "Mr. Intermarry," "Paleface," "Honky," "Color-Blind," and "The White Tornado," each one to bursts of applause from the tape; indeed, the only purpose or reality of the white husband's existence seemed to be as a butt for Sanford's jokey snarls.

Anger as stage business runs through nearly all Norman Lear's comedies, but it is a curious, modern, undifferentiated anger, which serves to provide the little dramas with a kind of energizing dynamic—sometimes the only dynamic. At the beginning of an episode of *The Jeffersons*, George Jefferson enters his new apartment already angry—vaguely and generally angry. Maude, in *Maude*, appears to be angry at Walter, in one particular instance, for eating too much, but clearly—clearly to the audience—she is just *angry:* it is a state of being, interrupted periodically by stage-business jokes or stage-business sentiment, or sometimes stage-business problems. What is notable here is that anger in a Norman Lear comedy isn't something isolated or set apart—as with, say, Sheridan Whiteside in George S. Kaufman and Moss Hart's *The Man Who Came to Dinner*, or in the traditional routines of "insult comedians." It has become part of the spirit of the occasion, like music in a musical comedy. Also, as with the characters themselves, who, despite their fits of problem-solving and self-awareness, return each week to the same unserial starting point, it is a rage that rarely extends much into the future, or even into the present. An individual outburst of temper may sometimes produce a concrete result, such as the disruption of a dinner, but for the most part these acts of the new anger are strangely actionless, and, in any case, are soon automatically defused and retracted. King Lear's rage has traveled, by way of Sheridan Whiteside's irritability, into the release-rhetoric of the psychotherapist's waiting room.

Modern, psychiatrically inspired or induced ambivalence may, indeed, be the key dramatic principle behind this new genre of popular entertainment. A step is taken, and then a step back. A gesture is made and then withdrawn—blurred into distracting laughter, or somehow forgotten. This seems especially true in the area of topicality—topical themes—which is supposed to be where Mr. Lear's chief contribution to new forms of comedy lies. For it is in Norman Lear comedies that the mass-entertainment public has first been persuaded to deal regularly with serious contemporary social subjects such as racism (*All in the Family*), alcoholism (*Maude*), black middle-class striving (*The Jeffersons*), and black lower-class problems (*Good Times*), and with a hodgepodge of traditionally unacceptable social and sexual situations (HOT L BALTIMORE). With or without the help of contemporary trends, what Mr. Lear has done in this regard is no mean achievement. He has taken a lot of the subjects that people privately talked or thought about, in between watching game shows, detective shows, and stand-up comedians, and put *those* subjects into mass-entertainment programming. His shows don't explicitly claim to be constructive or dogmatic, although the writers (and presumably Mr. Lear) are not averse to throwing in periodic doses of social democracy, but they do implicitly claim to be topical.

As things work out, though, it is a curious kind of topicality. The subject seems to be there—for instance, financial problems stemming from the recession, in a recent episode of *Maude*—but the actuality of the subject soon dissolves into the texture of the aforementioned vague anger, or else into a new type of ambivalence, which has been effected by employing fast cutting and the claque sound track. For example, in a recent episode of HOT L BALTIMORE the main drama concerned the breakup of a long-standing homosexual menage involving two hotel tenants—the middle-aged George and Gordon, with George clearly the "wife" in the pair—as a result of George's decision to spend two evenings out of each week studying law. Interestingly, the roles of George and Gordon were cast with a fair amount of sympathy and contemporary realism; at least, the actors and their parts were several cuts above the traditional mass-entertainment depiction of limp-wristed effeminacy à la Billy De Wolfe. The tilt of the drama—rather more a vignette—seemed human, and even serious, but then the mood would suddenly shift, almost in middialogue, into an old-timey gag or a cheap laugh played off the invisible audience. At one point—supposedly a key moment—the youthful and well-intentioned but dopey hotel manager appears on the scene to try to patch things up between the two separating roommates. The scene requires him to shake hands with George. George, quite dignified, extends his hand. The camera cuts to the hotel manager mugging his straight-arrow distaste. Then we see George, playing it seriously. Then back to the hotel manager, alternately rolling his eyes, shuffling his feet, and continuing to mug he-man embarrassment while the sound track variously giggles, sniggers, guffaws, and breathes a chorus-like sigh of relief when the handshake is finally consummated. What seemed unusual about the scene was that the other actors onstage were directed to play it seriously. In other words, the caption on the picture, so to speak, said that we were watching a human, realistic, albeit comedic treatment of a contemporary "social problem," but in fact the figures in the portrait were dissolving into images of our own (and perhaps their creator's) anxieties and ambivalences: into a caricature of the homosexual's role in our society, which the "caption" was attempting to deny. Similarly, in a recent episode of *The Jeffersons* the dramatic vignette concerned a tenants' party in the family's new apartment, in a predominantly white, upper-middle-class building, which George Jefferson had decided to give in order to show off to his neighbors and impress an important white banker with his cultivation. Predictably, the party was a social disaster. A funny "colored maid" went screaming around the room. When an effete, English-type tenant asked for "a

Scotch—neat," one of the Jeffersons said, "Don't worry, you'll get a clean glass." George Jefferson had ordered, sight unseen, a grand piano, which none of the family could play, and it was delivered into the middle of the living room, so that everybody tripped over it. And so forth. But none of the people onstage batted an eye. If the real point of the story was that the Jeffersons were pushy, *arriviste*, inept, but unfortunately *there*—in fact, were uppity—it was not a point acknowledged, or even touched upon, except very slightly, by the rest of the cast. There were no haughty looks and contemptuous sneers from the other posh tenants—the way the ritzy people used to look at Charlie Chaplin when he stumbled into the wrong salon. The only way you'd know that the party was an embarrassment was from the sound track, which, with its shrieks and giggles at the awkward moments, keyed the real audience: Yes, the Jeffersons *are* uppity. We can't say it too loud, because that would be wrong. In fact, we're going to play it on the level with those other stage tenants, perhaps—Lord knows—encouraging real tenants somewhere to play it on the level with real Jeffersons. But in the meantime let's let our anxieties and ambivalences work up the real drama, and let's have a laugh.

Even so, if what could mainly be said of Norman Lear's comedies was that they were on the cheap side, playing serious topical subjects for easy laughs—with a few jokes and snarls and much professional expertise thrown in—that wouldn't be very new or very interesting, and I don't think it would account for Mr. Lear's enormous success. It may well be that Lear does more with topical humor than comedians and comedy writers before him have done, but topicality isn't his invention, nor is exploiting it a new device, recently discovered. Indeed, American mass-entertainment producers have exploited audience "seriousness" for generations, as with the *Classics*-comics pageantry of Cecil B. De Mille, or with Stanley Kramer's "message" films, or with *The Defenders* on television, or even with the slick good-think of the Smothers Brothers and the political wisecracks of Bob Hope and *Laugh-In*. Topicality doesn't really seem to be what Mr. Lear does best—nor does comedy seem to be his strongest card. After watching a great many of Mr. Lear's six shows this past season, I suspect that what is most fascinating about the works of Norman Lear is that they are our first true "media" dramas.

Consider briefly how American mass-audience comedy has evolved in the past fifty years. For much of this time, comedy—both in print and onstage—was trapped within the joke: the one-liner, the two-liner, the set piece, the funny bit. From these beginnings, with the joke presented as separate or disconnected from ordinary life, came the more expansive—albeit still disconnected—narrative joke or funny story: *Nothing but the Truth; Bringing Up Baby; Abbott and Costello Meet Frankenstein*. On television, the funny story survives in such now old-fashioned programs as *Hogan's Heroes* and *Gilligan's Island* (as, indeed, vaudeville one-liners still survive with Bob Hope), but, for the most part, during the last generation television—as if it had prenatally digested *The Pickwick Papers* or at least *Life with Father*—has expanded humor from the isolated joke into the so-called family comedy. In *I Love Lucy* and *The Honeymooners* and *The Beverly Hillbillies* and countless other shows, the surface emphasis was still on jokes—Lucy finds a wallet, wins a contest, loses a handbag—but the joke sector of life had been enlarged to include not merely a comedian onstage talking about farmers' daughters but much of ordinary family life, if a rather stylized version of it. Lucy at first was not a real woman, though she had many of the appurtenances of a real woman—modest house, noisy kitchen, gossipy neighbors—but she ended up actually having babies and bringing up children. More recently, Dick Van Dyke and then Mary Tyler Moore expanded the terrain of family comedy further, replacing the home family with the job family, and fashioning, as in the case of the current *Rhoda* and *The Mary Tyler Moore Show*, more or less "real" people to go with the "real" problems and comedy situations. Still, *Mary* and *Rhoda* have remained by and large in the conventional mold of *families* dealing with *family* situations—either home family situations, such as boyfriends or dieting or mothers-in-law, or job family situations, such as office misadventures or employment rivalries.

The comedies of Norman Lear are probably new in that they seem to depend mainly neither on jokes nor on funny stories, nor even on family—although they often give the appearance of depending on all three—but on the new contemporary consciousness of "media." By this I mean that the base of the Lear programs is not so much the family and its problems as it is the commonality that seems to have been created largely by television itself, with its outpouring of casual worldliness and its ability to propel—as with some giant, invisible electric-utility feeder line—vast, undifferentiated quantities of topical information, problem discussions, psychiatric terminology, and surface political and social involvement through the national bloodstream. Thomas Jefferson, it is said, wrestled for a lifetime with the dark, felt concerns of intermarriage and miscegenation, and it is high time that Americans should be able to deal freely and rationally with such historically taboo matters. But lately in the space of a single week, in two Norman Lear shows, the subject of mixed marriage twice breezed blithely by, accompanied by the usual defusing jokes and the laughter of the sound track. Have we come this far so suddenly? In which case, who are *we?* Doubtless we are the same people who, as informed adults and media children, discuss, with all the appearance of passion and involvement, events that have occurred in places we have no knowledge of and had no previous interest in, and with implications we have rarely examined, or tried to connect backward or forward to other events—but events that now sit there and *exist* in the new consciousness in the manner of found objects, tuned into by interested and uninterested parties alike.

Mr. Lear is surely not the first explorer to have stumbled on this pool of media-informed consciousness, but he is the first man, as far as I can tell, to have so formally and so successfully tapped it for the purposes of mass entertainment. It is perhaps not a step higher, but it is a step forward. Ancient drama, one might say, was concerned primarily with the act as act—as the dynamic of drama.

Modern drama has gradually interposed motive and guilt as the kinetic forces. Now, maybe, we are treading dizzily into a new phase, where both act and motive have blurred or receded and what we are left with onstage (or on-screen) is the strange dynamic of a ubiquitous, unfeeling, unknowing, discursive collective consciousness. Beginning with the comedies of Norman Lear—as Aristophanes might have been the first to appreciate—we have finally become plugged in to our own Talk Show: connected to nothing except the assumption of being connected to something, which for the time being appears to be our new bond and our new family.

The Eyes and Ears of the World

On a recent evening, the *CBS Evening News with Walter Cronkite* presented, as usual, what it considered to be the key news stories of interest to the nation. As is often the case these days, they were focused mainly on domestic politics and economics. There were stories on the House Judiciary Committee's confirmation of Nelson Rockefeller as Vice-President, on Governor Jimmy Carter's candidacy for the Democratic nomination for President, on President Ford meeting with automobile leaders, and on pollution in Pennsylvania's drinking water, and there were several stories on the economic situation in the country—notably, an interesting examination by Washington correspondent George Herman of the recent rise in wholesale prices, and a fairly lengthy look at inflationary pressures in the lumber, cotton, and beef industries. Just before the final news item—a more or less lighthearted report from Texas about food being given away in a local supermarket—the camera turned to Walter Cronkite, who read three brief announcements. One was that the oil producers' cartel was meeting in Vienna; another was that Britain's trade deficit had risen; the third mentioned an air attack by several Israeli jets on a Palestinian compound near Beirut. These three announcements, whose reading consumed perhaps thirty seconds of air time, constituted the total foreign news broadcast by the *CBS Evening News* that day.

I mention this not to fault CBS for a surprising error of omission but to point out what has been obvious to many people for a good while: that foreign news as a broadcast commodity has been in a steady decline of late years, to such an extent that it now often seems to be thrown into a network's regular news productions as a kind of afterthought. I should say, in fairness, that this particular program contained a smaller amount of foreign news than is usual, even for these times. Both CBS and NBC—the two networks that have traditionally maintained substantial foreign-news operations (ABC was a late starter in the news business)—claim that on an annual basis the foreign-news content of their major news broadcasts averages from 20 to 25 percent. Still, even this modest figure has generally been filled out by two rather narrow types of international reporting: semi-official accounts of the overseas travels and meetings of our own Presidents and Secretaries of State, and a largely reflexive, military-oriented coverage of combat situations—as, recently, in the Middle East. Organic, ongoing, interpretive coverage of the world as a whole by United States broadcast journalism seems right now to be at a minimum, and—despite the profitability of the three networks—shows no signs of becoming more ambitious. For example, CBS, which has for the last several years employed roughly seventy-five full-time correspondents to cover the continental United States, currently employs fourteen correspondents to cover the rest of the world. NBC has for the last several years posted roughly fifty-five correspondents around the country but has posted full-time correspondents and camera crews in only twenty foreign cities, from which they must cover, and "correspond" about, the whole of Africa, Asia, Europe, and South America.

The networks are far from being uniquely deficient in this respect. In fact, they have been doing no more than go along with a prevailing trend in American journalism, which for some time has been to withdraw from international affairs and concentrate on problems and events at home. Thus, journalism has been only mirroring, or trying to mirror, the inner-directed mood of the American people, which perhaps first proclaimed itself in President Kennedy's nationalistic space program and then appeared more visibly in the rhetoric and the modest legislation of President Johnson's civil-rights and urban-reform programs, and which has more recently found expression—or, at least, the semblance of a form for itself—in the much-mentioned national introspection that resulted from President Nixon's Watergate imbroglio and lately, and more significantly, from the troubles of the domestic economy and the demand for "self-sufficiency" in oil. Indeed, it has become almost a commonplace to assert that the inhabitants of the nation are no longer interested in the international scene—certainly that they are not as much interested in it as they were, presumably, in the years right after the Second

World War, when the United States was involved in the rebuilding of Europe and in the tangled and dramatic internationalist neuroses of the Cold War. Nowadays, politicians appear to try to outdo each other in stressing their concern about purely local matters—the "plight of the cities." Bright college graduates who a generation ago might have cast an ambitious eye on the Foreign Service with a view to eventually holding a post in an important NATO country, or on organizational journalism with a view to landing a glamorous job as foreign correspondent in London, Paris, or Rome, now turn their ambitious eyes on running for state assemblyman, or on reporting the passage of a new strip-mining bill. It is a trend that, however temporary it may be, or may have to be, is not without its own deep logic; and for a commercial news organization to go entirely against it would be foolish. After I learned the figures for the foreign-correspondent staffs of CBS and NBC—which struck me as low, even for the present mood—I got in touch with Harrison Salisbury, a former associate editor of *The New York Times* and a veteran international reporter, to find out the present level of the *Times*'s foreign staff. Salisbury came up with a rough total of about forty correspondents around the world. I asked him if the number of overseas correspondents on the paper had been declining, and he said no—that it had stayed at around forty for the past ten years or so, except that there had been temporary increases in Vietnam at key moments in the war. Furthermore, he said he thought that the *Times*'s number of foreign correspondents was "about right," because there was no point in having more correspondents abroad when you couldn't get more foreign news into the paper. The last ten years, he said, hadn't been good from the point of view of getting foreign news—except possibly from Vietnam—into the paper.

The *Times*, to be sure, is exceptional among newspapers, both in its relatively international-minded readership and in at least the ubiquity of its foreign coverage. On the morning after the news program on which CBS presented thirty seconds of foreign news, the *Times* ran twenty-two stories with overseas datelines in its first fourteen pages, not counting United Nations coverage and a brief account of heavy weather on the Caspian Sea. Yet the fact that the *Times* currently employs forty worldwide reporters to serve its roughly one million clients, whereas CBS News employs fourteen worldwide reporters to serve its roughly twenty million clients, isn't really the main point—although doubtless it's a comparison worth noting. For if the *Times* has long had an international bias in its news pages, so has CBS News—a comparatively recent organization that developed largely out of the overseas staff of young reporters, such as Edward R. Murrow, Larry Lesueur, William L. Shirer, Charles Collingwood, Howard K. Smith, and Eric Sevareid, that covered the Second World War in Europe for CBS Radio.

Nor, of course, is the point that there is some sinister conspiracy on the part of newspaper editors or television executives to keep foreign news out of the paper or to limit network international coverage to 20 or 25 percent. The point, I think, is less easily definable and is probably in the long run important, having little to do with hidden motives or assignment schedules, or even with percentage figures. Something about it, in any case, was brought home to me by two recent events. One was the death of Walter Lippmann, at eighty-five. The other I can't really call an event, for it was merely a news item concerning the passage through town of Vincent Sheean, the once dashing and well-traveled journalist, who is now a gracious old gentleman of seventy-five. Lippmann's name and reputation are well known to most literate people in this country—though I wonder how many people know, as I did not, that Lippmann's original push into journalism came about through an apprenticeship with the great muckraker Lincoln Steffens. Vincent Sheean is today less well known, but it seems to me that he, too, has been one of this country's great journalists, and that his *Personal History*, published in 1935, still stands as a classic of intelligent and involved reporting—in this instance, of the politics and psychology and appearance of Europe as it drifted toward the Second World War. The names of Lippmann and Sheean impressed themselves on me the other day, and I mention them here not simply out of respect for two admirable journalists but because it seems to be more than a coincidence that some of the very best American journalism has been the journalism written by Americans who perceived the profound connection between America and the rest of the world—who not only perceived it but insisted on it when the American public, for various reasons, was more inclined to look to its own garden. Even in his earliest columns, written in the inward-turning America of the post-First World War period, Lippmann spoke steadily for the logic of American involvement in Europe and in the postwar settlements. Fifteen years later, with America assertively uninvolved and the postwar settlements undone, Sheean—in a different, more personal voice—drew masterly and evocative sketches of the larger world that was then collapsing and fragmenting behind the Wirephoto pictures of smiling Prime Ministers and dictators.

By the time this collapse had entered its final stage, American radio journalism had matured to the point where it was broadcasting occasional, largely unsponsored, five-minute news "analyses" by such men as Elmer Davis and H. V. Kaltenborn (who in 1936 had been compelled by CBS to pay his own travel expenses to cover the Spanish Civil War). With the development of shortwave radio broadcasting, and with the growing public concern over affairs in Europe, the two networks (although chiefly CBS) began laying the groundwork for an international news operation. Edward Murrow arrived in Europe for CBS in 1937, to provide shortwave news broadcasts as well as arrange concert programs for CBS's *American School of the Air*. Shirer was already in Berlin. On March 13, 1938, as Erik Barnouw recounts it in his book *The Golden Web*, Murrow broadcast his first news report to American listeners: "This is Edward Murrow speaking from Vienna. It's now nearly two-thirty in the morning, and Herr Hitler has not yet arrived. No one seems to know just when he will get here, but most people expect him sometime after ten o'clock tomorrow morning . . ." Later, from London, Murrow initiated the series of broadcasts that, as much as anything did, brought home to Americans the reality of that not so distant war. "Today, I went to buy a hat," he began a broadcast in September 1940—at around the time that Franklin Roosevelt was beginning his campaign for a third term against the isolationist-backed Wendell Willkie. "My favorite shop had gone—blown to bits," he went on. "The windows of my shoe store were blown out . . . The windows of the barbershop were gone." Barnouw writes: "Americans were hearing from many orators that Britain was decadent, a spent force. Murrow did not argue with them; he merely reported. But his words left little doubt that Britain would fight on." Still later, after America had entered the war, network-radio coverage became better established and more popular—attuned to the drama of combat and the chauvinism of our participation in the "great crusade." But it was to Murrow's credit, and to the credit of many of his colleagues at CBS and NBC, that in that prewar time, when even Lend-Lease was a moot issue and powerful currents of isolationism were running at home, the network journalists overseas conveyed to Americans not only what was often a far from popular picture of European disintegration and the early stages of the war but also—with Murrow's restrained tone and American voice—an unavoidable sense of implicit American involvement.

After the Second World War, it seemed that Americans became determined internationalists. There was our interest in the United Nations (which met first in San Francisco and then in New York) and in the Marshall Plan. General Eisenhower's wartime Allied Headquarters was approvingly expanded and institutionalized into NATO.

There was the "challenge" of the Cold War, and the "challenge" of rebuilding Europe. Even Wendell Willkie, who had once accepted the fiercely isolationist support of Martin, Barton, and Fish, had written a book titled *One World*. All the while, American business continued its spread overseas. And American news organizations increased their foreign staffs—imperially establishing bureaus across Europe and, to a lesser extent, in the Far East. In the postwar years, news from Europe was on the front pages of the important American newspapers almost daily, and represented (according to network estimates) roughly 50 percent of television's evening newscasts—which, as it happens, until September 1963 were only fifteen minutes long. Still, ironies abound in history, and surely they did then, in this formally internationalist period in American history. Thus, Americans in the 1940's and 1950's, as if to make up for their past mistake of self-absorption, increasingly directed their energy and interest to Europe and the Far East—so that European politics, the Cold War, Berlin, and Chiang Kai-shek appeared to be the main objects of American attention, and were so orchestrated by the news organizations. Meanwhile, the complexities, tensions, and injustices of American life remained intense but largely invisible, because they went unreported, until, in the 1960's, they finally exploded in a series of eruptions across the nation—in the Deep South, in the Northern cities, in black ghettos and white ethnic neighborhoods, in the lives of women, in the young, in long-dormant, unexplored areas of sexuality and politics—and American journalists rushed home to cover them. Much as the invisible, because unreported, phenomena of Europe in the 1930's had suddenly turned into facts that required a wrenching effort to deal with, so the unattended-to phenomena of postwar America suddenly turned into facts that required an equally extreme effort, of a different kind, to set in perspective.

It is surely a deep-rooted human trait to have difficulty in observing, let alone comprehending, two separate matters at the same time—say, a football game and a baseball game being played simultaneously. And so perhaps one shouldn't be surprised that public interest flickers back and forth in this cyclical way between foreign and domestic concerns, and that editors, news executives, politicians, and others attuned to the public mood invariably follow it. Still, it's an unfortunate situation—given the implicit relationship of communications to modern societies—and a result of the kind of modern carelessness that persons in power persist in explaining away as it not being their "job" to do otherwise. This is not to say that if the American people had been led to know of their real involvement with Europe in the 1930's to the extent that they were led to know of, say, the virtues of Pepsodent toothpaste, Hitler might have never come to power, or a war of some kind might never have occurred. But almost certainly it would have happened differently. Nor is it to say that if in the 1960's the news organizations of the nation (whose previously far-flung correspondents, camera crews, and "task forces" were then belatedly discovering Watts and Selma) had made any serious attempt to glance overseas and communicate what was happening in Southeast Asia—to measure the extent of our largely invisible, because unreported, involvement there—a war might never have occurred in Vietnam. But it, too, might have happened differently, and the descendants of the early purchasers of Pepsodent toothpaste, to say nothing of the rest of the American people, or the Vietnamese, might be more fortunate in a number of ways than they appear to be now.

The present, it is true, is a difficult region to be wise about—certainly for modern television journalists, whose Muse all too often floats low to the ground, laden with market surveys, public-opinion samples, advertising budgets, and various deadline imperatives. All the same, one doesn't have to be a foreign-news expert to be aware that there are several major ongoing foreign matters that Americans are at this moment inextricably involved with, and are being further involved with each day, and that remain largely unreported on television, save for occasional, disconnected, crisis announcements on the evening news. At the top of this urgent list one would have to put the Middle East situation, an enormous and complex "problem," which compels American attention on a number of levels, including the moral as well as the economic, and which is usually presented to the television public in the form of distant, episodic scenes of combat: dark planes in a blue sky flashing low over hills and rooftops; thin columns of smoke; ghostly sounds of gunfire. In many ways, it is the Vietnam television scenario, except for the absence (to date) of American generals, advisers, Special Forces troops, and optimistic interviews with the Ambassador. At any rate, granted the difficulties of communicating the Middle East situation to the American public as a whole, the response of television journalism so far has been sketchy and crisis-oriented. When something visibly dramatic happens, television covers it. The rest of the time, which is most of the time, *nothing* is presented as happening in this crucial, not so distant part of the world; little coherence is given to the historical and human complexities of the situation. Beneath the periodic film clips of swooping planes and official pronouncements, our involvement ticks forward every day—largely unwitnessed.

The United States is obviously now involved in nearly every part of the world—perhaps more so, in our present time of national introspection, than ever before. Less topical and "hot" a subject than the Middle East, but one that over the long run is probably even more relevant to the American future, is the "story" (and one might well call it that) that has been hinted at, suggested, and increasingly documented in several studies—the most recent being by Richard Barnet and Ronald Müller—of the worldwide role, and especially the American domination, of so-called multinational corporations. This is not the place to discuss the merits or demerits of American global corporations; one need merely note that the growing literature on the subject points to an already enormous and generally unreported involvement of American business with the economic and political fortunes of much of the rest of the world. And not only of American business, which for many people in this country still has a remote, elitist sound to it, but of the inevitable components of American business: stockholders; workers, employed and unemployed—the public. For example, "it is sometimes argued that the dependence of the United States on the world economy is exaggerated," say Barnet and Müller, who then show that "some thirty per cent of total United States corporate profits can now be . . . attributed to overseas operations," and, further, that "for many of America's major corporations, foreign profits mean the difference between operating in the black [and operating] in the red." And, in case that still seems too corporate and elite, after analyzing the effect of global operations on the American work force they conclude: "When more than a fourth of the payroll and the managerial energies of the leading industrial concerns go to workers outside the country, it is not surprising that the federal government finds it difficult to develop an effective employment policy."

The mostly untold and, so far, managerial-oriented story of American global corporations, then, seems to be a story of the American public's inextricable involvement in the wider world, and also—as a consequence of American corporate policy overseas, especially in the undeveloped nations—of the American public's substantial involvement in the lives and affairs of other *peoples:* a kinetic involvement, for all its invisibility at home, which has already produced counterthrusts, and is bound to produce still sharper ones. From South America, for instance, unconnected news stories have appeared from time to time about political unrest, or workers' strikes, or violent changes in government, accompanied by killings and by torture of the survivors (". . . were held for interrogation"). There have been scattered, largely unpursued accounts of C.I.A. involvement in the political affairs of several South American countries. The United States business "presence" in South America has been occasionally mentioned, guardedly discussed, and often romanticized, but it has almost never been seriously examined by television and mass journalism. In fact, at the moment CBS News maintains not a single full-time correspondent in the whole of South America.

Admittedly, it used to be a truism that the public wasn't "interested" in South America, and doubtless that's still so to a considerable degree. Neither was the public "interested" in Europe in the early 1930's, or in Southeast Asia in the middle 1960's, or in the complexities of the Arab world for much of this century. The public, one is told, prefers football games, craves entertainment, and is obsessively concerned with its own neighborhoods–and all that is true. But, on a deeper level, this is the same public that sent grain to Lenin's Russia, and died on French and Italian beaches, and airlifted supplies to West Berlin, and trudged through Philippine, Malayan, and then Vietnamese jungles–and at all times it has counted on *others* to provide it not just with snippets of information but with a coherent picture of its real connection to the larger world. In our time, these others have been mostly journalists, and, lately, television journalists, and too often the picture they have provided has been less than coherent, has been tardy, and has been mainly deferential to an obsolete idea of what is popularly dramatic. "There's no story *there*," says an assignment editor in 1965, looking at a news film of Vietnamese refugees filing by an American adviser team, and thinking back wistfully to newsreels of a commando raid in the Second World War. "There's no story *there*," says a

New York desk man today, reading a dispatch about a social revolt in Chile and comparing it to films of the Tet Offensive six years ago. Then, finally, one day, the "story" —the event, whatever it may be—bursts upon us, emerging, as it were, from its chrysalis, its size and impact invariably enhanced by our earlier ignorance or inattention, and at that point film crews rush off to cover it, and we are informed.

It seems odd, and almost arrogantly reckless, for grown men and women to admit to satisfaction with such a process, but on the surface they appear to. Thus, today we are ensnared as never before in the overseas world, and involved at least as much as ever before with our fellow man—and not merely in a fine-sounding, humanist way but, increasingly, in a bread-and-butter, world-recession, energy-crisis, Middle East-*Realpolitik*, and South American-class-war kind of way—and yet we are pretending that we have scant interest in learning about much beyond the price of lumber in Oregon and the condition of drinking water in Pennsylvania. Naturally, our merely learning about these "foreign" matters will not make them disappear. The point is that it will be a sign of the maturity and responsibility of our broadcast news organizations when the de-facto involvement of the American public with the rest of the world is no longer treated as an episodic, unconnected sequence of superficial events. For some time now, this involvement has been no secret to anybody else.

The Holiday Dinner: A Fable

MOTHER SAID THAT ON ACCOUNT OF WHAT THE PRESIdent had announced the other day about there being a recession, perhaps she ought to cut back on the holiday dinner this year. But Father said he wouldn't hear of such a thing. Father said that a holiday wasn't a proper holiday without one of Mother's special holiday turkeys, with her homemade stuffing on the inside, and a platter of her fresh-baked sweet potatoes on the table and one of her fine homemade pies for dessert, and Little Margaret and Eddie Jr. agreed. Father said that what Mother should do was to "shop around" and find the "best price." Father wasn't sure what the "best price" was, but he said that he knew that Mother would find it, and that that was the way to fight Mr. Ford's recession.

The afternoon before the holiday, Mr. Carmody didn't let Mother out of work until nearly four o'clock, but then Mother shopped around quite a bit and finally found some good buys out in the new supermarket near Wildwood Meadows. Mother came home on the last bus with a fine turkey, some sweet potatoes, fresh carrots, cranberry jelly, flour, butter, onions, parsley, the right bread for the stuffing, and two cans of filling for the pumpkin pie. Father said that it was too bad that Mother had had to shop so late and so had missed Andy Williams's guest appearance on the *Doris Day Holiday Special*, but Eddie Jr. pointed out that Doris Day would soon be appearing on the *Andy Williams Holiday Special*, and Little Margaret reminded Mother that she had already read all about the show in *TV Guide*, including about the comedy skit where Andy and Doris kid around with the twelve Spanish-speaking reindeer. When Mother realized that she hadn't really missed anything, she told Father not to feel badly about it and that she would start getting the kitchen straightened out. Father said that he would go into the living room, where the color set was, and make sure that there was nothing else on that Mother might be missing, and that Little Margaret and Eddie Jr. should help Mother put away the holiday groceries and be quick about it. Little Margaret put the jar of cranberry jelly on the stove. Eddie Jr. picked up the loaf of bread and put it on top of the pile of laundry. Little Margaret opened a Coke from the refrigerator and asked if there was anything else to do. Eddie Jr. moved the loaf of bread to the top of the stove and then remembered that the *Children's Holiday Special* was about to start. He asked Mother if she would like to watch the program while he and Little Margaret tried to figure out where the rest of the groceries should go, but Mother said that she would take care of the groceries and that he and Little Margaret could go and watch the television for a while.

Mother had to work late in the kitchen that evening, preparing the sweet potatoes, and getting the bread and onions and parsley chopped right for the stuffing, and fixing the piecrust for the pumpkin pie. After the *Children's Holiday Special*, Father and the children watched the *Charles Dickens Holiday Showcase*, which featured a special reading, by a leading astronaut, from the original manuscript of *A Christmas Carol;* and *Holy Journey*, which featured a personal tour of the Sea of Galilee by the middleweight champion of the world; and a rerun of the award-winning "Plum-pudding Homicide" from *Kojak*. During commercial breaks, Father made it a point to go out to the kitchen to have a chat with Mother. Father said that he was keeping an eye on the TV to make sure that Mother wasn't missing anything, but that all that was happening now was that Detective Kojak was trailing a homicidal maniac through an abandoned toy store. Father said that nobody made piecrusts the way Mother did. Father offered to open Mother a beer, but Mother said that first she would finish the stuffing and that Father should have a beer, if he would like a beer, and go back to his detective show. Father said that he might do that.

On the morning of the holiday, the alarm clock rang very early, which woke Father and made him irritable, but Mother said that there was no need for him to get up just then. Mother said that she had to start getting the turkey into the oven, and cleaning the platters, and getting the table ready, and Father said that in that case it would be better not to get in her way. When Father came downstairs later, Mother had the table all set, and the turkey was sizzling in the oven, and Mother was putting cranberry jelly in the jelly bowl. Father said that there was nothing like a holiday morning to bring out family spirit. Father said that no matter how hard the times might be, no family of his would ever go without a traditional holiday dinner. Father tasted the stuffing and asked Mother if perhaps she had put in too many onions. Mother said that she didn't think so, because she had made her special homemade stuffing the way she always did. Father sat in the kitchen and sipped at a cup of coffee. Father said that it was funny that the stuffing tasted so strongly of onions. The sound of a marching band came from the television set in the living room. Father got to his feet, and yawned, and said that he might very well step in there and see what was going on.

Little Margaret and Eddie Jr. were in pajamas on the floor of the living room, watching balloonlike cartoon characters float down a city street. "Isn't this the most exciting parade you've ever seen?" a woman announcer said to a tall man in a fur coat. "It sure is, Linda," said the man. An enormous balloon version of Mickey Mouse wafted by. Except for the remainder of the marching band, and two television trucks, there appeared to be only a handful of people on the street. "Wow, isn't that Mickey Mouse?" said Linda. "That's right," said the man in the fur coat. "That's Mickey Mouse, all right." Father reached forward and switched channels. A different city street appeared, with bright sunlight this time. Another marching band went by. An announcer's voice said, "That's the Pollard Junior High School marching band." A second voice said,

"That's right, Bob. They're one hundred and twenty-eight strong, and they've been participating in these festivities for seven years." A float featuring floral replicas of cartoon characters moved slowly down the sunlit street. "Say, isn't that Snow White and the Seven Dwarfs?" said the first announcer. "That's right, Bob," said the other voice. "And, right behind, that looks like Dumbo the Flying Elephant! I'd call this a magical time, wouldn't you?" Little Margaret appeared to be poking Eddie Jr. with her foot. Father asked Little Margaret what she was doing with her foot. Little Margaret said that she wasn't doing anything with her foot. Suddenly Eddie Jr. reached out and hit Little Margaret in the stomach. Little Margaret howled. Father kicked Eddie Jr., and Eddie Jr. began to cry. Mother called from the kitchen to ask what was happening. Father called back that everything was under control. Father told Little Margaret and Eddie Jr. to go upstairs and get dressed or he would knock their heads together. Father switched channels to where a man in a turtleneck sweater was seated at a desk in front of a blackboard on which the word "Defense" had been written. Or, rather, it had been written as two words: "De fense." "The name of the game in today's N.F.L. is *de*-fense," said the man in the turtleneck sweater. There was a film of a football player running and being tackled. Then of another player running and being tackled. Then of a third player running and being tackled. "They don't come any better than Roger Conboy," said the man in the turtleneck sweater. From the kitchen there was the sound of a plate breaking. Upstairs, Little Margaret shrieked. The doorbell rang. "I'll get it," said Father.

There was another film, this time of a quarterback dropping back to pass. As he stepped backward, three enormous tacklers ran in toward him. The quarterback started running to the side. He threw the ball—a long, arcing pass. A man juggled it, caught it. Began to run. At the door, Mother greeted Aunt Sarah and Uncle George. Cousin Phil helped Grandmother into the house—at least, as far as the bench in the hallway, where she sat down to rest.

Aunt Sarah and Mother went out to the kitchen. Uncle George and Father and Cousin Phil stood in front of the television set and watched highlights from last week's Kansas City–Oakland game. Little Margaret and Eddie Jr. came downstairs. Father said that they should go out and help Mother, instead of always hanging around. Eddie Jr. asked why Grandmother was sitting on a bench out in the front hall. Uncle George and Cousin Phil went out to the hall, where Grandmother was asleep, and reminded Grandmother that it was the holiday, and brought her into the dining room. Father and Uncle George and Cousin Phil stood in the living room and watched highlights from last week's Pittsburgh-Cincinnati game and from last week's Dallas-Washington game. Mother said that dinner was ready.

Everyone agreed that Mother had never produced a better-looking turkey than she had this year. Even Aunt Sarah, who was Father's sister and was a stickler for tradition, pronounced it as fine-looking a bird as she could remember. Father suggested that Uncle George should "do the honors" in carving the turkey, because, as Father said,

Uncle George really knew his stuff when it came to carving, and Mother's turkey deserved the very best. Father stepped into the living room, where, on the television set, two football teams were in position for a kickoff. A whistle blew. The ball sailed into the air. "Hardy takes it on the five," said the announcer. "He picks up blocking. The fifteen, the twenty. He's brought down by Dobson and Gilpenny." Father sat down in the chair in front of the television set. "It's a pitchout to Owens," the announcer said. "He gets to the twenty-six, where he's brought down by Mayes." And "Johnson steps back to throw. It's over the head of tight end Walter Jethroe. Jethroe has been plagued by injuries this year. Lew, I think he's still bothered by that hamstring." And "It's third and four. Johnson will put it in the air. No, it's a draw to Enderby." And "Lew, just then we saw a change we didn't get a chance to comment on. I think I better comment on that now. Willie Smith, defensive end, is in there playing for Eddie Naismith." Mother called to Father that his turkey was ready, and Father said that he would be right in. Father sat down at the table and smacked his hands together. Father said that certainly looked to him like a plateful of turkey. Father said that Eddie Jr. should stop scooping up all the cranberry jelly and leave some for other people. Uncle George asked if there was any score yet. Father said that there was no score yet but that Johnson's arm was still cold. Little Margaret said that she thought football was a stupid game. Mother said for Little Margaret not to talk to her father that way. Father looked at Little Margaret. Father cleared his throat and put his napkin on the table. Father said that what was stupid for some people was not always stupid for other people. Father said that some people were not always in a position to judge what was stupid or not. Father said that in his opinion somebody who had spent his or her entire life watching reruns of *Gilligan's Island* and *McHale's Navy* while talking to pimply adolescents on the telephone might be such a person. Father said that *McHale's Navy* wasn't even accurate about the war. "What war?" Grandmother asked. "Oh, *Grandmother!*" Aunt Sarah said. Cousin Phil said, "There isn't any war." Grandmother started to cough. "I hope you're pleased with yourself," Aunt Sarah said to Father. "Pass Grandmother some more candied sweet potatoes," Mother said. "Grandmother, don't you want more of those candied sweet potatoes?"

Father got up to get some cider for Mother from the kitchen. On his way back, he thought he just might pass through the living room. Uncle George and Cousin Phil were standing in front of the television set. Uncle George said for Cousin Phil to sit back down and finish his dinner. A mass of green-and-white and red-and-white players were at the center of the field. "Henderson gets no farther than the twenty-two," said the announcer. "The first medical reports on Gilpenny have just come in," said another announcer. "He's torn the ligaments in his knee." "That sounds like the right knee, Lew," the first announcer said. "Loomis drops back to pass. He's got plenty of time. He fires. Right on the button to Billy Van Edwards, who is upended on the thirty-six-yard line by Harry Widcombe."

Father and Uncle George sat in two chairs. The announcer said, "Enderby bangs up the middle for three." And "Johnson pitches out to Owens. He goes out of bounds on the forty-two." And "Let's take another look at that. Here's Johnson moving to his left. There's Big Ed Fogarty coming down the middle. Third and long yardage. Johnson goes back and throws. It's over the head of Otis Farney."

Mother and Aunt Sarah cleared the dishes after the main course. Aunt Sarah asked Eddie Jr. what he was doing underneath the table. Eddie Jr. said that he wasn't underneath the table. Mother brought in the pumpkin pie and the dessert plates. "Billy Van Edwards was out there in the flat, but the pass was wide," the announcer said. "That was great protection, Lew." And "Now Bengston gets back to kick. He hangs it high. Rowen is under it. He's hit hard by Delmonico and Harry Widcombe." And "Enderby bangs for two yards down the middle." And "Enderby gets the call again. Three, maybe four. Lew, you'd have to say the middle of that line is tough." Mother called to Father that his favorite dessert was on the table. Father and Uncle George went back into the dining room. Uncle George said that that was what he would call a piece of pie. Father smacked his hands. Mother said that she hoped that Father's team was ahead. Father said that football was not such a big deal with him that he would pass up a piece of pie like this one. Father told Eddie Jr. to go easy on the whipped cream. Grandmother said that she was reminded of the time she once visited her sister in San Francisco. Her sister was married to a man who had a telescope on the back lawn. She thought his name was Harding or Todhunter—she wasn't sure. A cheer emanated from the television set. Father said that he would be back in half a moment.

The announcer said, "Johnson throws deep to Walter Jethroe." And "Simmons pitches out to Henderson. Henderson gets to the thirty-five." And "Owens goes in for the score." And "Harry Widcombe is getting up slowly." And "Talbot just made it 27–10." And "Enderby goes nowhere up the middle." Aunt Sarah brought two cups of coffee into the living room for Father and Uncle George. After a while, Father switched channels. Men in green-and-yellow uniforms were running after a man in a red-and-brown uniform. "That's some kind of day Larry Temple is having," said the announcer. Mother brought out the plate of pie that Father hadn't finished, and put it on the table beside him. Two men in red-and-brown uniforms fell on a man in a green-and-yellow uniform. "They're going to have to figure out a way of containing Elroyd and Luchetti," said the announcer. Father told Mother that he had never tasted such a fine pumpkin pie. Uncle George said that he would certainly go along with that. A man in a green-and-yellow uniform threw a pass into the sideline. "Oh, my!" Mother said. Father asked if Mother would like to watch for a bit, but Mother said that she had better clear up the dinner things first, since otherwise she would only worry over them. Father said that if that was what Mother wanted to do, Mother should feel free to do as she pleased, and Uncle George said he would go along with that, too.

At half-time, Father came out to the kitchen to get two beers for Uncle George and himself. Mother was washing the dishes. Aunt Sarah was reading one of Mother's recipe books. Father asked where the children were. Mother said that they were helping take out the garbage. Father went upstairs and found Little Margaret, Eddie Jr., and Cousin Phil watching the *Holiday Cartoon Festival* on the upstairs television set. Father said that they should go downstairs and help or they would all be in big trouble. "I did the clearing, but Eddie Jr. didn't," said Little Margaret. Eddie Jr. and Cousin Phil said that they hadn't known that any clearing was being done. Little Margaret stuck out her tongue at Eddie Jr., and Eddie Jr. hit her on the neck. Father went downstairs. "Let's watch that fake again," said the announcer. "Here's Joe Don Nevelson on the inside. We still don't know what the penalty is." And "Grigsby cracks over the right side for three yards." And "Bendix fires one to Larry Temple. He's upended by Wally Hindenburg on the thirty-six." Aunt Sarah came in to say that Grandmother was asleep at the dining-room table. Aunt Sarah came back in to say that it was time for Uncle George to leave, in order to drive Grandmother to the bus station. Uncle George and Aunt Sarah had an argument. "Purvew and Carraway are wide," said the announcer. "Simmons hands to Patterson. He makes six. I think Vic Luchetti was in on that one, Bill." Aunt Sarah, Uncle George, Grandmother, and Cousin Phil made ready to leave in Uncle George's car. It was dark outside. Aunt Sarah said that they were going to be late to the bus station, on account of the traffic. Uncle George said that there wasn't going to be any traffic. Cousin Phil forgot his windbreaker and had to go back in to look for it. Mother gave Grandmother a package of candied sweet potatoes wrapped in tinfoil. Father waved goodbye and told Mother that she should get back inside, on account of the cold.

Back in the house, Father said that if Cousin Phil didn't get his head screwed on properly, one of these days he was going to lose it. Father picked up an ashtray and an empty can of beer from the hall table and carried them to the sideboard in the dining room. In the living room, the sunlit football field glowed yellow-green. "Simmons fires to Murdoch," the announcer said. And "Trezevant reaches the midfield stripe." And "Snelling goes wide. Simmons rolls to the right and fires. Incomplete." Father went out to the kitchen, where Mother was drying the glasses. Father said that he didn't know where Mother got all her energy. Father said that since it was a holiday and Mother had all the dishes nearly put away, maybe she would like to go to a show or something, or maybe go bowling. Mother said that that was a very nice invitation, because she had certainly enjoyed the time she and Father and Mr. Van Ness had gone bowling last summer, but she thought that she might prefer just to sit down as soon as she was finished and watch some television. Father said that that was a very sensible idea. Father said that there was no point in driving all over town on a holiday evening, even if Charlie Van Ness and a good bunch of fellows were likely to be at the bowling alley. Father picked up one of the glasses Mother had dried, and held it for a moment, and then put it down on top of the washing machine. Father said that he would be out in the living room.

On the television set, there was a blur of people streaming out of a stadium. "Ted, I think you'd have to say that the key to today's upset was that Bob Bendix was never able to get his running game going," said the announcer. Father switched channels. A man in a pink denim jacket, with a guitar, was singing "Ave Maria" in a Southern accent. Father switched again. Football players in orange-and-black uniforms were lined up against football players in blue-and-white uniforms. "Third and a long six," the announcer said. "Hawkins gets back. He throws. Travis Dobson takes it on the forty-one and is knocked out of bounds by Dover Welling." And "Hawkins throws deep to Domrich." And "Langthorne gets four across the middle." And "That was great second effort from Marvin Langthorne. Now second and seven. Moncrieff is blitzing. Hawkins throws incomplete to Homer Hayden." The football field shimmered in the darkened room. There was a closeup of six girl cheerleaders in cowboy costumes. A man in a leopard suit stood on the sideline. A mass of players converged at the far end of the field. "That was some kind of catch," said the announcer. "Let's take a look at the move that Travis Dobson made on Sonderby." During half-time, Father went upstairs to see how Mother was getting along. Mother was in bed asleep. The dim sound of gunfire came from Little Margaret's room. Father looked in. Little Margaret and Eddie Jr. were face down on the floor, also asleep. On the small television set, a black policeman was carrying a white policeman out of a burning house. Father turned off the set and poked Little Margaret and Eddie Jr., who both started to cry, and told them to get to bed. Father went back downstairs. "Second and seven," said the announcer. "Phillips goes back. He's looking downfield. He throws to Wally Binton on the thirty." Father went out to the kitchen, where he opened the refrigerator and took out a can of beer. The remains of the turkey were under a layer of tinfoil on the bottom shelf. Father reached under the tinfoil and wrenched off a drumstick. Father closed the refrigerator, and took the drumstick and the can of beer back into the living room, and sat down in a chair. "Carraway is upended by Billings," the announcer said. "Second and six. Henderson and Bonfils are wide. Foster hands off to Noonan, and Noonan bangs up the middle for about two." There was the sound of a toilet flushing upstairs. A man in a Santa Claus costume came on to sell car batteries. "Let's take another look at Big Manny Enriquez," said the announcer. "Here he reads the draw perfectly and cuts down Speedy Tompkins at the line of scrimmage." Father took a bite out of the drumstick and a sip from the can of beer. There was a closeup of the man in the leopard suit dancing with one of the cheerleaders. Father leaned forward and turned the color knob so that the field was the right shade of green. "Henderson is stopped at the forty-five," the announcer said. Two men in orange-and-black uniforms stood motionless upon the field of green and then began to run diagonally. A whistle blew. A car door slammed far down the street. "Veronis was offside on that one," the announcer said. The house was dark and still, except for the glow of the football field and the voice of the announcer. Father put the drumstick on the table and held the can of beer on his knee.

The trouble with some people, Father always said, was too much holiday.

Snapshots from Operation Attleboro

THERE HAS BEEN A KIND OF QUIET ABOUT THE TELEvision news lately—almost a silence—though one knows that there are plenty of stories being reported on, and that this quiet doesn't necessarily imply an absence of event or significance. Maybe it's that, as one watches the figures on the screen, one knows that we ourselves are part of the drama—but how does one know *which* part? And how is the connection to the drama made? The other night, for instance, I skimmed the channels for the evening's news: surely this is one of the more pleasurable sensations of modern technological life—to thus sit before a working piece of machinery and summon reports from Olympus about the day's doings. Hello, John Chancellor, Harry Reasoner, Walter Cronkite! What an odd fate has bound us all together: these Newsmen, in their working-reporter clothes, with their sensible faces and steady voices, and we —*the News*—each night heaved up on kitchen beaches across the land, attending vaguely to kids and wives, opening a beer, shoving the bills behind the breadbox, and watching with half an eye for these nightly certifications of our shared existence.

The news that night was, as it often is, fast-paced and various. CBS showed film of a reprisal by Israeli townspeople against a Palestinian attack. ABC reported on an attempt to kidnap the Philippine ambassador in Washington. CBS said that sugar prices would drop next year. NBC showed scenes of auto workers standing in unemployment lines in Detroit and said that Chrysler was shutting down five of its seven assembly plants. Since President Ford was in Japan that week, all the networks strove to provide scenes and documentation of the Presidential visit. Emperor Hirohito was shown—at a distance—toasting Mr. Ford. Mr. Ford was shown—also at a distance—toasting the Japanese. "President Ford toasted the ties that bind the two countries," said an invisible correspondent. Back in New York, ABC reported that former President Nixon's lawyers had agreed to permit a court-approved physical exam. CBS showed scientists gathering for an ecology conference. From Tokyo, NBC's John Chancellor appeared in closeup, against a tree-lined street, and said, "The historical importance is that the President of the United States was welcomed in the Japanese capital by the head of the Japanese state." NBC showed film of the Israeli reprisal against the Palestinian terrorists: a stark scene of bleeding bodies and contorted, angry faces. CBS reported on a strip-mining bill, and Eric Sevareid talked about the "economic warfare" that now threatened to undermine the world. ABC showed President Ford in Japan, receiving the Order of the

Golden Pheasant from a group of Japanese Boy Scouts. And so it went.

It's hard to say what seemed so strange, or quiet, or *off*, about this news. It certainly wasn't a matter of a decline in television's routine professional competence. Granted, network news is usually too official and too much concerned with official happenings, but that wasn't what seemed wrong about it. I could say that I had the feeling from watching the news that something had been left out, though that also seems too simple a view to take. Besides, if there were a "thing" that one could leave out of news, what would that "thing" be?

Then, on a certain morning recently, as I walked to work—a cold and gray morning, with damp in the air, and the feeling of concrete beneath one's feet—I was struck by an odd sensation, almost a kind of flashback. I mention the quality of the morning not to try to be poetic but because it was one of those gray urban moments that invite cheap philosophy and thoughts of mortality. There was also something oddly quiet about the city at the time. I've walked this particular stretch of street many days of my life, but on this morning I found myself suddenly remembering that it was *there*, at such-and-such an intersection, that eight years ago I had watched one of the first anti-war parades of the Vietnam period, and it was *there*, at that Park entrance, that in 1966 I had heard a man denounce the war as "murder," until he was driven off by the police. Right where I now stood, in early 1967, I remembered watching one of the pro-war parades march by. There had been an elderly Legionnaire being pushed in a wheelchair, holding up a placard: "It's Your Country! Love It or Leave It!" Two longhairs—"hippies," they were called then—had tried to distribute anti-war leaflets on the sidewalk and had been rushed and beaten by a number of the marchers. Such a curiously textured, distant time! Often the city had seemed quiet then, too. I remembered an old friend—a kindly, thoughtful man—telling me, one evening in the sixties, "Yes, I feel the war is wasteful. But I'm not *sure*. And we can't just pull out now, can we?" Some years later, I think, he flew to Washington with members of his law firm to protest the bombing of Cambodia.

Now, as I reached my office—on this more recent and quieter morning—I found myself wondering what the television news had really been like in those days, when so much had actually been going on, and when so many people in the country knew so little about it—and in so many cases were so desperately unsure of even what to feel. It happens that I used to keep notes of certain news programs that I watched. I don't think that I'd ever expected to use the notes again, and I had stuffed them into two old boxes, along with canceled checks and health-insurance forms. Anyway, here is a rough outline of the *CBS Evening News* for a random fall day—November 24, 1966:

The lead story that night was about United States maneuvers in the United Nations General Assembly to defeat the proposed admission of Red China. Walter Cronkite had two reports on this subject. President Johnson was home in Texas after an operation, and there was a report on how he was being kept informed of the U.N. situation. Vietnam:

Walter Cronkite said that an American patrol had been overrun by Vietcong in the Ia Drang Valley. From Saigon, a correspondent was shown standing in a field of tall grass beside some helicopters, and he reported on the progress of Operation Attleboro, one of the army's "sweeps" against the Vietcong. "The men of Operation Attleboro are using heavy firepower from artillery and also coordinated air strikes in order to clear out the enemy," said the correspondent. In New York, Walter Cronkite said that a conference of Roman Catholic bishops had approved the war. Jordan was asking the U.N. to condemn Israel. The Haitian government denied an invasion rumor. There was a story from Germany about the neo-Nazi Party's success in a recent election. There was a film of Robert Kennedy visiting his brother's grave, and talking with Secretary of Defense Robert McNamara. There was a film of Governor Rockefeller and George Romney vacationing together in Puerto Rico. Lester Maddox attacked the A.C.L.U. Vietnam: Morley Safer had a story about soldiers going on leave to Hong Kong. "One assignment no G.I. is ever late for is a trip to Hong Kong for R. and R.," said Morley Safer. Walter Cronkite told of a Bulgarian airliner that had crashed after takeoff, and of a pilots' strike against Qantas Airlines. He said that so far six thousand United States servicemen had been killed in Vietnam. In Mississippi, a man pleaded guilty to the shooting of James Meredith. Vietnam again: a CBS correspondent explained the "complex problems" that the military encountered in getting Thanksgiving turkeys to the troops in the field. Jordan announced a call-up of able-bodied men . . .

What does one make of such a trip into the past? On one level, it was quite poignant. That passing image of Robert Kennedy! Or the almost boyish assurance of the CBS correspondent who reported on Operation Attleboro! Had Robert Kennedy been real? Had Operation Attleboro been real: all those Operations, with the whirring helicopters, and the men fanning out against the buffalo grass; and all those correspondents who had stood in fields or outside canvas tents—a microphone in one hand, a cameraman in front of them—as they composed the American involvement in Southeast Asia into film clips for the evening news? But on another level it was not poignant at all. For although Operation Attleboro had been real, the news about it had not been real. The shipment of Thanksgiving turkeys had been real, but the news about it had not been real. The G.I.s cheerily boarding military-transport planes for a seven-day furlough in Hong Kong had been real, and, as it turned out, Morley Safer's personal disapproval of the war they were being furloughed from had been real. But the story he told had pursued a different logic. The event might have been real, as an event. But the story in the end, on a deep level, had not been true to its own imagery or implications.

Certainly there are differences between the way the networks dealt with news then and the way they deal with it today. For one thing, an American military involvement overseas now wouldn't be likely to elicit benign majority approval from the nation's citizens, or the same kind of assured—and, on the whole, benign—reporting from the nation's television newsmen. For another thing, after Presidents Johnson and Nixon, after Vietnam and Watergate, it has become increasingly acceptable for news organizations to take a skeptical attitude toward official authority. Lately, there seem to be signs of slightly greater sophistication on the big news programs. There's less lofty didacticism on the part of studio newscasters, and more opportunity for reporters in the field to occasionally insert a personal or human note. Sometimes, now, newsmen even ask tough questions. As occurred the other day when ABC's Harry Reasoner, ensnared for fifteen minutes in one of those numbing Ed Murrow-*Person to Person*-type interviews with the high and mighty—in this case, a tour of Camp David with President Gerald Ford—finally sat himself down before the President and said, "I suppose the basic criticism is that your Administration so far seems rudderless . . . Is there something in that?" And "Can you *grow* into this job, sir?" The President answered both queries in a vague and amiable manner, asserting that he was "moving the ship of state right down the middle," and so forth; and perhaps he hadn't quite understood the questions. It was an odd moment, though. For years, journalism critics have censured television reporters for not asking tough questions. Tough questions were supposed to untangle complexity and create truth—and doubtless they can when they are not fired into the bland pudding of a chief of state. At any rate, here were tough questions—being swallowed up by pudding. But could one have imagined a network newsman even *asking* such questions of a high official back in 1966? *General Westmoreland, there have been criticisms that your military campaign is rudderless. What do you say to that, sir?*

It's tricky, obviously, to draw too strict a sense of déjà vu from a comparison of the evening news this fall with that of eight years ago. Too many things everywhere have changed. We are no longer concerned with trying to keep Red China out of the United Nations, or with President Johnson's operation, or with Lester Maddox, or even with Vietnam. Instead, we are faced with great quantities of people out of work, with challenges to the world's foundations of trade, with threats of war and the evidence of hunger and starvation in many areas of the globe. Our position is clearly in a state of flux. Geologic shifts can be observed increasingly beneath the surface of government and authority. Change is either in the air, or beckons all around us.

But some things haven't changed very much. Television, for example. Neither the structure of television news nor its basic approach nor the note struck by it seems to have altered appreciably in the past decade. There have been surface changes in procedure. News is now more popular, and efforts are made to present it more attractively and personably. Camera and transmission techniques have been improved. But the system remains the same, and this should concern us, because, by and large, the collection, the selection, and the *form* of the news beamed by American television to the American public are essentially similar to what they were ten years ago. By that I mean that the same system of communications which gave this country its sense of itself, and of the war, during the Vietnam period gives us our sense of ourselves, and of our difficult situation, today. By that I mean that the tendency of network news to fragment and trivialize events and flux (which it calls "news") has become virtually automatic. Suppose one asked, What is the important story of the time? Is it a military engagement in Southeast Asia? Is it a precarious conflict of interest in the Middle East? Is it the deep dissociations and inequities forced on a nation during even a partial economic collapse? Suppose one then asked, Now, if *you* had such a story to tell, and thought it *important*, would you contrive to tell it only in bits and pieces—say, an item before dinner, and then some further observations between dessert and coffee, and perhaps a "windup statement" before putting the cat out for the night?

It seems to me that the crucial failure of television news during the Vietnam period was not its early bias toward the government (which was somewhat understandable, given the conventions of the time) but that it abused its own powers. Pierre Mendès-France once observed, "To govern is to *choose*." One could add that to inform, to communicate, to give the news is to choose. As a device, television can communicate virtually anything. It can reveal people—which is why so many politicians have tried to control it. It can reveal processes, even the most intrinsically boring of processes, and make them clear, unfold their coherence: senators reading from testimony in a committee hearing room; men waiting for hours on an aircraft-carrier deck for a parachute to appear in the sky. Admittedly, there has to be a willingness on the part of the public to watch the people or to observe the processes, but—what is surely just as important in this other-directed era of "priorities" and image—there has to be a willingness on the part of the communicator to communicate *this* particular story, to put his bets on *this* particular event. To choose to make *this* process clear. I remember, in the fall of 1967, talking with a network-news executive who was about to leave for a quick trip to Saigon. "It's the most important event of my generation," he proclaimed, "and I have to see it." In fact, we both expected the war to be over by that winter. "Why don't you run more about it on the news?" I asked. He looked at me. "The public wouldn't stand for it," he said. He was right, of course, in that the public wasn't keen on watching an endless unfurling of one-minute film reports on Operation Attleboro, or of officious interviews with General Westmoreland, or of scenes of ghostly, distant combat in unexplained jungles. But the public was never given anything else about the war to watch, or any other way to watch it. When a few "news specials" were made about the war, they were made from the same semi-official, disconnected point of view, and they were usually aired late in the evening—past "prime time." For most of the time on television, the Vietnam war was rarely *prime*. It was chopped up for us. Fragmented. Sensible men with steady voices doled it out to us in bits and pieces. And for nearly ten years the American nation was adrift, tangled in this seemingly remote and deadly matter, and also detached from it, and not so much misinformed by television reporting (although there was that, too) as indulged in its own distractedness by television-news leadership.

And so this fall, as I said, it seems strange to be *again* in a hard time—a hard, quiet time—and watching the news. In its measured, far-off delivery, the news speaks about "layoffs at Chrysler." About "work forces." Percentages. Was it five plants shut down, or seven? Were they Palestinians screaming in the courtyard in Beit Shean, or Israelis? Which man held up the knife? Who made the speech? The Philippine ambassador is kidnapped. The Philippine ambassador is safe. Here's some weather. A new strip-mining bill. Here's President Ford. Isn't that the Japanese Imperial Palace off there in the blur? "The Imperial Palace sits within a kind of 240-acre estate," John Chancellor said. One imagines that John Chancellor himself must feel pretty distracted, chatting up the Imperial Palace in distant, war-torn Tokyo. No, Beit Shean, in Israel, is war-torn. Tokyo is fine, except that its economy (according to the *Times*) is close to collapse and the government is expected to fall. President Ford is fine, too. John Chancellor is fine. We have a few problems, of course, but everything is fine here, too. Good night from Saigon. Good night from Tokyo, New York, and London. Good night from Vladivostok, Beit Shean, the Houston Astrodome, and Chrysler. Good night, good night. Later, we'll find out how it really was.

The Cold, Bright Charms of Immortality

In the modern world, death breaks into our lives suddenly—as it were, by surprise—even though it remains a fact that most men and women in this country still die in their beds of what used to be called old age. A death occurs in the family! Long-distance telephone calls crisscross through the night. The survivors—uneasy with a sense of uniqueness, their separate grief imprisoned in their separate civilities—stand about in suits and overcoats while tiny explosions detonate inside their heads, and then start for home.

The Sioux, I'm told, placed their dead on platforms up in the branches of trees along the Platte River—companionable treefuls of dead Sioux. The Crow made sure to show their grief by cutting off part of a finger. The Arapaho acknowledged death's imminence by singing a song to it; an abandoned warrior, dying, would brace himself against a rock and sing the Death Song until he died. Generally, nowadays, we do things differently.

An uncle of mine died a few weeks ago—a kind and modest man whom I much cared about; he was seventy-three at the time of his heart attack, which, as my sister insisted, had come "out of nowhere." His dying naturally made me think of death—at first, in the usual manner, whereby for a while after the death of a close friend or relative harsh winds of mortality gust with a sudden, temporary significance through the heads of those remaining. Then, perhaps because he had been such a calm, methodical, gently purposive man, and there had been something calm, methodical, and—yes—gently purposive about his death and the manner of its arrival, I found myself feeling the moment quite differently. For an instant, death itself seemed almost like a modest, commonplace event—perhaps like what it was. In his fine book *The Lives of a Cell,* Dr. Lewis Thomas has written: "There are three billion of us on the earth, and all three billion must be dead, on a schedule, within this lifetime." Just then, from inside one's modern, individual isolation, one could nearly sense the dim, communal, ordinary idea of a mortality that was beyond us, and that human beings sometimes reached for—without attaining. And so afterward, mindful of the invisible community, I thought of television, and wondered what—were I to watch it steadily for a while—I might find that this pervasive communicator was telling us, or not telling us, about our mass, ongoing, connective activity; about death.

I picked a finite period of one week to study, and therein I watched, with reasonable fidelity, ten or twelve hours each day. I wrote down only references to death or dying, as follows:

FRIDAY: On *The Edge of Night*, there were two references to the earlier murder of a young woman named Taffy Simms. On *Days of Our Lives*, Bob said, "Phyllis, you almost died." From the NBC local news: "A mine disaster in northern France has claimed forty-one lives." And "Eighteen persons were killed in Brazil this morning as a train crashed into a bus." And "Fifteen died today in Portugal when two passenger trains collided outside a railroad station in Lisbon." And "Eighteen people were reported strangled in the Ethiopian city of Asmara. This brings the total number of deaths by strangulation to forty-five." The death of Jack Benny was reported, accompanied by a photograph of Benny during his early days on radio, when he worked for NBC, and prominently displaying the NBC microphone. There was a film from Darwin, Australia, that briefly showed a dead victim of the Darwin cyclone being carried away on a stretcher, and also presented an interview with a survivor. "What happened to your wife?" the reporter asked. "My wife was killed," the survivor said. The CBS network news mentioned the forty-one mine-explosion deaths in France, and the fifteen Portuguese who had been killed this morning in a train crash "just outside Lisbon's main railroad station." There was an item about Jack Benny: "Benny Kubelsky, better known as Jack Benny, died in his home today of cancer. For half a century, Jack Benny made people laugh by laughing at himself." On *Kolchak*, a score of people were murdered by a vampire. In the movie *The Last Run*, a man fell to his death; another man was shot and then burned up in a car; two men were killed in a gunfight. On *Police Woman*, the dead body of a man was found in a car trunk, and four men were killed in a gunfight.

SATURDAY: There were no deaths in any of the entertainment programs. From the NBC network news: "In recent months, more than twenty thousand people have died of starvation" in Bangladesh. And "Doctors have said that more tests will be needed to determine the cause of the fall last evening which resulted in the death of columnist Amy Vanderbilt. Miss Vanderbilt was an authority and author of several books on etiquette." In an ABC documentary, *Crashes: The Illusion of Safety*, there were references to numerous plane crashes, in which a total of forty-eight hundred people had died. On the NBC late news, there was an item about a retired policeman who had been shot and killed. And "There still appears to be some mystery surrounding the death of columnist Amy Vanderbilt. Police have indicated the possibility of suicide, although her husband has said he knows of nothing to indicate that motivation."

SUNDAY: On *World of Survival*, a reef crab was killed by an octopus. "A very sad day for the crab," said the announcer. From the CBS local news: "Pakistani authorities have estimated that over three hundred people have been killed in an earthquake in northern Pakistan." And "Nicaraguan guerrillas killed three guards yesterday." And

"Three persons were killed in a four-car accident at the corner of Barlow and a Hundred and Thirty-ninth Street." CBS News (whose parent company, CBS, had hired Benny away from NBC) provided an hour-long *Tribute to Jack Benny*. There were brief scenes of Hollywood celebrities arriving in cars. "This was the day of his [Jack Benny's] funeral, and all of Hollywood was there," said correspondent Charles Kuralt. A 1967 CBS tape showed the late Ed Sullivan. "It's true that Jack Benny spoke his first words on the air on an Ed Sullivan radio show," said Mr. Kuralt. Benny's former CBS announcer, Don Wilson, said, "Jack, above all, was a great human being . . . Jack was a very normal person . . . He never went to a psychiatrist–he never had to." There was a tape of Benny's recent appearance with Dinah Shore on CBS's *Dinah!* "One of the last times he made us laugh was just this fall, when the premiere of the new Dinah Shore program had a walk-on guest," said Charles Kuralt. Milton Berle said, "We've lost an institution . . . It's like the sinking of the Statue of Liberty." CBS board chairman, William Paley, was interviewed and spoke of Benny's "professionalism that was unique and outstanding." There was a tape of Benny doing a skit with his violin. "The violin is stilled," said Mr. Kuralt. On *Kojak*, an old man was shot to death by gangsters, and two men were killed in a gunfight. On *Columbo*, one woman was strangled to death, and another woman was drowned in her bathtub.

MONDAY: On *The Edge of Night*, there were two references to the murder of Taffy Simms. In a Popeye cartoon, a bully was pushed off a tall building and fell into an open coffin, which was hammered closed. From the ABC local news: "A sniper, armed with a rifle, has killed three people in the town of Olean, New York." And "The dead are still being counted at the scene of the massive earthquake in northern Pakistan." From the ABC network news: "Authorities in northwest Pakistan say the death toll from an earthquake there has reached four thousand seven hundred, and is likely to go higher." On *Gunsmoke*, two men were killed in a gunfight. On *Born Free*, a man was killed by a leopard. In *Frankenstein: The True Story*, seven corpses were disinterred.

TUESDAY: From the CBS local news: "Twelve fishermen are feared drowned after two boats capsized in heavy seas" off the coast of southern Italy. And "An Israeli patrol reportedly shot and killed three guerrillas as they were spotted crossing the border." On *Hawaii Five-O*, a man was murdered with a hara-kiri knife, and another man was shot and killed in a gunfight. On *Barnaby Jones*, a man was killed in a gunfight.

WEDNESDAY: From the NBC local and network news: "Twenty-three persons were feared dead as a busload of holiday skiers plunged into a lake near the town of Omachi, north of Tokyo." And "Two policemen were killed this afternoon in an auto accident as they were driving in response to an emergency call." On *Cannon*, one man was killed in an overturned car, and another man was shot to death by a rifle. On *The Manhunter*, one man was killed by being pushed out of a tall building, and another man was killed by a pistol shot.

THURSDAY: On *The Edge of Night*, a character referred to "the tragic death of Taffy Simms." Three bandits were blown up by dynamite in a Popeye cartoon. From the ABC local news: "Word from the National Safety Council is that this year's Christmas holiday death toll is down by 20 percent." From the ABC network news: "Four Arab civilians were killed by Israelis in a raid across the border early this morning." On *Ironside*, a judge shot to death a man who was trying to kill him. On *Harry O*, an unknown man was shot to death; a woman was beaten to death; another man was shot to death, and the man who shot him was killed. From the ABC late news: "Fire killed a two-year-old girl and injured several members of her family. Indications are that the victim, Carmen Allen, had been playing with matches."

It's hard to know what a "survey" of this kind proves, beyond the obvious, which in this case is that we are a violent people—seemingly entranced by violence—and have no serious regard for death. Also, I'm not at all sure what can be conveyed in prose of the experience of watching television for its acknowledgments of death. Twelve hours or so of television for seven days adds up to roughly eighty-four hours of more or less continuous broadcasting—the equivalent of around a half million words. How to convey the *absence* of death—real death—from this daily torrent of supposedly realistic narrative and imagery?

On the whole, a study of death on television turns up few surface surprises. After all, it should be no surprise by now that half of American network prime-time entertainment programming seems to be crime-oriented, and employs death by murder or in gunfights casually and routinely, as a simple plot device. (In fact, in most detective programs nowadays—as if they were following a prescribed ritual—there is usually a key murder of an unknown but significant figure within the first five minutes; there is sometimes a throwaway murder of a secondary character in the middle; and there is invariably a gunfight, which kills off one or two secondary or unknown characters, within the last five minutes.) Nor, in the area of news reporting, should it be much of a surprise that the detached and captionlike quality of the networks' regular news coverage is generally carried over into their accounts of death in the nation and across the world. Thus, snippets of information about the death of Brazilians in a bus crash or of Frenchmen in a mine disaster are blithely transmitted between snippets of information about factory layoffs in Detroit or gold speculation in London.

Perhaps, in the end, the surprise is that one is so little surprised. We accept the fact that death is mentioned so rarely on television—and usually in such a relentlessly offhand and stylized manner—because we apparently accept the idea that, as a nation, we have no wish to confront death, or deal with it, except by euphemism and avoidance. Doubtless, to a considerable extent this is true. It doesn't seem to be true of most of the rest of the world, especially of the poorer and less advanced countries, where—despite enormous populations, and the contrary expectations of many Western military experts—people appear to care hugely about human life and death, but perhaps it is more true of technologically progressive countries, or, at any rate, it is becoming true. Still, even here in America—with our Forest Lawns and pet cemeteries—our proverbial avoidance of or uncaringness about death often seems illusory or skin-deep. In private lives, for example, there are surely myriad explosions of grief, incomprehension, and deep human response taking place literally all the time in the isolation of families where death occurs. And in public America—though the surface appears impervious to death—it was, ironically, television that, some time ago, on the occasions of the deaths of the two Kennedy brothers and Dr. Martin Luther King, helped the American people break through their apparent fear of death and death's imagery, and assisted in creating a nearly national rite of passage.

To be sure, the deaths of the two Kennedys and of Dr. King were extraordinary events—touched not only by public and private loss but also by high drama and by a kind of national guilt. (That is, if we had been more aware and sensible of death, we might have been less bland in letting these three notable, high-profile men walk prematurely into theirs.) One might, then, say that television respects death only in the famous. But this misses the point. First, if it were generally true that television (or our public society) respected death only in the famous, that would be at worst a commonplace of life; art alone, which can draw a Sancho Panza as vividly as a knight of La Mancha, seems consistently to skirt class differences. But, for the most part, even when television attempts to deal with the death of famous persons what it commonly does is to attend briskly and meretriciously to the *famousness* of the departed, and to leave the death, and everything that humanly has to do with death, at arm's length. Thus, at the death of Jack Benny—a man who had clearly been much liked in his lifetime, and whose dying had doubtless produced many true feelings of loss and change—the texture of his leaving us was somehow cleaned up for television. No grief appeared on camera. The chairman of the CBS "family" spoke about "professionalism." Taped highlights were shown of a man who had existed ten or twenty years before. As for the death of the less famous Miss Vanderbilt, her accident popped in and out of the news for a day and a half not as the real death of a real woman but as hoked-up "mystery."

The point seems to be that television—this great communicating force—has settled into a role of largely ignoring the reality of death. It does this in part by simply not mentioning it, as if, despite the fact that folktales since ancient times have been filled with the reality of human death, it had lately become—for our "mass audience"—an irrelevant subject. And it does this, perhaps inadvertently, by asserting that the whole reality of death is violence. In entertainment programs, for example, a woman is matter-of-factly drowned in a bathtub; two unknown men are killed in a gun battle; a character—possessed of no past, present, or future—is shot to death by fleeing burglars. In almost no instances of fictional death on television do the dead victims, or their deaths, have any depth or meaning—or, sometimes, even identity—for the audience. (Indeed, one could state it almost as an axiom that no one in a popular television drama who has a fully developed character ever dies.) And when death occurs it arrives invariably through violence, though it is usually a casual, spurious, stage violence, unconnected to personality or feeling, either among the characters or in the audience—a ubiquitous, toy violence. On the news programs, where deaths are regularly announced, these, too, are generally the result of violence or catastrophe, are similarly anonymous, and take place in the unconnected remoteness either of a brief factual caption or of a distant, meaningless locale. In a sense, one might say that the standard news broadcasts, with their nightly accounts of the deaths of fifteen identity-less Portuguese in a train crash, or of a dozen persona-less Italian fishermen in a shipwreck, come close to representing the actual scattered randomness of death as it occurs on this planet. But, once again, these real deaths are treated as if they had no meaning—except as the statistical by-product of some disaster. Death is usually reported to us in the sterility of numbers—"body counts"—and on the few occasions when a person has been found who is humanly connected to real death (as with the two-sentence interview of the man who had lost his wife in Darwin), the cameras, or editors, move gingerly in their treatment of the situation, compressing or squeezing out the humanity and skipping quickly on.

The matter of violence on television has been much discussed recently, though its connection with death seems mainly to be a specious and distorting one. Certainly there has been a plenitude of violent action in commercial broadcasting, and, quite plausibly, there have been a number of surveys, studies, and pronouncements dealing with the subject. Critics, on the whole, have said that there is too much violence on the airwaves, and that violent entertainment tends to breed violent citizens. Telefilm producers have replied that the citizens were violent to begin with, and that everyone knows that detective or Western programs are only fiction, and that, besides, the audience loves a good gunfight. Probably this is a situation in which both sides are to some degree right. Clearly, there is an oversupply of violence, and, also clearly, the majority of the viewers don't take the stuff very seriously. The trouble is that death is not the same as violence. Death is not inseparable from violence. It's true that crimes of violence have increased in this country in recent years, as it's true that the reporting and communicating of crimes of violence have increased in recent years, but in most of its occurrences in the world and in America death is (how else to say it?) *itself:* supremely ordinary, supremely deep. Each week, across the seven continents of the earth, roughly a million human beings die, and most of them die from a classic confluence of age and state of health and the vagaries of life. In other words, to shy away from death because it has been glibly associated with violence—and with stage violence, at that—is like throwing out *King Lear* along with the proverbial bathwater of trivial detective stories. For example, I've read approving comments lately from consumer groups and certain network executives on the decline in the "level of violence" on children's programs, and, basically, this is bound to be an improvement. On the other hand, in the entire week of television that I watched I never once saw death appear in human form on a children's program (I discount *Popeye*, which seems in this regard no worse and no better than *Hawaii Five-O*.) There is a time in childhood when we first become aware of death—when we try to open our eyes to it, have bad dreams, and ask strange, tactless questions. It seems regrettable, at the least—especially considering the frequent presence of death in the great children's stories—that our television fathers and families just won't talk about death to young people.

But it's not only children in our society who are isolated from death by our communications organizations. Virtually all the rest of us have been left to shift for ourselves in dealing with this great, commonplace matter—have been made enemies of death, terrified and stricken by its seeming uniqueness, frozen at gravesides into our separate overcoats. One has heard it said that everyone must deal with death on his own, and perhaps that's true in terms of the physical act of one human being's dying. But for much of history both the dying and the survivors (soon to be the dying) have devised systems—tribal custom or religion—whereby it was possible to place death where it belonged, as part of the continuous, collective cycle of human life. In our era, television has pushed its way into the void left by the fading presence of religion and tribal authority. Television is, if not a formal system, at any rate a huge, cool authority, and also a kind of family, and juggling act, and troupe of players—and priesthood. Indeed, once, with the Kennedy deaths and the death of Martin Luther King, it showed what it could do in incorporating into the community not just a particular or famous death but *death*. Since then, however, it has been mainly silent on the subject. We do not die, apparently, except in numbers, or in Rangoon, or with blank faces in a gunfight. The institution of television often claims to be a mirror reflecting our society, and often many of us are agreeable to thinking that this is so. Perhaps it's more and more worth realizing that it is a mirror that reflects only a part of us. Our deaths, at least—that mass collective act—are not yet part of the reflection.

Icons of War

THREE DAYS AGO, ON TELEVISION, I WATCHED A FILE OF South Vietnamese refugees trudging south along a narrow asphalt road. Two days ago, on television, I watched a different band of South Vietnamese refugees trudging south along a similar gray road. Yesterday, also, there was a 30-second film clip of the flight of South Vietnamese civilians from the northern cities of Quang Tri and Hué toward Danang. This morning, on the news, there were still other refugees, on the same road and framed in the same scene. It has become a familiar shot. The cameraman stands in the road ahead of the oncoming Vietnamese. They walk toward him—grave Asian faces, numbed with fatigue or wretchedness. Some turn to look at him. Some carry small children—sometimes small bloodstained children. Then the cameraman swivels and follows their retreating backs: men and women in scraps of clothing, trudging slowly down a narrow asphalt road that points to an unseen destination.

For weeks, we have watched on television news the encirclement of the Cambodian capital of Phnom Penh and, more recently, the results of a new North Vietnamese offensive against the northernmost urban centers of South Vietnam. That is, we have watched film clips of artillery firing, of smoke rising from far-off buildings, of children bleeding from dreadful wounds, and of refugees trudging down a narrow gray road. I don't mean to deprecate the enterprise of those men and women of American television who at risk to themselves sent back such brief messages as we received during ten years' engagement in Indochina when I say that such iconlike scenes are now dreadful mostly in their sameness, and in the obscenely facile way in which they are still being fitted into our daily newscasts.

The Vietnam war is finally, as the saying goes, winding down—though our soldiers are no longer fighting in it. In nearby Cambodia, a different encounter, between our "national interest" and Cambodian politics, is also winding down. Clearly, it is the end of the affair; something terribly important is happening. But it appears that television—our eyes and ears—will not really have it so. It has been business as usual on the television news. This morning, in addition to the film clip of refugees along the road there was a scene of artillery firing in Cambodia: four howitzers drawn up in a row. Then there was a discussion of congressional action on income-tax legislation. Then a view of Mr. Kissinger in the Middle East. President Ford, it was reported, planned to get away to Palm Beach by the end of the week for "a little golf." Even Charlemagne would probably have taken time off for a little golf, had it been available. Even "business as usual" is not a bad way to go about things, if one is in business—or, at least, if one knows what business one is in. But which business has this nation been engaged in overseas in Southeast Asia for the past decade, and how is it that now—at this sad and terrible point in its denouement—we still know so damn little about it? Was it the domino business? "You had a row of dominoes set up," said President Eisenhower in 1954, "and if you knocked over the first one and what would happen to the last one was the certainty that it would fall over very quickly." A child might have pointed out that dominoes, like nations, are played flat, and that only children stand them on their edges, but then a child wasn't asked. Later, President Kennedy's and President Johnson's Secretary of State, Dean Rusk, was concerned that in not facing up to the Communists in South Vietnam we might "lack credibility" in preventing future wars. Were we in the credibility business? In due course, there was "Pacification" and "Vietnamization." There were "strategic hamlets" and "search-and-destroy missions" and "free-fire zones" and, of course, bombing: air strikes, air missions, raids against the North, against heavily entrenched positions, against enemy strongholds, against hidden base camps, against carefully camouflaged supply depots, against enemy shipping, against missile sites, against railroad yards, against warehouses, against suspected troop concentrations, against enemy enclaves, against cities. In January 1973, after a final spasm of punitive bombing raids against North Vietnam, President Nixon and his national security adviser, Henry Kissinger, standing before the placidly observing lenses of the television cameras, proclaimed a peace settlement in Vietnam. Now, two years later, after still more deaths and misery in South Vietnam, the business (whatever it has been) is closing down, and before the same cool, passive lenses.

Recently, a journalist I know who had himself spent

several years in Vietnam during the 1960's remarked, "They're all heading back for the showdown." I've noticed that Malcolm Browne, who won a Pulitzer Prize as an Associated Press correspondent in Vietnam in 1964, is now back in Saigon for *The New York Times*. Likewise Bernard Weinraub, who was there as a junior reporter providing "color" stories in 1967. The television networks have been flying in additional correspondents and film crews to cover a war that has mysteriously "heated up," though, in fact, the temperature of the Southeast Asia crisis has remained at a consistently dangerous level since the Pax Kissinger, and it is only we and television news who have been cool to it—with perhaps this curious exception: that, after an absence of regular news broadcasting from the area for well over a year, scenes of the continuous savage fighting in Cambodia began slowly filtering back to American televison screens a few months ago, around the time that the Administration was attempting to push its emergency military-aid bills for South Vietnam and Cambodia through Congress. At any rate, the phrase "déjà vu" has appeared a number of times over the past few weeks in televised commentary from Vietnam—even, on one occasion, from a correspondent who had not been there before. Indeed, the *Times* headlined its lead article in Sunday's The Week in Review section "Indochina Déjà Vu." Ironies doubtless come readily to journalists at times such as this; at least, they provide a certain distance, or the semblance of perspective, to someone trying to confront a wretched situation. But it's doubtful whether irony alone can communicate a story as dark and painful as that of our Vietnam experience.

I think what might help is this: for television, finally, to make an honest attempt to have us look at what was happening all along in Southeast Asia. We have been treated like children too often in our national news broadcasts, with our little boredoms and anxieties and attention spans so quickly and tactfully attended to. Are we boyish? Then show us an icon of an airplane or a gun firing. Are we sentimental? Then show us an icon of a bleeding child. Instead of language—even film language—we have been shown pictographs. But, all along, we were never children. Neither the parents of the American men who died nor the men who died nor the survivors were children—only grown men and women who (in the fashion of grown men and women the world over) will sometimes express childlike qualities unless they are summoned beyond these qualities to more difficult terrain. But who was to summon us? Not our politicians, wrapped in their remote fantasies of power, and their subjective, rearward visions of history: Beware the Great Depression! Beware Munich! The Sack of Troy! The only voice that spoke to us from outside ourselves during this long time was television, which spoke to us each day, all through the day, each evening, every morning—the voice of television.

The voice of television has dealt us a cheap hand, I think. It has been pleased, for its commercial purposes, to play the role of benign adult toward us simpleminded children—has been quite agreeable to assuming the dramatic posture of "giving the public what it wants," of not taxing our frail anxieties with too much worry, of not wishing to bore us with too much complex discussion or frighten us with too stark a vision of mortality. But when the presence of a true adult has been needed—that is, of a man or a woman who will take responsibility for his or her position in the world—the voice of television has faded, waffled, chatted of this or that, shown us half a dozen things at once, been charming: has ducked out.

It seems to me that it is time for television to assert itself on the matter of "the news." Television, after all, is merely a word describing vast enterprises that are run by human beings. *Somebody* is there. One has heard amply about organizational responsibility to stockholders or to the F.C.C. or to various doctrines of fairness and balance. Still, there must be some *person* there who carries a sufficient measure of the classic virtue of pride to be able to say, I am *most* responsible: I have eyes and ears, and my eyes and ears tell me such-and-such, and I will now tell you—as straightly as it is possible. If it is true, as many believe it to be, that the central fact of American life since the Second World War has been our involvement in Southeast Asia—first Laos, then Vietnam, and now Cambodia—it is not too late to salvage some element of truth and self-understanding for this nation from what has been a largely uncomprehended experience. We remain a people who have never been bombed. We have never trudged as refugees down a highway, heading north or south. There are some things we can never truly know, and the perhaps well-intentioned but meretricious symbol-pictures of wounds and refugees will not bring us closer to any truth—except, perhaps, the truth that we are a nation that more and more transforms experience into symbols. But there are other things, many other things, that we *can* know—and were these to be told to us coherently, in the spirit of truth, or at least of a storyteller believing his own story, we might look and listen to them, and some connection might take place within us. Something in us might change. Something in us might even feel loss and hurt and pain. For if a misfortune or tragedy has been taking place so far away, across the world in Southeast Asia, and yet so near to us, it is surely our misfortune or tragedy, too. And what chance have we to realize and deal with this experience if the experience is kept from us or tidied up or simplified—processes that amount to the same thing?

It seems to me that we have seen enough of these film clips of guns firing and of smoke rising and of refugees fleeing—because these images, however real, are no longer to the point. We have seen enough of propaganda—whether pro-war or anti-war. Someone on television must begin to tell us where we have been and where we are now—and must do his level best, must use the medium's skills of attraction, to get us to look at it. Admittedly, television, for all its power and wealth, is not a logical place to expect to find such a synthesis. With one or two minor exceptions, American television in ten years has produced no notable "literature" on the subject of Vietnam or Asia. Indeed, our vaunted television-news era has so far been rather like the early era of manuscript literature under the clerics—a period of dry orthodoxy beneath a timid, powerful authority. But the denouement of our adventure in Southeast Asia is the terminus of a great, tragic human saga—one worthy of the best storytellers. It is a story that demands to be grasped, and not avoided or relegated to late-night news "specials" or two-minute film clips sandwiched in between the day's comings and goings. For ten years now, television news has provided us with these bits and patches—disconnected visual glimpses or isolated snatches of dialogue, as if from some massive ongoing novel, whose core the novelist has somehow omitted or not yet dealt with. How, then, is it to provide the missing core or meaning of this great story? By means of "specials" or "documentaries" or "closeups" or "expanded news coverage" or "investigative reporting"? I don't believe I am being offhand when I say that I don't think that this is the main question. Whenever there is an important story to tell, a form will usually evolve for telling it; the story will shape its own form. Consider, for example, what Marcel Ophuls eventually did for the French people with *The Sorrow and the Pity*—and without howitzers or sentimental imagery. The crucial question is about commitment: Will television now undertake even to grasp the story? Will the people in television face their deeper responsibilities and grant to their communication of the tragic narrative of the American expedition to Southeast Asia a priority and a prominence that accord with the actual dimensions of the story—and so enable the people of this country to see, feel, and, if not fully know themselves, at least comprehend their passage through recent time? It is a matter not of providing more combat footage, or more snapshots of human misery, or even more routine documentaries on corruption in Saigon but, rather, of acknowledging the true scope and texture of the subject, and of finding the talent (whether from outside or inside the present news establishments) to master it: either as a great single work—television's equivalent of an epic film or novel—or as several linked, separate works adding up to a coherent whole; or, at least, one wherein the terrible magnitude of the subject might for once be meshed with the commitment of the faceless but powerful network authorities. It is a very large opportunity—not least of all for television to achieve something that its professionals might be proud of, and that its audience finally deserves. So far, the omissions from the story have been more noticeable—and somehow louder—than television's skimpy and fainthearted narrative.

Waiting for the Storyteller

I WAS STANDING ON A CITY STREET CORNER A FEW DAYS ago with two of our children when, with a wail of sirens, a couple of police cars emerged from the tangle of traffic and shrieked their way past us, heading uptown.

"What do you suppose is happening?" I said.

"Must be after a robber," said the younger child.

"More likely a dope raid," said the other.

"You don't use sirens on a dope raid," said the first.

"You do if the suspect is getting away. Lieutenant Kojak uses sirens all the time."

"Anyway, it's some kind of an adventure," said the older child, who is ten.

We all agreed it was probably some kind of an adventure. Later, as we were walking uptown ourselves, I asked, "What do you think an adventure is?"

"It's something scary you don't have to believe in," the older child said.

I have been thinking lately about adventure on television, not just because of the two police cars and the children's response to them (the moment framed by a television scenario: the detective; the squad-car chase; the adventures of Lieutenant Kojak) but because it seems increasingly true that this is an awkward, self-conscious time for adventure in our culture, and that television is probably the single most important source of adventure narrative that remains to us.

Did adventure die in the trenches of the First World War, or perhaps in the advance of science and technology? At any rate, what we call the spirit of adventure seems to have disappeared or receded from modern life—almost discredited, as it were, along with adventure's protagonist, the hero—to reappear from time to time in the relentless, prosaic professionalism of the astronauts or in the new adventure metaphors of our moneyed culture: the retired businessmen and their wives who travel up the Amazon on tour or visit the Galápagos Islands on a cruise ship, or the sensibility-prone young who backpack in Nepal or do somersaults above the ski slopes of Colorado. The other evening on television, in fact, I saw two advertisements that seemed to conjure up the new adventurism. One was for a beer. It showed two attractively raffish American men pushing their way through a throng at a South American river port. Each has a backpack and a stagy, well-traveled look. They board a river steamer. The captain seems to be a bearded exotic figure. "Where you fellows from?" he asks. "Omaha," one says. "Hey, I was in Omaha once," the captain says. He laughs. They laugh. They guzzle some beer. Small world, small world! The other ad was for a credit-card company and showed a modest-seeming man in a plaid jacket. "Do you know me? I'm one of the astronauts who walked on the moon," says the man, whose name is Charles Conrad, Jr. "But when I walk in here to rent a car, they don't always recognize me." That is why, he explains, he always carries this credit card wherever he travels. The ad seemed sad, and also truthful: as if we had fashioned such a tight-fitting suit of anti-heroic professionalism for these moon explorers that there was now no way they could escape it, even in car-rental offices.

Intellectuals in America make much of their disdain for television—for regular television programming. And the mass of people make much of their disdain for intellectuals and their artifacts: notably, serious novels and serious films. One wonders if the absence or misdirection of adventure narrative isn't at the heart of some of these conflicting disdains; which is to say that since ancient times people have wanted stories, and the stories they have most wanted have been adventure stories. Indeed, it isn't pushing a point to claim that since the period of the Attic bards adventure narrative has formed the basis and the dynamic for most of the great stories of Western literature. Consider the skein of adventure that runs from the *Odyssey*, through *Don Quixote*, to *Robinson Crusoe*, *David Copperfield*, and *Moby Dick*, and perhaps, finally, to that other odyssey *Ulysses*. But with James Joyce's great novel modern literature appeared to withdraw its interest from what had theretofore been regarded as adventure—the largely physical exploits of heroic characters—in favor of stories of human sensibility and of psychological exploration (some still might say adventure) within the human consciousness. The traditional adventure narrative was, so to speak, abandoned by serious writers and passed down to the literary subculture of the detective story, children's stories, "cheap fiction," and the new, popular form of the movies, where, in heroic dramas of the American West, of gangsters, of spies, and of two world wars, it remained the prime source of mass entertainment until the last generation. But movies, too, have "grown up," in part abandoning and in part abandoned by their popular clientele. True, adventure narrative still remains in movies, but it, too, is more and more that of a subculture, with an occasional thriller or faddish "disaster" film, a plenitude of black-oriented "cheap fiction," and now and then a successful modern adventure, such as *The Sting*, that draws in both the elite and the mass audience because of its parodic ambivalences. The serious trend in movies, as in literature some time ago, is mainly toward explorations of sensibility and psychology, toward symbolism and episodic narrative—with the result that at present the place where adventure narrative survives most consistently and with the greatest appearance of its own importance is on television.

Even so, it is often a bizarre and anachronistic presence. Consider some capsule descriptions from a recent *TV Guide* of current adventure-type programs:

> AVENGERS: Steed's only lead to the death of an agent is a department-store sales slip issued on a day the store was closed.

> EMERGENCY!: The paramedics rescue a man trapped in the ooze of a gushing oil well.

MANNIX: Hired to find the straying wife of a politically ambitious publisher, Mannix finds the pay very generous and the case suspiciously easy to solve.

PROTECTORS: A deadly chase over stacks of concrete pipes results when the Contessa faces a treacherous kidnapper.

STAR TREK: Kirk (William Shatner) and three crew members try to reverse the effects of a storm, which swept them into an incredibly savage universe.

ADAM-12: Malloy is held hostage by young criminals, who demand the release of a prisoner convicted of killing a pimp.

What does one make of such a list, or of the stories that these codelike captions fairly accurately describe? Consider, for example, the extravagant variety of the adventures to be unfolded: the death of an agent; a man trapped in a gusher of oil; a missing woman; bribery; a deadly chase; kidnapping; a storm in outer space; abduction by criminals; murder. But we know, too, that this seeming extravagance doesn't necessarily mean anything, for the same capsule spirit that wrote the captions will animate the stories. Not only will all end well—which is true of many adventure stories—but nothing importantly affecting will happen en route. The detective will collar the criminal by the end of the drama; in the process he may be threatened, or an assistant may be killed, or someone may scream or crack up in a car or be drowned in a bathtub. But the logic of the modern television adventure will have dominated these events, as if the events hardly existed. This logic often has the appearance of "classic simplicity"—of lean, simple narrative. But in reality it is almost never the textured, artful simplicity of classic narrative, or even of fairy tales, with their intimations of tensions and shadows beneath clear surfaces; rather, it is the denuded simplicity of the detective story or of police-desk journalism—of the simple declarative sentence. *My name is Mulligan. I'm a cop.* To be sure, some of the television adventure programs are better than others. *Columbo* and *Kojak*, for example, seem superior to the run-of-the-mill cops-and-robbers shootouts, but this is mainly because the producers populate the stories with interesting minor characters. That comes down to being mostly an improvement in sensibility or in character acting. The adventures remain insistently conventional. There is little genuine excitement, except in the sense that a ride on a modest roller coaster is said to be exciting—a roller coaster where the safety of the trip is known to be absolute, and the only surprises are a series of predictable (and therefore unsurprising) tossings and turnings. At a tense moment in *Kojak*, the camera reveals a homicidal rapist crouched behind a garbage can as the great detective strides toward an alley. We experience a brief, mechanical tic of apprehension while waiting for the members of the detective force to appear on the scene, and so startle the criminal, and so shoot him; but it is likely to be a response not so much to this particular encounter in this particular alley as to a literary or movie memory of ambushes that somehow made us care more. Why does one care so little now? *Kojak*, after all, is an adult-oriented program; adults are fascinated by adventure fully as much as children are—

witness the successes of John le Carré and Alfred Hitchcock. It seems to me that even the large, neglected adventure-hungry audience recognizes instinctively that these modern television adventures don't really *apply*. Not that all the programs or dramas are totally beside the point, for the telefilm storytellers are clever and have new (mainly cinematic) visual techniques to assist them, together with the public's current fascination with topical detail. Still, modern television adventures seem to be both popular and somehow unremembered, as if a storyteller had crept into our house and told a story—with many declamations, and much eye-rolling and firing of toy pistols—and then had left without a trace, and we had waked up the next day without even a visceral memory of his tale. What, for example, does anyone remember of the great, long-running adventure *Dragnet*, except the theme song?

In an intelligent and interesting book called *The Adventurer*, Paul Zweig has remarked on the pivotal position of Daniel Defoe's *Robinson Crusoe* in the mainstream of Western narrative literature, finding in the character of Crusoe the prototype of the modern anti-adventurer—the point of his adventures being, after all, that a man might survive on a desert island neither by heroics nor by gallant action but by the steadfast application of English domestic virtues. Zweig also points out that with Defoe's novels of early-eighteenth-century London life begins a new, formal, literary view of the city as an arena of adventure, with crime or criminality as its principal field of play. He goes on to trace the evolution of narrative adventure from the eroticism of Casanova, through the Gothic novel, to the recent journeys of hallucinogenic voyagers, but it often seems as if most television adventures had remained rooted in the concepts of Defoe—with their relentlessly practical men inextricably involved in the criminal substructure of societies. Even when the setting is shifted to the American West or to outer space, a similar obsession with domestic practicality plus criminality seems to persist. Captain Kirk, in *Star Trek*, for example, is himself a Crusoe-like character, resolving complex and threatening hazards of intergalactic travel with down-home rationalism, while his Man Friday, Mr. Spock, though he is alleged to be equipped with magic telepathic powers, in fact employs them chiefly in the service of sound, earth-bound common sense.

Admittedly, someone might say that television adventures, then, are at least true to the real adventures of life, for it has turned out that our real space explorers have necessarily been practical men, anti-adventurous in the Crusoe manner, and, if not actually weeping with terror at the sight of a footprint on the moon, at least surpassingly proud of their capacities for teamwork, responsibility, and common sense. Furthermore, there is no denying that the theatricality of cities and of criminality has amply remained with us since the time of Defoe. But I suspect that these are surface relevances or comparisons. At the root of the difficulty of creating effective storytelling for the mass audience (by which I mean stories that induce not only ratings but memory) are, I imagine, two problems. One is the essential insincerity of the stories; it is hard to accept the premise that our mass-media storytellers can themselves believe in the stories they are telling us. After all, most of them appear to be intelligent and educated men and women, who come from the kind of cultural background that has been schooled in the anti-adventure and anti-narrative tendencies of twentieth-century literature. Given an association of Attic bards who didn't care much for gods, or fate, or heroic action, or even the Trojan War, it would have taken more than the appearance of a Homer to produce the *Iliad*. Still, this is mainly a guess as to the personae of our modern storytellers, and even if correct it can account only for the detached, rhetorical, borrowed quality that one finds in so many television dramas—the sense of being given only the shell of an adventure. I suspect that where television stories go wrong—in terms of not really speaking to the audience—is in what lies under the shell. This is a difficult substance to isolate, for it seems to be many things. For one, it seems to be simple narrative—a good story. But there is rarely a good story on popular television; the stories are nearly always the same, or have the same feeling and the same balances. Then, there is much talk of mythology. Detective So-and-So is a "mythic hero" —as are various Western sheriffs or saintly medical men. But what does "mythic" mean except "pertaining to myths," and what are myths except dramatic organizations of the varieties of human life? Nearly everyone is mythic to some degree, including the elevator operator who takes the mythmaking television writer to his office every morning. Orpheus descended to the Underworld from a surface world consisting of a complex set of relationships between himself and his conscious and unconscious environment—the gods. Detective Mulligan descends to the Times Square subway station, but it will take a lot more than mood photography and portentous dialogue to make him "Orphic." It seems to me that what lies under the shells of our mass-audience adventures is neither story nor myth but mainly the surviving embers of nineteenth-century pietistic morality.

In recent months, there has been much official and public discussion of violence in television programming, with both television executives and consumer groups seeming to agree that there is too much of it, and that scenes of mayhem and gunfighting have a deleterious effect on the youth of the nation. As I think I've written before, one can't in good conscience take a position in favor of the sort of random, gratuitous violence one so often sees on the television screen, though I leave the argument as to whether meretricious depictions of gunplay incite the citizenry to act likewise to the no man's land of sociological debate, where I think the question belongs. But I have a feeling that what is corrupt—or, anyway, amiss—with so much of the narrative one sees on television isn't that there is either too much or too little violence but that most of the action that takes place on the television screen is somehow blurred, muted, transposed behind a gauzy screen of pietism and morality. No matter how much killing or shooting takes place in a detective or Western program, the one note that seems to reverberate through the action is the moral position of the detective or sheriff and the moral position of the program—our storyteller. On the simpler programs, the morality is infused in relatively simple fashion: noble, rational, pro-society figures against wicked, antisocial, if often romantic, criminals. On the more ambitious programs, such as the aforementioned *Kojak* and *Columbo*, among many others, a more complex moral tone pervades the narrative—usually an ill-meshed combination of bogus Freudianism and leftover Christian pietism. Characters can hardly move without being "understood," though it is rarely a deeply felt understanding but, rather, a rhetorical note of moralizing. The criminal acts because of a wretched upbringing, which is never shown but simply told us, often by the detective in pursuit: "The fellow had a wretched upbringing," mutters the mythic detective, speeding uptown in his police car.

In a fine essay titled "On Misunderstanding the *Oedipus Rex*," the great classics scholar E. R. Dodds attacked the nineteenth-century English critics for undermining the strength of vision of the early Greek dramatists by interpreting the dramatists' noble works through morality-conscious Victorian eyes. Oedipus didn't meet disaster because he had a tragic moral flaw, said Dodds. He met it because an oracle had prophesied that he would, and, being of heroic character, he chose to meet it. That is how the ancient Greeks conceived of the world. Americans in the late twentieth century conceive of it differently, but if their lives—and their periodic explosions of personality and consciousness—are any gauge, they no longer conceive of it in terms of Christian pietism, though they seem often to be trapped beneath the weight of that. Adventure, after all, is escape. But how then to "escape" from a private, nearly abandoned pietism into a remote, official, televised pietism? How to "escape" from an evolving national consciousness that is attempting quite bravely, for example, to redefine its concepts of criminality and society—into story-dramas that still insistently present a frozen, fairy-tale world of cops and robbers? In short, television storytelling seems to speak to us from a void, appealing to the mass audience's need for stories, but then furnishing unfelt and idealized versions of ourselves—and using ideals that are mostly rear-ward-facing and discredited. As for the actual stuff of our mythology, our own Trojan War—our space missions, our explorations of the subconscious, our proud battles beneath the skin with our own selves and bodies—these are adventures that television scarcely attends to in the organizing form of stories; and does little more than hint at beneath a screen of moralizing journalism, which is the same as not attending to. The story-minded audience remains out there, perhaps uncertain of its evolving relations with the gods. This is a transitional period, apparently, in which we are waiting for tales of new adventure and for new storytellers, and are meanwhile making do with Robinson Crusoe in science-fiction dress or the sly pieties of law-enforcement heroes.

Still, I think that, by chance, there remains one small area in popular television entertainment where a dim echo of non-moralizing adventure storytelling persists. I came across it the other evening while looking over the shoulders of my children as they watched filmed scenes of animals prowling across the television screen: one of the nature documentaries that the networks show every so often as family entertainment. In this instance, the program was about hyenas in the Ngorongoro Crater of East Africa, and was produced in what has become the conventional manner for such studies; that is, with views of much splendid natural scenery, many striking, almost surreally intimate scenes of wildlife, and a kind of modest, firm, unapologetic thread of narrative. Then, as I listened to this narrative—describing a scene of hyenas on the prowl after a herd of zebras—I thought I heard another voice:

> A zebra is separated from the herd.
> Isolated, she becomes the prey.
> She is no match for the hyenas.
> She is doomed.
> The hyenas have powerful jaws that can crack bones in a single stroke.

It seemed to be the clear, simple voice of the storyteller. And all the while there had been something beautiful in the flight of the zebra and, in a way, something equally beautiful in the pursuit by the fleet and terrible hyenas, and something straightforward, and even (perhaps because it was on the animals' terms) meaningful, in the end of the chase: the death and destruction of the zebra. After a moment, I thought, What can I care for hyenas and zebras? But it seemed to me then that I had cared more about them—about this brief, honest story I had watched and heard—than about most of the insistent dramas of detectives, spies, and space police that I had watched for many months on the same screen. I looked at my children. They were silent now, watching the hyenas lope across the plain, and, I suspected, wrestling within their youthful minds to reconcile the vivid artistic impact of the scene and the prevailing learned-by-rote morality: Never kill a living thing. One imagines sometimes that only the nation that dropped the first two atomic bombs could (or would) later go backpacking into the wilderness muttering, "Never kill a living thing."

Since then, I have watched a number of these nature programs: about bees, and wild dogs, and even jellyfish. Doubtless there is a limit to anyone's capacity for dramatic sympathy with four-legged creatures, to say nothing of bees and jellyfish, so it seems a curious irony that it is here—with these "family entertainments" of natural life and death, of objectified action, of the playing out of existence against fate and felt imperatives—that the ancient, receding craft of non-moralizing adventure storytelling should come temporarily to roost.

For instance, I made the following notes from a documentary about bees, which showed an extraordinary battle between members of the hive and an attacking army of wasps, and, later, a stark and pitiful scene of the expulsion of resisting drones in order to safeguard the rest of the colony.

> Honeybees have many enemies. The worst is the wasp.
>
> After a battle, the wasps often carry back the slaughtered bees as food for their larvae.
>
> Here the entire honeybee colony fights off an attack. Some of the wasps are killed, but the sacrifice borne by the honeybees is always greater.

When there is not enough food to feed the bee colony, some of them must die.

The drones are banished from the colony.

Try as they might, the drones are not allowed back into the hive.

As winter begins, workers are born in great numbers to keep the colony alive. They cluster together, waiting for spring.

Are these, then, our modern epics? One wouldn't want to push the point too far. Still, these wildlife narratives exist on their own plane of adventure and of truth. On the one hand, it is easy to view them as a withdrawal from man and his complexities; on the other hand, possibly they are the beginnings of a new extension of storytelling man into the objective world. At any rate, no one has yet piously complained of too much violence in the Ngorongoro Crater or tried to shroud a beehive in pop psychology. So perhaps we should enjoy them while we can.

The View from Highway 1

WALTER CRONKITE SAID: "GOOD EVENING. COMmunist gunners in South Vietnam were busy on four sides of Saigon today, shelling the sprawling U.S.-built Bien Hoa airbase, and, farther from the capital, the cities of Xuan Loc, Tay Ninh, and Cai Lay. At Bien Hoa, fifteen miles northeast of the capital, three explosions—seen and felt in Saigon—tore through a bomb-ammunition dump. It's not known whether artillery fire or sabotage was the cause. Near Xuan Loc, forty miles east of Saigon, there was sporadic, sometimes heavy fighting around Highway 1. Government and Communist reinforcements were being moved into the area, which military strategists in Saigon see as the next crucial battle. For more on the military situation around Xuan Loc, Bob Simon reports . . ."

It has been an eerie spring in America. The threat of general financial collapse and rampant inflation—so stark last winter, when economic stories urgently filled the newscasts—has not yet materialized, and though there are still many men and women out of work, business and government experts profess to see a "turnaround" in the economy: another light at the end of another tunnel. Meanwhile, a truce persists in the Middle East. At home, a railroad strike has been averted. Car sales are up. Green shoots of plants and foliage have begun to appear around the country; even in concrete-bound New York, some hyacinths have popped up in Central Park. The days are longer and are warmer. And it has been toward the close of these long, sweetening days, with the pale sun still lighting the spring sky, and the shades not yet drawn, and the sounds of children outside again on the street, that those millions of us Americans who watch the news each evening on television (there are about fifty million of us now) have been watching the fall of Indochina to the Communist armies of Cambodia and Vietnam.

It is not, one imagines, a spectacle that can be regarded in a too simple fashion, even secondhand, or from American living rooms. A few weeks ago, at the beginning of the Communist offensive, when I wrote a piece criticizing the television networks for not providing a more coherent and ambitious depiction of the state of affairs in Indochina, I received an intense and angry pencil-written letter from a reader in Quincy, Massachusetts, who said, in effect, that in years past she had been compelled to look at more scenes of Vietnamese warfare than she could stand, and that she could see no useful purpose served in television's now dwelling at even greater length on these distant miseries. I have no idea of how many in the vast television-news audience share this view, but I suspect that a great many do. At any rate, it is not a response that one should brush aside carelessly, or out of one's own impatience, for it seemed to me that the main note that reverberated through this long letter from my correspondent in Massachusetts was—despite her tartly reasoned call for television's disengagement from Vietnam—her own, perhaps classically ambiguous American involvement. "For your information," she wrote, "we have already seen too many scenes of horror *to be borne*." It's hard not to sympathize at least with the emotional basis of such a sentiment, though for myself I think I'd alter the expression to read, "We have already seen too many unfelt and disconnected scenes of military activity and random human misery to try to make sense of them." Even so, what has had weight for me in her remarks was not her "argument"—pro or con, too much or too little—but the sheer humanness of her connection. For if it's true that television news has been remiss, or strangely helpless, in its communication of information about our ten-year engagement in Indochina, it is also true that network television has brought the mass of people of this country face to face with war in a way that has never happened before.

Vietnam scenes from the past merge in one's memory: a more than ten-year-long television serial. In the beginning, there were the "military advisers"—tall, crew-cut Americans, standing at a slight distance from grinning South Vietnamese troops. The South Vietnamese generals and their (our) tanks and airplanes. Scenes of Vietnamese leaders and our ambassador: the ambassador visits the Presidential palace; the President and the ambassador tour the new airbase. Then there were the American soldiers beginning to fan out across the fields of dry, waist-high, and (on our black-and-white television screens) whitish grass; we came to learn that it was called buffalo grass. There were the great navy carriers floating at sea. Delta-winged airplanes in the sky. There were important places, with no locatable existence: the Central Highlands, Hill 880, the Ia Drang Valley. There were the rhythmic, abrupt landings of helicopters, with the kickup of dust and dirt, the wind-blown grass, and the men in uniform scurrying into the woods—"the tree line," it was called. American generals were periodically interviewed. They drank from canteens in the field and spoke of "the need for training." Visiting congressmen toured Saigon. Bob Hope was pictured in Danang. George Romney visited the ambassador. There were a number of rotten stories: for years, until the mood of the country turned, or became ambivalent, the network news programs went out of their way, or so it seemed, to portray the air war—the heavy bombing, the light bombing, the deadly "gunships"—as romantic and ennobling. I remember one hour-long special, *Vietnam Perspective: Air War in the North*, that consisted largely of film provided by the Air Force, extolling its exciting planes, and of straight-faced, R.A.F.-beer-hall-type interviews with several pilots, who chatted of "strikes" and "missions," and one of whom, I recall, spoke heartily of gunning down "gooks" and "suspected Cong" as they ran across an open field. There were also some examples of first-rate combat journalism. I think of John Laurence reporting for CBS from Con Thien;

of the coverage by all three networks of the Tet offensive; and of various, seemingly isolated moments of actuality which broke through, as it were, the generally impersonal, unquestioning ritual of network Vietnam coverage—such as certain scenes I still remember that were filmed one May week in 1967 by NBC's fine Vietnamese cameraman Vo Huynh, of a company of our Marines under fire in what seemed to be almost a New England wood. One man was badly wounded and kept calling out to his comrades, "My leg is bust!" (The sound equipment by then was good enough so that you could pick up his words.) Eventually, they got to him—with Vo Huynh not far behind—and brought him back. There was another young Marine, I remember, who had apparently panicked, or was close to panicking. A huge black sergeant held him by the arm, half soothing, half furious. "Git up there!" he said. "Now, git on up there!" Vo Huynh caught that, too.

Bob Simon said: "Military movement and civilian uprooting have always gone together in this war. Route 1 today is no exception. But at least right now, in distinction to the disasters of the past few weeks, the soldiers and the refugees are moving in different directions . . . A few miles up the road—the last government outpost. It's a little less than five miles from Xuan Loc. The Communists have cut the road between here and the city. The men here have been holding this position for six days."

The truth is that the natural bias of television news has been for action and immediacy. At its most professional, television covers fast-breaking news more vividly than any other form of journalism. It is even widely understood that this single-track ability of television to communicate objective events directly has served almost to heighten an instinctive public tendency to associate "news" only with objectified happenings. Thus, it is a modern truism of sorts that, for example, an American city's tensions or injustices or misunderstandings are rarely treated as news until a riot "explodes," which act somehow certifies the city's situation as news and permits a brief ex-post-facto examination until another event, elsewhere, takes precedence.

But the question is, to what degree is it excessive and willful to find fault with such a system, inasmuch as this system surely reflects human nature—or, at least, the traditional difficulty that men and women experience when they try to focus on something other than objective action? This spring, for instance, in Indochina, as the Cambodian capital of Phnom Penh was being surrounded by the Khmer Rouge, and the South Vietnamese capital of Saigon was being threatened by the North Vietnamese and the Vietcong, CBS correspondent Bob Simon (quoted above) was assigned to correspond with the viewing audience in America on the subject of refugees along Highway 1 as well as on such familiar matters as the firing of howitzers ("The government is moving heavy artillery into positions alongside the road") and air strikes by the South Vietnamese Air Force ("F-5 fighter-bombers from Bien Hoa are in action, hitting suspected Communist positions"). All things considered, however, one would have been hard put to suggest where better, or even where else at all, he might have stationed himself. For it was as if the war that television had for so long insistently reported to us—the shooting war, the war of fighter planes and guns and distant pillars of smoke—had finally become real. Not that previous scenes of combat hadn't been real, or that there hadn't been planes in the air or glimpses of war-weary Vietnamese peasants beside the roads, but that finally this activity seemed to be about something that was palpably credible. Unfortunately, one felt (with the ambivalent involvement-detachment of someone who has watched a badly narrated story for too long), the "wrong" side was winning and the "right" side was losing; all the same, it was this kind of winner-loser "victory" that we had been attuned to for so many years, and now here it was. There was something almost artistically appropriate in the final televised depictions of our Indochina involvement—as if that "bang-bang" footage which network assignment desks had made so much of in the past had at last achieved its point.

In certain ways, this is probably a good time in which to be wary of blaming television for too much. For sometimes in recent years it has become a kind of badge of embattled individualism to blame commercial television—or "the mass media"—for the flaws and errors and imperfections of our society. If it weren't for television—so various arguments run—our children would be more responsible; our minorities would be less demanding; our middle class would be more serious; our politicians would pay more attention to issues; our popular values would be somehow higher; and, as a nation, we would not have been so sadly and unsuccessfully involved in Indochina.

The truth is obviously that the audience shapes its television and that television also shapes its audience; but this kind of unmeasurable truth becomes murkier than usual in the matter of television and its audience and the Vietnam war, because for all concerned it has been an entirely novel experience. "Good" and "bad," which are always difficult terms to apply in questions of communication, become even more relative and subjective in regard to America and Indochina. To what does one compare American television's coverage of Vietnam and Cambodia? To the print coverage of the Second World War? To the example of other nations? In the early days of television, for instance, the French fought an unpopular and unsuccessful war in Indochina; televised coverage in France, via the government-controlled news channel, was slight, fragmentary, and officially biased. Our new international-trade partner, the Soviet Union, has had experience both in television technology and in politico-military involvements; however, one hardly looks to Soviet broadcasting's handling of the Hungarian uprising or the Sino-Soviet schism for a model of communications possibilities. By a number of standards of comparison, American television's coverage of Indochina has been fairly good. The network camera crews have not gone everywhere, or even very far from officially certified events; still, they have pushed their way into an astonishing number and variety of places—the more surprising when one considers the number of persons (three) and the amount of equipment they need in order to work. And if the articulate, politically liberal element in the nation has often been impatient at commercial television's timidities—

notably in waiting so long to report even skeptical opinions about the conduct of the Vietnam war—one should keep it in mind that during most of that time the majority of the nation (and of the audience) actively favored, or clung to, the government's consistently confident and optimistic pronouncements. But questions about television's coverage of the Vietnam war go deeper than this, and it seems to me that the reason they remain important is that they still don't appear to be admitted, even as questions, by the persons who are most concerned: the public and the broadcasting establishment. It is true that the public frequently expresses an undefined anxiety about the generality of broadcasting, and mostly in demonological terms: attacks on the political leanings of news commentators, and the like. And the broadcasting establishment, for its part, either engages in counter-propaganda ("The audience is the boss") or attempts to allay the public's uneasiness by similarly treating it as a political issue—employing rightist commentators to balance leftist newsmen.

But the problem, one suspects, is not so much political as social. That is, it lies in the context of social intimacy in which we have placed our television receivers—our sets—and thus our whole television experience. Previously, as we know, there have been huge popular audiences for theater, circuses, vaudeville, cinema, and so on. There have been popular audiences for newspapers and radio. Yet there has never been anything like the intimate relationship of a people to a "communications source" which has existed for some time between the American people and its television broadcasters. It is new ground. As a result, a lot of public criticism of commercial television has a way of foundering or of disappearing into thin air—especially criticism that complains of network television for merely existing in its present form, or wishes vaguely that "it" were some other way or that "it" might somehow act toward us as if there were a different set of rules in force. The truth is that there are no real rules governing television's deep relationship to the national audience, because there has been very little acceptance of the extent to which that relationship exists. In fact, American television is at present largely defined by various quasi rules, which are determined not by the actual, evolving, functional relationship of broadcasting organizations to their audience but by superficial considerations of marketing and, even in the matter of news, by the rigid and anachronistic profit-and-loss conventions of an entertainment industry.

In the last few weeks of crisis in Vietnam and Cambodia, for example, *The New York Times* has supplied an average of twenty-five thousand words of information each day about the military, political, and human situation there, together with continued commentary on related developments in Washington. The *Times* is owned by the New York Times Company, which last year had sales of $390 million and a net income of over $20 million. In these same weeks, each of the major networks has presented a maximum of around three thousand words each day on the Indochina situation. The networks have also—as the main feature of their news reports—presented numerous brief news-film accounts (such as Bob Simon's from Highway 1), of which some have been dramatic and immediate, and others disjointed and routine. They have also (as a group total) presented two or three "special reports." About ten days ago, NBC presented a thirty-minute "special report" on Cambodia, which consisted mainly of a wrapup of NBC's regular news footage of the previous week by the New York commentator and was shown on Saturday afternoon. Over two weeks ago, CBS presented an hour-long, altogether conventional "special report" titled *Indochina 1975: The End of the Road?*, which featured a narration by Charles Collingwood (about four thousand words) and was shown at ten o'clock in the evening, in competition with the Academy Awards ceremonies. There have been no further "special reports" on Indochina by CBS, though network officials say that one may soon be forthcoming. The point is that CBS Television, whose News Division produced fifty-three minutes on the Indochina crisis on the night of the Academy Awards, is a part of CBS Inc., which last year had sales of $1.75 billion and a net income of $108 million. The question that, it seems, no one will yet attend to, because it is not yet real, is: To what extent is it important, or even necessary, in a communications society—in which citizens-as-businessmen receive a constant stream of telephoned or Telexed "news" throughout the day as an accepted function of their business role—for citizens-as-citizens to receive information of a similar quality and texture as a function of their perhaps more important role?

On previous occasions, I have sometimes written to a similar point; namely, the question of the responsibility of television news organizations to communicate information more seriously than they have in the past. And each time, invariably, I have received letters in reply accusing me of being "unrealistic" in these criticisms—one correspondent lately finding me "dishonest" for talking of television news in terms of possibilities that do not exist. The reason I bring up this subject once again is that it strikes me that—with the fact before us of the collapse of our Indochinese position—the question of what is "realistic" or "unrealistic" in television news communication could perhaps begin to be glimpsed in a new light.

A few days ago, at the time of President Thieu's angry resignation speech, I read in the paper that since the beginning of our involvement in Vietnam 56,000 of our own men had been killed; 156,000 of them had been gravely wounded (which is to say, often maimed for life); and we had spent roughly $155 billion of our national treasure. I said earlier that I think television often did an extremely competent job in reporting scenes of immediate combat. But I think, too, that network television news—as a voice—almost never reported the true, full story of what at any given time was happening either to the Vietnamese or to us in Indochina. In the beginning, this voice talked to us about the brave South Vietnamese government—when reporters knew of its corruption and weakness, and knew that the point, anyway, was not its virtues or lack of them but our government's strategic ambitions. The voice told us about the "military advisers"—when reporters knew that the advisers' efforts were being devoted largely to turning the South Vietnamese into a conventional army with which to fight what was then a guerrilla war. The voice told us of our hundred and fifty thousand soldiers, and then our three hundred thousand soldiers, and then our five hundred and fifty thousand soldiers, and about their "sweeps" and "missions" and "patrols" and "reconnnoiters" and "air support" and "captured ammo dumps" and "reinforced perimeters"—when the story was what these young soldiers could not do, what could not be done. Our troops played touch football at Thanksgiving. President Johnson put his arm around President Thieu. President Nixon put his arm around President Thieu. Toward the end of the story, the voice announced to us that there was peace—when all too many knew that there could be no real peace, and that it existed under a South Vietnamese government that all too many knew could not govern for long.

All of us in this country, to say nothing of the citizens of Indochina, have lost a great deal in the course of the narration of these false—or, at least, surreal—stories. And yet the real stories were no great secret. There were reporters who knew about them—many of them reporters working for television. As an odd irony, I noticed in Bob Simon's report from Highway 1 the statement "Military movement and civilian uprooting have always gone together in this war." Simon, who seems to be an able and enterprising young man, spoke this phrase in the spring of 1975 as if it were part of some accepted knowledge—as if we all knew this of Vietnam. The fact is, though, that while Simon might make such a casually accepted statement now, when the point is past, his predecessors, for eight or nine years, almost never did so, when the point might have counted. What were *we* doing to the South

Vietnamese, with our "strategic hamlets" and "free-fire zones"? That was certainly one of the key stories from Indochina. And, though television belatedly acknowledged it—for the most part, as ironic texture, one of those "facts of war"—it never really broke the story or made a point of it, despite the networks' vast resources and numerous correspondents. In regard to this and other evaded stories, I have several times heard network executives remark on the considerable government pressures that were brought to bear on their companies as a result of the few critical news reports they did present in the Vietnam period. There is no denying that Presidents Kennedy and Johnson (to say nothing of President Nixon) were congenitally unpleased by journalistic criticism, and often tried to throw their weight around with company officials. But one wonders what might have happened—not just in terms of the nation's understanding and support of the war but in terms of the public's long-term respect for television news, for "the mass media"—if the networks had chosen to seriously acknowledge their role as journalists, as something more than transmitters of certified events, and had given their correspondents honest reportorial missions and then had stood behind them. After all, was Lyndon Johnson's hold on the warrior spirit of the nation so secure that he would finally have compelled a network *not* to report, say, the chaotic forced uprootings of Vietnamese that so disastrously occurred from 1966 to 1969? Did the businessmen of the nation (who are still reeling from the effects of our Vietnam-inspired inflation) have such an irrational stake in our Indochina adventure that if NBC, CBS, and ABC had said, "Look, it is different from what the politicians and generals say, and from what you think or hope; technology will not win this war; more often, too, we are destroying rather than creating," they would have ceased to sponsor network programs?

Such might-have beens! The networks never stood up, at least not for long, and, for all their billion-dollar resources, almost never gave their reporters honest, enterprising reportorial missions—except into direct combat, which was mostly a false story. Each night, the great orchestration of the evening news went on, with its parade of surreal or superficial stories, and the vast audience traveled through time in its strange company. I think it is wrong or foolish to imagine that television news in some idealized form could have somehow "solved" the problem of Vietnam for us. But I think it is evasive and disingenuous to suppose that, in its unwillingness over a space of ten years to assign a true information-gathering function to its news operations in Washington and Vietnam, American network news did much beyond contribute to the unreality, and thus the dysfunction, of American life.

On a recent evening, on NBC, I watched another televised scene of South Vietnamese civilians and soldiers fleeing in trucks and on foot—this time down the highway that runs south from Saigon toward the seacoast town of Vung Tau. From some years back, I could remember a news program (though on which network it was shown I've long forgotten) that included a story about the American contractors who had then just rebuilt the old French highway to Vung Tau. They seemed to be mild, efficient-looking men in short-sleeved sports shirts. I remember there were some South Vietnamese political figures on hand; also a general, though I don't recall whether he was American or Vietnamese. There was a speech. I think even a ribbon was cut, and some troop-carrying trucks sped down the new gray asphalt highway.

In the end, I think, there has been something deeply moving in the American public's muted, ambiguous response to the final days of our engagement in Indochina: our Indochinese war. I talk about the American public's "response" as if this were a tangible object, which it isn't, or as if I knew exactly what it is, which I don't. Still, it is possible to feel *something* about this, even from the television screen each evening (glowing now in color) as the network correspondents—so many of them new to this long war—try somehow to meet an invisible, unspoken national question with at least a professional response. Helplessly and methodically, they risk their safety by hauling their triad teams and their equipment into the few remaining artillery emplacements or close to the ever-constricting "front lines" or in the path of the continuously fleeing refugees. We are still supplied with the same simplistically informational scenes of firing guns and diving aircraft, but more and more, we could fill in the rest. Evidently, something was dying. But was it a nation, or was it the irrationality and superfluity of our presence?

At any rate, it seems not too much to say that television news was crucial—in its commissions and omissions—to the

American public's comprehension of our Indochinese involvement. Now, perhaps in the manner of a family that has watched some of its members and goods destroyed in the burning of a house that turned out to have been faultily fireproofed–and that had been posted with signs that turned out to have been either inaccurate or about some other house–the rest of us (when we have finished shaking our heads, and setting up charities for the next of kin, and commiserating with the fire commissioner for having such a hard and lonely job) may, as the saying goes, have learned something. If not about anything else, then about what is "realistic." After all, has anyone, *anywhere* (for the question still persists), been well served by navigating from this past "reality"?

Neutrality at the Empty Center

IT IS HARD TO DESCRIBE ON PAPER THE TELEVISION PERsonality of Howard Cosell, the media celebrity whose heavy-voiced sports announcing is already familiar to many people from ABC's *NFL Monday Night Football,* and who has lately inaugurated a variety show, also on ABC, called *Saturday Night Live with Howard Cosell.* In appearance, Cosell is a tall man, seemingly not very athletic, but nonetheless a man whose presence conveys a certain sense of bulky power. His voice is deep, and on camera he speaks in a kind of slow-motion, High Brooklyn version of what used to be called Winchellese (after the late *Daily Mirror* columnist and radio celebrity Walter Winchell, whose portentous, staccato phrases—"Good evening, Mr. and Mrs. America, and all the ships at sea!"—were once considered a model of assertive broadcasting delivery). Cosell speaks slowly and clearly, in a fashion that Marshall McLuhan might describe as "cool"—as opposed to Winchell's "hot" style of speech. "Now, *tell* me, Muhammad Ali," Cosell will intone, as if to a metronome, "when you *heard* . . . that *bell* . . . at the *start* . . . of the *seventh* round . . . you *knew* . . ." But the essence of Cosell's wide appeal does not seem to lie in any McLuhanesque property of coolness, nor, surely, does it lie in his alleged expertise in sports or in his ability to "tell it like it is"—qualities that, by and large, remain public-relations virtues and exist mainly in contrast to the sheer inanity of most other sports announcers. "Up to *this* point, *Washington* is really *defensing* the run," Cosell observed sonorously the other evening—an observation that could doubtless have been anticipated by any grandmother who had been following the game. Even his occasional penchant for criticizing a player for having missed an obvious block or dropped an easy pass ("Mel *received* that *ball* and *ran* stupidly") speaks less of some vaunted Cosellian savviness than of the uniformly childish and uncritical sanctity with which sports in this country have been generally presented by broadcasting.

In any case, as with most TV announcers and personalities, what is interesting about Cosell is not what he actually says on camera but how his presence (the voice beneath the personality) connects with the audience—what he really tells the people who watch him. In this regard, much has been made—usually on the level of a show-business *shtick*, as with Jack Benny's "stinginess"—of Cosell's "ego" and of his tendency to become overbearing. And, in fact, his public personality frequently is that of a bully. At times, he bullies his sports-announcing associates, Frank Gifford and Alex Karras; at other times, he has been known to bully some hapless (and distant) sports figure down on the field—a few weeks ago, for example, singling out Terry Bradshaw, of the Steelers. On his new variety show, Cosell has so far been fairly restrained in his overbearingness (and as a result, in a strange way, the show has seemed generally inert and artificial); but it is in the becalmed, empty waters of the sports announcer's booth that a sportscaster's personality (or lack of it) flourishes, and it is here that Cosell's brand of popular and telegenic sadism seems to have scored so heavily. "Big Mouth!" say the hand-lettered placards that fans hold aloft in hopeful derision at football games, and that the ABC cameras cheerfully photograph. The talk is of ego and mouths, but the electricity, one feels, is directly connected to a psychology of hurting. As with the proverbial man at the party who throws his weight around without actually hitting anyone, the focus of Cosell's public personality seems to be on what he might say, or finally might do; it is not so much on anger or violence itself as on anger or violence temporarily held back.

Cosell is by no means the only performer on popular television these days whose public personality has strong sadistic overtones. Johnny Carson has sometimes indulged in cruelties on *The Tonight Show*, and so has Dick Cavett from time to time on his show—though with both these stylized "hosts" the occasional instances of cruelty seem to have been more a matter of inevitable human rudeness (taking the form of malice with Carson and withdrawal with Cavett) than a formal assertion of personality. Also, many of the so-called game shows and their M.C.'s are notably sadistic, in some cases deliberately stirring up the insecure and exposed contestants into paroxysms of desire, only to drop them flat, perhaps with a smile. (In one recent instance, a young woman was encouraged to go into an extended fever of anticipation under the impression that she had just won a Rolls-Royce. After a while, the M.C. calmly handed her a package of rolls and a box of rice, and said she had been foolishly mistaken; the prize had been rolls and rice. The camera observed her distressed and unbelieving face, and then switched to the next contestant.) As a matter of fact, a case could almost be made for the existence of an informal division of daytime television into arenas of sadism and masochism, with the audiences of the game shows—guided by the M.C.'s—waiting chiefly to observe the hurt or humiliation visited upon the contestants or else to be stirred into secret rage at the undeserved good fortune of the lucky winners, and then, seated in another cube of time, perhaps the same audiences—but now guided by the familiar storybook figures of the soap operas—passively suffering the relentless disasters and miseries (those "everyday human problems") of the prototypical mothers, fathers, lovers, alienated children, and so forth.

In a sense, then, even with the appearance of Howard Cosell's bullying personality as a popular television art form, one might say that there is nothing much new going on in the psychology of popular entertainment. From Punch and Judy through Jiggs and Maggie and then to the "insult comedians," quiz shows, game shows, and soap operas of recent years, theatrical models of sadism and masochism have been around on a folkloric level for as long as there have been audiences to watch them. But in addition to watching and listening to the portentous Mr. Cosell, I have lately been watching a man who occupies an entirely different—or perhaps one should say a traditionally different—area of public attention: Tom Snyder, who made a popular reputation in Los Angeles as host of the *Tomorrow* show (a very-late-night talk program), and who was brought to New York last year by NBC not only to continue his role on *Tomorrow*, which also moved to New York, but chiefly to serve as a key news announcer on *NewsCenter 4*, the much-watched two-hour local-news program that is broadcast by WNBC each weekday from 5 to 7 p.m. It is Mr. Snyder's role as a news announcer (a news announcer, one imagines, of potentially greater eminence than *NewsCenter 4*) that seems worth looking at and trying to think about, because there are some disturbing similarities between the public personalities of the two men.

In appearance, Snyder is an altogether different type from Cosell. Where Cosell (who is in his fifties) resembles the archetypal New York taxi driver, Snyder (who is thirty-nine) is very contemporary, trim, and Californian. He expresses efficiency, assurance, and also a certain surface "coolness." In a TV serial he might play one of those successful young architects or doctors, or an engineer connected vaguely with the space program. Where a similarity to Cosell creeps in, I think, is in the quality of "edge" that both men appear to have—at least, in their public personalities. "Edge," of course, is a contemporary masking word, like "ego" or "drive." For what distinguishes Tom Snyder is surely not the pitch of his careful, neutral, accentless voice or the efficient manner in which he reads or introduces the news stories but a quality of abrasiveness and barely concealed hostility. This quality is hard to define precisely, and a television news program of even two hours' length doesn't quite provide the empty spaces of a sports announcer's booth. Even so, one has the definite impression that the man behind the neutral good looks, the neutral face, the neutral voice is not a neutral man. To the extent that I have watched him, the hostility, or "edge," has been mostly a matter of apparent nuance, of small intramural details. The other evening, for example, Frank Field, the station's science expert and a man of fifty-two, was scheduled to begin a report on the "Male Menopause." Each time Snyder referred to the coming story, he would throw in a remark such as "Frank Field, *himself* in his middle years . . ." Clearly, it was phrased as a joke, but it was not a joke. As the two hours wore on, Field's story was frequently referred to, and each time this stress was somehow placed by Snyder on Field's age and, therefore, his connection to the story. When Field finally appeared, just before beginning his report he turned to Snyder and said, with evident feeling, "You know, I'm only in my *early* middle years."

Now, the spectacle of a news announcer making casual, slightly malicious fun of one of his associates is not a matter of world-shaking importance, any more than was the needling by Howard Cosell of the Pittsburgh quarterback Terry Bradshaw. One could even say that, given the unearthly blandness of most television announcers, it somehow accords with a more realistic view of society to permit its broadcasting spokesmen to express some of the general aggressions and hostilities found everywhere in modern life. One watches both Snyder and Cosell, I think, with an implicit sense of waiting for the other shoe to drop, for there is something about these men, with their "edge," or "ego," or "authority," that serves as a magnet to the emotions. The calmly articulated tensions always appear to be about something (though *what* is never mentioned), and the controlled or implied angers always seem to be pointing in some direction (though *where* is never revealed).

I suspect that this never-never land of "emotional responses" is where the secret of Tom Snyder's and Howard Cosell's success exists, and where their importance to us can be found. It seems to me that, for all the solemnity or efficiency of their readings, the deepest, primary message of these announcers—these spokesmen—is of *non-involvement*. In a sense, the bullying, the abrasions, the sadistic texture are only part of a smoke screen. The reason the aura of tension is never resolved is that there is no source behind it, beyond the personality of the announcer. The reason the hostility never leads anywhere is that it leads only back into itself. As Cosell's gravity is uninvolved, so are his anger and bullying. "*Kilmer* has been having *trouble* all evening finding *deep* receivers," Cosell intones. There is a grudging, edgy quality buried in the voice—a sense of blame being placed (on Kilmer? on the deep receivers?), of belligerent emotions being slipped into this unimportant sentence, as if somehow to blow it into life and conceal the emptiness at the center.

With Cosell, the subject at hand is mainly sports—or "only sports," if that is one's viewpoint, though the reason for the man's celebrity is the importance so many Americans attach to athletics and to sports figures. With Snyder, however, the subject at hand is news—this history of ourselves and of the world which the giant broadcasting corporations furnish us each day as a stylized adjunct to their entertainment business. In a perceptive book called *Television: Technology and Cultural Form*, the British critic Raymond Williams discusses what he calls the "mediating" role of television in English and American society, by which he means the classic role of authority in furthering its life views through the mediating (or supposedly "normal") channels of broadcasting. In England, this mediating role has been easier to spot, as a result of formal government domination of broadcasting through the BBC. Here in America, the mediating role has been much less clear, not only as a result of corporate ownership of broadcasting but also because national authority itself has been so divided between government and business. The textbooks continue to proclaim a "civics" in which the key checks and balances of national life are those between the legislative, executive, and judicial branches of government, whereas for some time now the important dynamic beneath the American surface has been the geologic shifts and countershifts between business and government. Thus, in foreign policy—for example, as regards oil in the Middle East or copper in South America—the interests of business and government have diverged, merged, and competed. And in domestic life, on questions ranging from industrial safety to the environment, the interests of business and government have diverged, merged, and competed. The theory remains that business is subservient to government: there are regulatory agencies and antitrust legislation to prove this. But the broadcasting industry itself is proof of the limited extent to which such a token subservience exists. In fact, through much of recent American history the self-contained dynamic of business (and its traditional acceptance by much of the populace) has increasingly placed it in a nearly independent orbit, pursuing its own logic and its own imperatives.

What this has to do with news broadcasting is simply that here, too, a theory exists—that "news" comes out of thin air, and is caught by ubiquitous or enterprising "newsmen," who relay it to "news stations," which then, via popular and neutral "newscasters," disseminate it to the nation. The facts are neither as just described nor entirely contrary. Not only is the "news" a product of careful selection by television news organizations (whose personnel themselves are carefully selected), but—what is as important—the context and the personality of its transmission are selected with equal care. All the skills that business has been able to extract from social science (audience-testing, sampling, marketing, and so on) are nowadays devoted to choosing the mediators—the men who "front," or "mediate," for the networks, and who thus create the context for the news. NBC, in fact, is supposed to have spent six months analyzing various "tests" and "data" before deciding on Tom Snyder as one of the anchormen on *NewsCenter 4*, and increasingly this sort of semi-scientific selection process precedes the appointment of key news personnel across the country. *After* the selection, a strenuous public-relations campaign is usually undertaken by the parent network to disguise the selection process and reinforce the myth or theory that the newsman or newsmen have been chosen for their connective human and individual qualities. Newsmen are thereby increasingly cast as actors—as friendly or funny or wise or gruff, or now as egoistic. They are instructed by the network authorities to "be themselves," and they are continually advertised (should anyone miss the point) for their personal characteristics: characteristics that appear to identify them, as individuals, with the audience—with us.

The fact is, of course, that they are not really us; they are models or mediators, often chosen for qualities we have no knowledge of, and only appearing to be us. A few years ago, this role-playing came to be understood—or, at least, detected—by elements of the minority audience, who began to look askance at the theatrically credible, solid-citizen news announcers, such as Walter Cronkite, Harry Reasoner, and the late Chet Huntley; though to this day the mass of people feel "trust" for "Uncle Walter," and with good reason in the sense that Walter Cronkite (to my mind a tough rather than an avuncular man) has been mainly and honorably following his own instincts—"being himself"—during the years that brought us into Vietnam, and farther in, and farther in, and farther in, and then perplexedly (and apparently triumphantly) out. As to why Walter Cronkite was chosen for the role—besides a basic professional competence—well, there is no exact or certified way of answering such a question, but it seems worth noting that in that extraordinary era, which began in a way with the interests of Big Government and Big Business appearing to converge, the guide and mediator for our news (a news of governmental adventure supported by business) was a man whose evident and implicit virtues were prudence, dignity, above all *coherence*, and a support for classic American values.

Many things have happened in the last ten years, not the least important of which has been a growing popular disaffection with the authority of government, which ostensibly came to a head around the Watergate crisis but in fact persists in the national mood and is played upon frequently in the nightly network news broadcasts. One might assume that it was the popular disenchantment with government in the late 1960's which produced the current anti-government bias in broadcasting; but the truth seems to be that broadcasting's espousal of the anti-war, anti-government cause was then slender to the point of nonexistence, and that it was only toward the latter part of the Nixon Presidency, when Big Business finally turned against the government, that this new, skeptical note of anti-government bias crept into routine news programs. At any rate, a decided shift in popular perceptions of authority has taken place in the recent past, and has been accompanied by two seemingly surface developments in broadcast-news operations. One is the emergence of the new generation of news "mediators"—those personable groups of informal and chatty and sometimes laughing newscasters—whose role seems to be that of playing-off on the news; the other is what seems to me to be an increasing bias on the part of these same news programs against government authority—a bias that is usually masked by an aura of "anti-corruption" reporting (as if corruption in government were the only kind of corruption worth emphasizing), and by a stylized post-Watergate "skepticism" toward the Presidency, which seems to appear and vanish and reappear according to broadcasting's mood.

And what, finally, of Tom Snyder, whose personality (like Cosell's) is somewhat stronger than the personalities of the other chatty announcers in his vicinity? It is probably a mistake to try to make too much of his particular news presence: he is a capable news reader, who clearly wishes to be a success; he is "being himself." But I think it would be equally a mistake to make too little—not of Snyder himself, but of his role as mediator. For what he gives us, not so much by his words (which are the standard TelePrompTer newsspeak of all television stations) as by some mystery or inadvertence of personality, is a message of disconnection from us. "Coolness" is another masking word and means nearly anything one wishes it to mean. The point is: What is at the center? Or is the center empty?

In any case, the important issue is not Howard Cosell or Tom Snyder. I imagine they can take care of themselves. Neither Snyder nor Cosell nor anyone else will "disconnect" the television audience all by himself; nor, surely, is anyone consciously trying to. But there is a disconnection already present in the country, and it is being nurtured. Much of our theatrical fantasy life is centered upon sports, and so it is worth noting that the chief mediator for our sports is a man who—pushing and bullying his silent audience—proclaims an implicit message of non-involvement. Noise and solemnity, yes; but emptiness beneath. And in our important and insecure civic life (which, it is a truism to state, is so heavily informed and activated by TV reports) it seems that, more and more, the men who mediate this area of life are speaking largely of its flaws and irrelevance—of its lack of importance.

In the meantime, as if to breathe away a supposedly "liberal" fear of the broadcasting business as Big Brother, a new concept has lately been put forward which asserts that commercial television is a merely neutral force. Thus, in *The Tin Kazoo* Edwin Diamond writes that TV has become simply "another utility, like the telephone." And in *Who Controls the Mass Media?* Martin H. Seiden goes even further, arguing that because of commercials, and the public's responses to commercials, it is the mass public that exerts the controlling force on broadcasting. There is some merit in trying to demystify television in this country, but that is not the same as saying that it is a neutral appliance—that neutral forces somehow combine and produce neutral sequences of information, which are then acted on subjectively only in our own heads. The fact we are all stuck with is that television is an authority, and the evidence of this century is that there has been no such thing as a *neutral* authority.

The New Season

(*AFTER A LOOK AT THE NEW SEASON*)

Top Cop

"People complain that television concentrates too much on violence in our country," says Omar W. Applebaum, the soft-spoken screenwriter-turned-producer responsible for last season's *S.P.L.A.T.*, "and I accept the criticism." That is why Applebaum Productions has gone *outside* the country for this season's new detective series with a difference, *Top Cop*, which is based on the true-life activities of Col. Renaldo (Sandy) Sanchez, former chief investigator for the Chilean Secret Police. "Of course, we are using location footage wherever possible," says producer Applebaum, who has been active, with wife Susi, in local Save the Herons campaigns, "but I think the main thing we have going for us is that our show is about *people*. Sandy Sanchez is just a copper, south of the border, doing his job like any other copper." For Ron Hockaday, the veteran Hawaiian-born actor who plays Col. Sanchez, *Top Cop* has been a chance to shuck the second-fiddle image he acquired while playing Wu, the bumbling anesthesiologist in *Hawaiian Doc*. "At first, I had trouble identifying with the part of Sandy Sanchez on account of his being five feet three and a Taurus, while I am six feet two and a Capricorn," admits the popular Hockaday, "but I have always wanted to do a series for Om Applebaum, and besides director Les Conboy lets me do most of my own stunts." In the first episode, Col. Sanchez is forced to cut short a long-overdue vacation when a gang of elderly, left-wing professors kidnap the crippled daughter of a major-oil-company executive and then threaten to poison the entire Santiago water supply unless their demands are met.

1720 Buena Vista

After the success of *Beacon Hill*, followed by *Murray Hill*, *Nob Hill*, and then *Shaker Heights*—and notwithstanding last season's flop *Pikes Peak*, produced under the mistaken impression that viewers were interested mainly in a new genre of "altitude comedy"—Belladonna Productions is back on the track with *1720 Buena Vista*, which has been described by Belladonna prexy Arthur Brinckerhoff, Sr., as a "totally candid, unsparing, yet affectionate look at the manners and mores of the American upper classes in the 1970's." The plot action centers on the saga of the J. Foxglove Mantee family, whose members reside in the spacious, heavily mortgaged comforts of 1720 Buena Vista Drive in the exclusive Sherwood Forest Estates area of Los Angeles, and on the Mantee family's deep, sturdy, though necessarily human relationship with their traditional cadre of "helpers": Irmgard Anschluss, the sixteen-year-old Swiss *au pair* who "helps" Kay-Kay Mantee take care of her five children and two adopted South Vietnamese orphans; Mrs. Emma-Louise Wilberforce, who "helps" Mrs. Mantee clean house; and Manuel Sanchez, who "helps" Mr. Mantee trim the camellia bushes and run the power lawnmower. In the first episode, a Mantee family crisis is narrowly averted, on the occasion of Irmgard's bringing a casual pickup (Walter Neame) home for "dinner—and anything else," by the uncompromising decision of patriarch J. Foxglove Mantee to eat *his* dinner out in the car. In further episodes, youngest son Lance Mantee II is threatened with expulsion from the Book-of-the-Month Club by a "mysterious phone call"; Kay-Kay "embarrasses" Manuel by asking him to pick her up at exercise class and drive her to Mexico; Mrs. Wilberforce threatens to "live in."

Hanging High

With a string of irreverent, topical comedy hits to his credit, dealing openly yet humorously with such heretofore sacrosanct themes as senior-citizen shoplifting (*The Petersons*), biracial eating (*The Larrabees*), middle-age circumcision (*Louie*), and ethnic driving (*Edna*), the time finally seemed ripe to Herb Muldoon, brainy, effervescent president of Muldoon Productions, for bringing out a new kind of irreverent, topical comedy about adolescent impotence. Thus the idea for *Hanging High* was born, centered on the characters of Ned and Gloria—two young people "getting it together" in the gorgeous San Francisco Bay area and trying to deal frankly and humorously with the problem of Ned's impotence as well as with Gloria's refusal to do "non-creative" work in a male-dominated society. The first episode, which started filming last summer at Muldoon Studios, shows Ned (Tyler Benedict) and Gloria (Miriam Moncure) having breakfast on their prayer mats after yet another difficult night. "Well, you can't win 'em all," says Ned shyly, still unwilling to deal with the problem, which he thinks is connected with faulty wiring in his quadraphonic tape deck. "That's cool," says Gloria, on her way to a new job at a Lapp metalwork boutique. Later that morning, Gloria returns home, having quit her job as a result of "being hassled" by customers, and she and Ned "try" once again, without success. Next, Ned and Gloria talk things over with Jim and Jemima, the biracial, bisexual couple next door, who suggest that Ned and Gloria go in for hang-gliding and "forget the whole interpersonal thing." Unfortunately, at this point in the filming, the networks' new "family-hour" code was enunciated, with the result, according to Mr. Muldoon, that "much against our creative instincts we were forced to abandon the heretofore sacrosanct problems of impotence, and concentrate on the hitherto rarely discussed problems of hang-gliding." At the end of the first episode, Ned unexpectedly traps a gang of quality-paperback rustlers by crashing on them from a height of three hundred feet.

The Iliad

A new treat for public television's culture-minded viewers is Independent Welsh Television's 120-episode version of Homer's mighty *Iliad,* which debuts this fall on most PBS stations under a grant from Mammoth Petroleum Corporation. Once again, a topflight cast of British (and Welsh) actors has taken hold of an ancient classic and, in the words of IWT chairman Lord Nairn, "has shown that Homer, whoever he or she might have been, could tell a rattling good story as well as the next fellow." Frederick Ffolke-Felspar, Brian Connaught, and Anthony Vere handle the roles of Agamemnon, Hector, and Achilles with that skill at ensemble playing for which the British (and, of course, the Welsh) have been so justly praised. Celia Ponsonby (whom American viewers remember as the stylish Little Eva in last year's BBC production of *Uncle Tom's Cabin*) plays an impeccable Helen. Hugo Trevor-Trevor is a jolly Ajax, with an eye for "the wenches" and a hearty appetite for Sarpedon's venison pie. Sir Christopher Sparks, Mammoth Petroleum Corporation Professor of Attic Studies at Stokes College, is "host" for the program, and describes the origins of Attic folk dance for the benefit of the American audience.

The Goobers

A heartwarming "family program" set in the Oklahoma of the 1930's, *The Goobers* relates the trials and tribulations (and periodic chuckles) of the large and somewhat demented DeWitt Goober family as it struggles to live and laugh its way through the difficult period of the "Dust Bowl." No expense has been spared by Creative Supervisor Cuthbert Milner in re-creating the "feel" of this historic and picturesque era, including the time-consuming tracking down and eventual purchase of the actual farm machinery used in the Twentieth Century-Fox version of *The Grapes of Wrath* as well as the construction—thirty miles east of Anaheim, Calif.—of a complete replica of a twelve-acre mismanaged, badly eroded farm, over which eight specially converted Flying Fortress engines blow 350 cubic tons of dust each day during filming. "Diction gets to be something of a problem, as well as scalp cleanliness," avers Ben Willoughby, the veteran actor who plays DeWitt Goober. "However, even the young kids on the show feel they're involved in something more important than just a regular sit-com—like learning where Oklahoma is, for example." In the first episode, bad luck seems about to overwhelm the Goobers in the form of the death of their remaining cow, the failure of the spring rutabaga crop, the abduction of Little Sister (Evelyn Markey) by Ponca City white slavers, and serious injury to Grandpa (Dennis Deterding), who has been stationed on the roof, trying to spot locusts; however, unexpected good fortune arrives when Young DeWitt (Greg Loin) wins a month's supply of coat hangers in a raffle. In subsequent episodes, Big Sister (Lori Mims) admits to a "crush" on Judge Tremayne (Fred Compote) and is shot in the heel; Ma Goober (Lucinda Marr) sends away to Oklahoma City for a new corduroy hat and is taught a lesson in humility when the grasshoppers eat it. In a special two-parter, Little Sister comes back home for National Safety Week dinner and brings some new rutabaga seeds with her.

Tom & Tessie

A husband-and-wife police team with a difference is Bulbar Productions' *Tom & Tessie*, which follows the activities of Tom (Derwent Fizdale) and Tessie (Gladys Galoon) Flaherty—a divorced-husband-and-wife team of airport security guards whose professional duties involve them in an endless variety of far-flung adventures. "Really, inspecting hand luggage for tubes of explosive toothpaste is only one segment of an airport security person's job," says Gladys Galoon, who in real life is married to William J. (Bill) Bulbar. Miss Galoon, a former Pecan Queen and a member of the La Jolla Little Players, spent several hours last summer observing trained security guards at work at the Bakersfield International Airport, where much of the action for the first episode was filmed. "So far, I'd have to say that Tessie's character is the more fully developed of the two, since in the opening show Tom gets his hand caught in the zipper of a homicidal retired admiral's mandolin case and so has to be shipped aboard the plane in the carry-on-clothing compartment," says Derwent Fizdale, who five years ago played Tug Rafferty in *Manhole* and who has recently been speaking out on the pro-heron bond issue. "However," continues the young actor, "I have great respect for director Hub Bathgate, as well as Bill Bulbar, and I am confident that Tom's character will have a chance to grow." In later episodes, Tom is instructed by his security supervisor (Lew Glyph) to enforce under-the-seat baggage regulations on members of the Berlin Philharmonic, and narrowly averts disaster when one of the cellos refuses to "fold." Later, Tessie catches the eye of a traveling Middle East "strong man," who invites her and Tom to come to his country and guard his new airport against undesirable charter-flight passengers.

Rookie Truck-Driving Doc

Bevis Dimbal plays Dr. Phil Hartigan, a brash kid with a slum background, a love of the open road, and a degree from Harvard Medical School, who, disdaining the usual opportunities for storefront medical practice in a big city, chooses instead to cruise the highways and byways of the nation in a ten-ton Diamond Reo semi, diagnosing "unpopular" symptoms at truck stops, mending broken hearts and broken bones as he speeds along the black-top, and sometimes good-humoredly operating in cases where the local medical structure has broken down. "I can really identify with Phil," says Bev Dimbal, who studied speech under the renowned Ilse Morris, and who admits that "frankly we were hurting until Bob Bannerman moved us into the eight-thirty time slot, right after *Grendel*." In the opening episode, Sue-Ann Wendover plays a rich widow afflicted with knuckle-cracking in a town whose only source of health care is a telephone answering service.

Mammoth News Specials

Sponsored by the Mammoth Petroleum Corporation, these specials carry forward a long tradition of public-service programs beginning with *Mammoth Kingdom*, *Mammoth Theater*, *Mammoth Playhouse*, *Mammoth Theology*, and *Mammoth World of Sports*. The opening program, "Let Freedom Ring," examines the attempt of a major American oil company to rid a South American village of savage, heron-devouring alligators by building an oil refinery on a nearby swamp.

Pervasive Albion

THE TIME IS AN ENGLISH SUMMER'S MIDDAY. THE year is 1912. The scene is London—inside the Bellamy town house. It's an ample and elegant place—old paintings and solid furniture. Great silent rooms. The Bellamys themselves are away for the weekend. The staff of six sits about in the kitchen, stirring tea, and hoping for a bit of Saturday quiet. But downstairs now comes young Captain James—James Bellamy, that is—about twenty-seven and already retired from the army. He's been lazing around all morning in his room, listening to new jazz records from America, and now he lazes his way past the library—blue blazer, white ducks, and nothing much to do—where he spots his father's new typist, young Miss Forrest, working on some papers. He asks her to lunch. Alas, not *out* to lunch. As Lady Marjorie later observes to James, "If you decided to invite Miss Forrest out to supper at a restaurant, nobody would object." But he asks her to lunch upstairs, in the family dining room. Clearly, the staff mind being routed up for a quick Edwardian light lunch—with the huge table to be set, and the proper glasses to be polished, and the vegetables to be washed, and the apples to be peeled and mashed into applesauce—a lot less than they mind the idea of Captain James seated in the family dining room with a working girl. "I'm sure Mr. Bellamy's typist is a perfectly *respectable* young woman," says Roberts, Her Ladyship's maid, "but she is not a lady." The whole matter comes to a head over the question of wine. James offers sherry before lunch. Then, trying to show off before Miss Forrest, he further demands from the butler a claret in the dining room—in fact, the best claret.

HUDSON: I'm sorry, sir, but I am not to serve the Château Brane Cantenac without special instruction.

JAMES: Why not? I know it's not been drunk. We had a bottle with our dinner last week.

HUDSON: There are certain *difficulties* . . . If I might see you, sir, in private.

JAMES: What is all this, Hudson?

HUDSON: I must point out I cannot serve the master's best claret. There are only two bottles left.

JAMES: I ordered one, Hudson, and I expect you to serve it.

HUDSON: I'm sorry, sir. I am not to serve the Château Brane Cantenac '93 without special instruction.

JAMES: Did my father forbid you to serve that claret?

HUDSON: He wouldn't wish it to be served at *luncheon*, sir. And not today.

As things turn out, Hudson reluctantly serves the wine. Miss Forrest—embarrassed at becoming an issue between the two men—makes her way back to the suburbs. And later, when the Bellamys have returned, Hudson brings up the incident and gives notice, which has the desired effect of upsetting both Bellamys—prompting Mr. Bellamy to ask

James to apologize to Hudson, and Her Ladyship to assert, despite her grief, that no son of hers shall ever apologize to a servant. In the end, though, Hudson rescinds his notice; Captain James murmurs a languid apology to the butler; and Her Ladyship departs on a scheduled visit to Canada aboard the R.M.S. *Titanic*. Thus concludes the year's first episode in what may be the best regular dramatic feature on American television: *Upstairs, Downstairs*—the British series that public-television stations in this country show under the program heading of Masterpiece Theatre.

There's no doubt about it: *Upstairs, Downstairs* is very good entertainment—and since it's as entertainment that it claims our attention, it's mainly as entertainment that one ought to consider it. The production is elegant, without being arch or showy. The ensemble acting of the British cast is of a high order. The writing has wit and style. Of course, there's something to be said for lines of dialogue which can be delivered with a "sir" in front of them. But the *Upstairs, Downstairs* actors rarely fool with this sort of thing—the way, for example, that Broadway Edwardians often do—and even in a bit of byplay such as the wine controversy, which is close to parody, the moment of parody itself is never reached, either in the mannerisms of the characters or in the language, whose literate, economic music gets played intact. The "period" business, too, generally manages to be right and satisfying—and properly sensual. Upstairs, the rich woodwork shines in the sun; the silver tea service gleams. Downstairs, the maids and footman work around the clock. But both worlds are caught—

are caught in the strange, subtle embrace that surely then existed between the classes, and without the usual intervening distortions of a modern consciousness, such as pervade either Gatsby's frozen salons or Arnold Wesker's Marxist kitchens. In *Upstairs, Downstairs*, the gentlemen and ladies, serving girls and butlers dance on the same stage but in different spotlights, and using different steps. The servants rise at dawn to dust and sweep and clean and polish the great house's objects–and the story tells us that they're not sustained in these hard lives so much by "knowing their place," or by some fuddled Hollywood sentiment, as by being observers of a larger drama: in some ways, a national drama. In short, class life and class tensions are revealed as theater: an oddly shared theater, in which the Bellamys naturally have the important roles–sweeping in and out of the most ordinary events (a lunch! a departure for the weekend!) while the downstairs audience, which makes the lunch, and staggers about under the suitcases, gazes on raptly, with as yet only a dim sense of its own theatricality.

On the surface, *Upstairs, Downstairs* seems to be devoted to explaining or portraying the almost exotic conventions of pre-First World War Europe. Thus, the convention of a gentleman's not entertaining the lower classes in his home, or perhaps of working girls' not stepping into the wrong spotlight, or perhaps the convention of the right claret at lunch. (Later episodes examine the conventions of a gentleman's income, of serving-class loyalty, of racial sentiment, and other matters.) All this is interesting, though in a rather recondite but entertaining way, and the themes are invariably handled with sensitivity and intelligence. What *Upstairs, Downstairs* is especially good at is revealing, almost uncovering, affection—the odd, intricate play of affections in this assured and often brutal era. Beneath the ballet and drudgery of the great house, there's a real and fascinating *fondness* that floats—most of the time almost invisible, like smoke—from downstairs to upstairs. The servants have their own passions and preoccupations. But they also really care about Her lovely Ladyship, and about her ministerial husband, and even about spoiled young Captain James. However, when Hudson plays his strong card and gives notice, Lady Bellamy's first reaction is that her house has been disrupted, and Bellamy's regret is that he'll have to spend several months without a butler. To be sure, a few moments later he gets around to remarking that Hudson is actually a very good butler—"He's served your mother and me well." But it's a tough, true moment, and it's handled with no false moves or harrumphing. Indeed, such has been the usual level of class melodrama (even when done by the British) that one keeps expecting each tough moment—each class dissonance—to somehow collapse on itself, or follow the traditional logic of stage sentiment. But nothing collapses. In that lunch scene with James, Miss Forrest, and Hudson, the sympathy of the scene never tilts too far toward Miss Forrest—the working girl who's in an awkward position. And James himself is a fine, affectionate, but unromantic portrait of a careless young blood—an earlier kin to Evelyn Waugh's bland and brutish Noble Lords, and even to Fitzgerald's Racquet Club aristocrats.

Still, since *Upstairs, Downstairs* is as good as it is,

there's no need to get carried away into thinking that it's television's answer to Ibsen, Shaw, and Beckett. It's an extremely well-done entertainment series, which is content mainly to re-create the feel of a certain historical period, and to be borne along by an episodic story line that frequently owes as much to the conventions of soap opera (as per Lady B.'s departure on the *Titanic*) as to the standards of serious drama. Its limits seem to be a certain sociological fussiness and a kind of snobbery. For instance, in the wine scene I know we're supposed to have fun at the expense of sophisticated conventions, but I suspect we're also supposed to feel a distinct pleasure at being let in on those conventions. It's skillful theater, but it's a theater of minor characters, who move with marvelous grace against a background that is sometimes sharp and alive, and sometimes rather too deliberately social history filled out with actors.

Also, it's so intrinsically *British*—British made, for British audiences—and this brings up another question, although perhaps more a political than an aesthetic one. For, at the risk of sounding chauvinist or parochial, it's worth asking: What is *Upstairs, Downstairs* doing here—and in the prominent place it holds on most public-television schedules? How does it happen that the best entertainment series on American public television is an essentially British import from England? Nor is it the only one. For probably the next-best entertainment series that's being shown on public television this fall is *A Family at War*—a finely made, somewhat more melodramatic, equally British view of the late 1930's and the Second World War through the experiences of a Liverpool family—which was produced by, and imported from, England's independent Granada Television. There's also a BBC comedy show called *Monty Python's Flying Circus*, which is now being shown mainly on the Eastern public-television stations.

This isn't meant as a criticism of imported programs, or, certainly, of the public-television stations that show them—since the obvious reason they run imports is that imports are the best quality buys for the money. But imports on public TV aren't quite the same thing as imported plays and movies. For many years, after all, some of the most successful and best-received plays on Broadway have been European—mostly transplanted from London. And American movie theaters—at least, in the big cities—regularly show the new films of Bergman, Fellini, Truffaut, and so forth, to the obvious advantage and pleasure of American audiences. In fact, if there was a time when Henry James had to move to Europe in order to rub shoulders with European culture, and Edmund Wilson, later, more or less had to carry back French and Russian novels between his teeth to the American intelligentsia, by now there is a plenitude of international culture around the country—and we could doubtless use more of it.

But television is different—different in its private, cultural impact (for most people don't regard it as "culture," or as outside their everyday experience), and different in its distribution systems. When a European play moves into New York, it takes up only one out of what are still several dozen theaters. Furthermore, most foreign theatrical imports are in the Big Hit category. *Equus* doesn't squeeze out Off Broadway. *Amarcord* is a great, artistic—and not merely Italian but international–film which doesn't supplant the work of original American filmmakers. The importation of foreign movies and plays is, on the whole, a happy event, because they're additions to an existing body of American work. There's room for all, since there's already an American drama and an American film; that is, playwrights and moviemakers whose plays and movies are regularly being produced.

But there's no such thing on television–at least, virtually no such thing. A long time ago, we signed over a large share of the public spectrum to the networks. The networks are closely tied to mass-market commercial advertising. Thus, on the networks, for the most part, there exists a middling level of commercial-entertainment competence, which only rarely rises even to a high level of commercial-entertainment competence. For example, a few weeks ago NBC showed an original telefilm called *The Law*, which displayed considerable virtuosity and style in its editing (no small matter, since the movie was trying to portray the complexities of an urban courthouse), and contained some capable acting in the key roles. *The Law* was as good a network drama as I've seen in recent years. But although it periodically rose above its slick, formula genre (especially in stretches of subtle, plain-spoken dialogue), still there was something soft and tricky at its center–a hokey story that was touched upon, then dwelled upon, as if the film's creators had agreed that its seriousness could be taken so far but no further. In the end, it was one of those well-made professional movies that don't leave you with anything to say about them as you walk out of the theater–or, in this case, wander into the kitchen. And, one understands, *that's* the way commercial television usually has to be when dealing with the mass audience.

But where's the alternative? There is supposed to be an alternative. It's called *public* television, and, as we saw, two of its best and most prominent entertainment features (on a thin schedule) are the British *Upstairs, Downstairs* and the British *A Family at War*, plus *Monty Python's Flying Circus*, which is fun, though even more British than the other two—a giggly-British. In a sense, I suppose, one could find this very ironic. After all, wasn't it as a part of the great postwar surge of American economic imperialism—with American companies buying up foreign companies, and American advertising agencies and consumer products spreading around the globe—that American telefilm producers also began flooding the world with American entertainment series, most of which had already earned back their costs at home and thus could be deliberately unloaded below cost overseas, so as to price out any potentially competing local product? In Canada in the 1950's, for instance, American Westerns were being sold for as little as two thousand dollars per half hour, at a time when the developing Canadian telefilm industry could barely produce a program of similar length for less than twenty thousand dollars. Similar stories were reported about Australia, South America, and elsewhere—with the result that *Dragnet, Restless Gun, Route 66*, and other such strident visions of American life have been visited upon much of the world, perhaps briefly gratifying a mass audience (which usually had no more alternatives than the original American audience) but also in the process stifling or diminishing the development of local television activity and the creation of a more locally relevant programming.

Has the worm (or telefilm) turned, then? Are United States "nationals" soon to be standing by helplessly while their impressionable small children utter their first words in giggly-British, or demand Edwardian silver tea services for Christmas, or call their fathers "Guv'nor"? That might be nice for a change, but it's not likely, and it's not the point. The point, I think, is that just about every government in the world has recognized the importance of a nationally expressive television—which is why, among other reasons, there have been so many complaints from weaker governments about American telefilm predominance. In our country, there's no doubt as to the nationalism that animates the big networks—nor any doubt as to *whose* nationalism or national spirit is carefully expressed, and tended, and continuously played upon in entertainment features as well as in advertising, not to mention those arcane "Star-Spangled Banner"s that are thrummed up toward the Goodyear blimp each weekend from stadiums across the land. It's not that commercial television is above receiving imports, but when it does—as in the case of another fine BBC series, *Till Death Do Us Part*—it shucks the Britishness, and then deliberately and expensively refurbishes the basic idea in a totally American set of clothes, and calls it *All in the Family*. When it comes to playing with national imagery, commercial television knows what it's doing.

But public television—well, that seems to be another story. It's not that public television doesn't know what it's doing but that it's an institution that is supposed to be supported by the government (and by other institutions), and while these distant forces have generally managed to keep it alive—padding around in bedroom slippers in the background, sometimes even going for long walks—it's clear by now that few important people want to give it enough money to make it strong and healthy: economically and artistically viable. Indeed, no one seems to seriously want a *strong* public television, except for a few foundations and the public—and much of the public isn't sure, or can't feel clearly about it, because public TV has never had the financial resources to show everyone what it can do. Not that the business-government establishment is against the institution per se—provided that it takes a certain form. The television networks, for example, vaguely encourage its existence, for otherwise, sooner or later, a new Andrew Jackson might happen along and decide to create another network from scratch, but they want it "educational," hence uncompetitive, hence weak. Big business offers individual stations occasional teaspoons, and sometimes tablespoons, of cash—in some instances tactfully, as in the case of Xerox, but often self-servingly, as in the recent case of Mobil Oil Corporation, whose "public-service" grant to station KCET, in Los Angeles, for producing *The Way It Was*, a sports series, has been exploited by the company in a nationwide advertising campaign. The principal obstacles to a strong public television, however, have been Congress and recent Administrations—the representatives of the public. Apparently, too many congressmen are too well tied to commercial broadcasters to permit the unleashing of a competitive "fourth network." And recent Presidents, such as Richard Nixon—whose interest in controlling mass media bordered on a full-time mania—have been content ostensibly to support public television's modest requests for funds, while making sure that, when it *does* get money from the government, this money is then diverted and scattered to the individual stations around the nation.

This last idea doesn't necessarily sound obstructive—although it certainly has that now familiar ring of jut-jawed, corrupted populism about it. But the way the process has been worked out, and virtually legalized (as the Public Broadcasting Financing Act makes its way through the Senate), is that what was formerly the central organizing and programming authority for public television—the Public Broadcasting Service—has been cut out of roughly half of the new federal moneys, which will henceforth flow to the 246 individual public-television stations. PBS, based in Washington, and successor to the old Educational Television network, has been the only central public-television organization with the capacity to back expensive, and sometimes controversial, programs, such as *An American Family*, and to orchestrate the two hundred-odd public stations into a kind of network. As the new public-television bill would work, PBS wouldn't have enough money to be more than an administrative organization. And the individual stations, which have never been famous either for production risk-taking or for being able to agree on common policies, will now have much greater buying power spread among them—but not *that* much, nor will it be provided in such a way that they are likely to regularly mount the type of professional, imaginative productions that might attract the public to its own still unformed network.

It would be an exaggeration to say that the situation is a total disaster. The new bill would provide federal funds to public television of $70 million in its first year, fiscal 1975. Also, the bill guarantees government funding for at least five years. Furthermore, public television's audience seems to be growing, and so does the level of individual citizens' contributions. New York's station WNET recently raised $372,000 from viewers in one of its quarterly campaigns, which lately have been supplying the station with 20 percent of its annual operating funds. But it would be an exaggeration to say that the public-television situation is enormously encouraging. PBS has been largely reduced to pushing paper. All too many station schedules are padded out with yoga classes, health instruction, burglar-lock advice, and countless Children's Television Workshop repeats. And in public "prime time," although there are often fine musical programs, and an interesting weekly news show, *The 51st State*, and irregular but well-done documentaries, there is something important missing from the center of the schedule—and perhaps it's the presence of these generally attractive British programs that makes one notice it so sharply. After all, it's not isolationist to suggest that an American public might feel a deep connection to an American *Family at War*, or to a saga of pre-First World War *America*—and that this public might be a good deal more substantial than the audience that now attends to the clever dance steps of Hudson and the Bellamys. At least, there should be room for both. There should be provision for both. There's really no honorable reason any more that the people of this rich country can't be given a sturdy *national* television production system—honestly informative, creative, unfettered by the imperatives of hucksterism, and unhampered by the self-serving theories of transient politicians.

Time, Memory, and News

MOST TELEVISION NEWS PROGRAMS HAVE BEEN GRADually switching over from monolithic anchormen to a more informal and comradely setup, but when the President wants to tell us something he still goes one-on-one against the audience. "My conscience tells me clearly and certainly that I cannot prolong the bad dreams that continue to reopen a chapter that is closed," said President Ford the other morning before proclaiming his pardon of Richard Nixon. President Ford's head stayed squarely in the center of the television screen, filling the picture—whose dim background was the Oval Office of the White House, into which a glimpse of sunlight and green leaves had been symbolically admitted at the start of the announcement and then, perhaps also symbolically, focused out.

The President, in the modern fashion, referred to dreams in his address to the nation. Equally contemporary were the television reporters who later tried to analyze Mr. Ford's action and who frequently found themselves employing the new twentieth-century language of relative time. Thus, Bruce Morton of CBS spoke of the likelihood—or, at least, the possibility—that the repercussions of the pardon might "in time blow over." On NBC, there were references (many expressed by members of Congress) to the President's "gamble" in supposing that the public would "wish to forget" and to "move on to other things." Everywhere on the airwaves, there were allusions to "time's healing" and the "healing processes of time," but perhaps it was in print that the essence of this view was most clearly stated, when Peter Lisagor of the Chicago *Daily News* wrote of the President's having "counted on a short public memory and the American penchant for responding favorably to an 'act of mercy.' "

In 1967, in a dour and compelling book titled *The Political Illusion*, the French social philosopher Jacques Ellul wrote: "The man who lives in the news . . . is a man without memory." By now, there is further reason to believe that news and its relationship to time and memory are more than casual concerns of citizens of our epoch—especially of those in this country, who are members of the most advanced broadcast audience on earth, and whose subjection (or attraction) to the news has come a long way since that not so distant period (no further back than 1934) when early radio stations were restrained by formal agreement from broadcasting more than ten minutes of news per day. In the past ten years, "all-news" radio stations have become a commonplace here. More recently, commercial television has discovered that television news is profitable, or can be profitable if it is suitably presented; and earlier this year WNBC-TV, the NBC affiliate station in New York, inaugurated a program consisting of two hours of continuous news each weekday evening—*News-Center 4*. In our day, the concept of "future shock"—by which is meant the effect on the individual of an increasing bombardment of change, of technical and communications stimuli—has itself proceeded rapidly from a danger recognized only in the academy to a truism, and on to the title of a best-seller, which was then sold to (or bombarded upon) customers in bookstores by means of book covers in six different colors. Evidently, we have seen the enemy and have tried to package it.

The proliferation of communications in our society, then, is a phenomenon peculiar to the past few generations, and in its explosive geometric rate of increase it has much in common with the proliferation of people—of world population—since the eighteenth century. With this difference: that the explosion of communications is generally regarded as "good" and the explosion of population is generally regarded as "bad." But perhaps with a certain similarity of approach on the part of the public, which is to say that much of the popular disinclination to deal seriously with either phenomenon seems to stem from an interior assertion, or hope, that both occurrences are somehow commonplace—that is, are not unique, are part of a trend. In the matter of population growth and world hunger, there have been numerous studies published which show that the extraordinary rise in world population since around 1750 has indeed been unique, and was not in any way a predictable extension of prior arithmetic progression. Yet the response of many persons to this phenomenon has been to take shelter, as it were, in the false impression that this is not actually so—that population growth is somehow part of a continuing human equation, that what is happening now has always happened, and that *that* concept itself will somehow take care of us.

So, too, with communications. In spite of the exponential growth rate of communications in this country within only the last two generations; in spite of the miles of cable, the transmitters, the satellites, the millions upon millions of telephonic and television receivers in homes, in cars, in boats; in spite of the kind of capacity which just over ten years ago enabled 90 percent of the population of this country to learn of the assassination of President Kennedy within an hour and a half of the event—in spite of all these—one constantly comes across a type of homespun characterization of these communications systems which serves mainly to reinforce a public belief that what exists now is merely an extension of a historical enterprise, part of an ongoing trend.

The press, for example, which, with the United States Department of Defense, owns one of the two most extensive electronic-communications *apparats* in the history of the world, is fond of referring to itself, or to its members, as "messengers" (often in the self-pitying context of "slaying the messenger"), as if its enormous array of equipment, its outpouring of "information," and our willing acceptance of it were but an up-to-date version of the town crier, a Phidippides jogging along a microwave beam to Athens. Mr. McLuhan's term "global village," with its askew conception either of village life or of the modern citizen's relationship to homogeneous commercial broadcasting, has noticeably remained with us, becoming an accepted part of our idiom, and, in doing so, implying (an implication not lost on commercial broadcasting, which often employs the phrase in advertising, to provide a touch of class) not merely a kind of popular coziness but also a free flow between audience and broadcaster. Indeed, the implication goes deeper, conveying the idea of yet another traditional continuity: if we are still in a village, as we were once in a village, then nothing too much has changed; we are safely positioned on our dot upon the parabolic curve; there are no new dangers.

These thoughts came to mind in connection with the President's recent appearance on television, and with the television reports and comment that filled the ensuing days, because both events—that is, the news of the Nixon pardon and the subsequent "news" of the reaction and comment—seemed somehow to frame an unusual moment: a moment-in-time. For it seemed then that we had reached a point where the common denominator that connected the President, the press, and us citizen-viewers was communications itself—not merely as a conduit for an announcement from our President and for comment from the broadcasters, but as a substantive part of the social and political process. In other words, news was now being broadcast to us at such a rate that public distractedness in the face of such information volume might be seriously taken into account in the political process.

Back in May, our previous President, Mr. Nixon, was

revealed in published transcripts of White House discussions to have also had an interest in relative time, at one point counting on the public's interest in Watergate to blow over within "a couple or three weeks." One mentions relative time in this connection because Mr. Nixon could then hardly have been supposed to be relying on a monumental, mystical act of forgetfulness taking place in millions of brains; more likely, he had in mind a kind of replacement—an inevitable (or so it seemed) supplanting of Watergate by the deafening onrush of other pieces of information. In this specific instance of communications guesswork, Mr. Nixon was wrong. He was not entirely off the mark, though, for in June, when it was possible for the White House to supply the communications system with information about the President's coming trip to the Soviet Union, which thus replaced information about Watergate, the public—deprived of one set of news, immersed in another—granted Mr. Nixon (according to the polls) a rise in popular support. Even so, the texture of Watergate was sufficient to remain intact within the public's memory.

But now (at least for an instant) we are in the present. Was President Ford also wrong in his appraisal of the public's "memory"? We won't know the answer to that for some time, though there appears slight chance that the Democratic Party will find the energy to break through the public's apparent distractedness on the subject of the pardon. But what a paradox it is that as this nation has achieved the supposedly desired end of rapid communication and a mass audience, the system should already seem to be turning on itself: each item of news implicitly created so as to subvert a previous item. Will the public (which is us) learn this new language of relative time—learn to sort out "input" and to reconnect the items of information which the news process has fragmented? Or will we, in the manner of the aged, many of whom retain new facts, addresses, telephone numbers only at the expense of forgetting old ones, soon sit before our videos, washed over by nearly continuous news, wondering vaguely from time to time which piece of information is replacing what?

As if in counterpoint to this scenario, a week or so ago, on CBS, Roger Mudd spoke almost matter-of-factly of the "tide of public opinion" which had apparently formed and expressed itself within a period of twenty-four hours, and had inhibited President Ford from pardoning the remaining Watergate defendants. Clearly, there are intimations these days that the airwaves and cables of the nation are beginning to carry the smallest traces of a *two-way* communications traffic: from us to them; from the receiving sets to the transmitters. At last, the hushed (or shushed) streets of the global village, which have been largely silent throughout history save for the sounds of loudspeakers blaring in the central square, may be slowly waking—with the first, faint electronic murmurs of villagers directly talking back. If so, perhaps it is the fact of *these* "messages"—startling, powerful, human, with effects still unpredictable—which will turn out to be the crucial political and communications phenomenon of our time.

Kidvid

WHILE IN CHICAGO RECENTLY, I TURNED ON THE television set around noon, in the hope of catching one of those Cheshire Cat late-morning news programs (whose announcers seem to vanish, grinning, into the thin air of game shows and soap operas scant moments after they have appeared), and instead, perhaps being a few minutes off the mark, found myself face to face with Bozo the Clown. This particular Bozo wasn't exactly an old friend, but he was familiar—and there was something decidedly familiar about the type of program. "Hi, everyone! And how is everyone feeling today?" asked Mr. Ned, the M.C., who was dressed as a ringmaster, in riding breeches, doorman's jacket, and a battered top hat. A studio audience of children of ages from five to fifteen waved their arms and made cheering sounds. "You feel fine, do you?" asked—or, rather, declared—Mr. Ned. "Well, that's great, that's *great!* I bet you're glad to be here." More scenes of arm-waving and sound-making. "Well, thank you, thank you all!"

It was a bit like being taken back in time, the way that listening to an old song sometimes takes one back. Not, in this case, to my own childhood, but at least to the early childhood of my children, when for an hour or so of peace and quiet each evening we'd place them before a television set showing one of those kiddie programs—often M.C.'d by men in funny hats, and disgorging endless, jangly cartoons, or the Three Stooges, or Superman, or Soupy Sales. Such addled, peculiar entertainments these were! I remember a young fellow dressed up as an old sea captain: Cap'n Dan. There was also an old fellow dressed up as a fire chief: Fireman Ed. Fireman Ed showed Popeye cartoons, in the spirit of a lifetime curse, and laughed spasmodically in a mirthless and furious fashion. "Well, kiddies, is *everybody* happy? Is everybody *really happy?*" he used to bark, like one of the Hounds of Fate. For a while, too, in the early 1960's, there was a species of Japanese-made cartoon that was much in vogue—or, anyway, was much in evidence—and featured bold, unabashedly erotic designs, much noise, and a kind of cheery sadism. Sometimes I used to watch with the children: the older ones alternately chortling or hypnotized, the youngest sobbing wildly, as their parent stood behind them in the doorway making vague, patriarchal murmurs. Scenes of family life, mid-century!

And so there again, or still, was Bozo. In Chicago, the program is called *Bozo's Circus,* and it is shown each day at noon on the station owned by the Chicago *Tribune.* In addition to Mr. Ned, there was, naturally, Bozo himself, a tall, ungainly clown who talked in a kind of falsetto Pidgin English, and a short, ungainly clown who giggled and fell down often and was called Cooky. Mr. Ned announced an obstacle race. A dozen or so children stepped listlessly in and out of tires, and then placed large hoops over themselves and then removed the hoops. A studio organ played "Roll Out the Barrel" frenetically. "Did you have fun?" said Mr. Ned. "Did you all have fun?" Bozo and Cooky stood dutifully beside the ringmaster, their arms laden with packages. "Guess what we have here. A Wood Sculpture Kit from Craftmaster! It's entertaining and educational, too," said Mr. Ned, handing over a package to a young boy who was standing with one foot inside a tire. There were cereal commercials. Then a Bozo cartoon—an ancient, barely animated wheeze. Then there was a strangely languid interlude of seemingly interminable pratfalls performed by Bozo and Cooky. The children remained mostly silent and amiable. An old Mr. Magoo cartoon unreeled itself: Magoo's Chinese houseboy got scratched by a cat; the cat stuck its tail in the light socket; the houseboy fell out of a bell tower. More commercials: a toy called Weebles Marina, and Count Chocula cereal. A trampoline was hauled into the center of the "ring," and a group of leotarded citizens known as the Jumping Jays bounced up and down on the trampoline in a leisurely way for three minutes . . . for five minutes . . . for close to ten minutes. "Now, boys and girls, and moms and dads," announced Mr. Ned, "the Jumping Jays are going to attempt something *extremely difficult*—a three-man balance on the trampoline!" They missed it on the first try. Mr. Ned stared into the middle distance. The organ played "Anchors Aweigh." At last, three Jays achieved a transient balance and bounced off.

After another flurry of commercials, the finale was announced. "All right, all of you moms in the audience, I want you to sit up nice and pretty, because it's time to play the Mommy Game," said Mr. Ned. "It's a game especially designed for moms, because Mom can be a winner, too—and if a mom wins today she'll be able to make her own home movies, complete with sound, with this new Kodak miracle camera! Now, the way you start the game is this: you see these marshmallows *here* and that jar over *there?* Mom, all you have to do is place a marshmallow on this knife and then run with it and drop it into that jar." Several women lurched about the studio with their knives and marshmallows while the children waved their arms and the organist attempted the *William Tell* Overture, then thought better of it and turned again to "Roll Out the Barrel." The winners were paraded in front of the cameras and burdened with more prizes. "Listen to this, friends!" said Mr. Ned. "A Hoover Dial-A-Matic! Listen to this! A Kodak miracle movie projector from McDade & Company!" Gradually, circus time drew to a close. There were a few more commercials. Mr. Ned and Bozo and Cooky waved at the cameras. The women and children in the audience waved. A placard was briefly introduced: GIVE A HOOT! DON'T POLLUTE! "All right, boys and girls," said Mr. Ned, "I want everyone, including moms, to stand and join us in our Grand March . . ."

The fact is that today there are not so very many children's television programs that resemble *Bozo's Circus*, with its particular spirit of carnival cheapness and its almost quaintly primitive exploitation of children and parents. To be sure, *Romper Room*—also brainless and overcommercial—persists in many areas of the country. There is a Bozo cartoon show on a UHF channel in the New York area. The likes of Popeye, Casper, and Felix the Cat pop up periodically in the swamp of afternoon programming which exists on most independent stations—like aging or fallen sports heroes who continue to play baseball in the Mexican provinces. But for the most part these old workhorses from television's first great Era of Captive Children—the Cap'n Dans and Uncle Dons, the funny costumes and scratchy 1940's *Looney Tunes*—have been retired. Fireman Ed has hung up his hat. Mr. Magoo has been farmed out to foreign television—doubtless to addle the minds of the Third World. Slowly, tentatively, we have been entering a new era.

I suppose one might call it the Era of *Sesame Street*, but that seems a bit unfair to *Sesame Street*, and also maybe somewhat too kind—or, at least, not very accurate—about what most of commercial television has been doing in the area of children's programming. Certainly the Children's Television Workshop, which produced *Sesame Street* in 1969 and *The Electric Company* in 1971, has been an enormous influence—both in its success in producing regular programs that on their own artistic merit attracted a large audience of children, and that proceeded to inform the children's viewing time with something "good," rather than nothing or something "bad," and in its demonstration to adults of the nation of what was possible. For the *Sesame Street* audience (based on Nielsen figures) now numbers around nine million children between the ages of two and five—not to count the many others, of all ages, who watch the program. Artistically, and also in terms of mass appeal, the Workshop productions have been a fine achievement.

Not that they are immune from criticism. Both *Sesame Street* and *The Electric Company* not only teach an unabashedly linear approach to literacy and education but, in addition, do so within a context of propounding what are generally called white middle-class values—perhaps one might call them *higher* white middle-class values. Why is it, a number of people have asked, that when we are dealing with such unformed minds and employing such effective instruction techniques, we are teaching the *Sesame Street* audience (which is often poor and black) *those* values? John Holt, an able and passionate writer on children's education, has frequently criticized *Sesame Street*'s implicit condescension to its poor black clients, and also its devotion to orthodox education. "The program asks, 'How can we get children ready to learn what the schools are going to teach them?' " Holt has written. "Instead of 'How can we help them learn what the schools may *never* teach them?' "

It's hard to deny the importance of Holt's question, especially as it pertains to the traditional approach to learning in this country. Indeed, there has been a forthright passion in much of the recent writing about American education—voices saying, "Can't you see? What we're talking about isn't radical but only *sensible*"—which has been creating as moving, and, one hopes, as prophetic, a literature as those equally righteous, impassioned novels about the possibilities of human sexuality earlier in the century. At the same time, given the situation of the moment, it's harder still to disagree with the perhaps more filtered, bureaucratic reasoning of the Workshop's producers. "Schools do need changing," wrote Gerald Lesser, *Sesame Street*'s educational designer, in his book *Children and Television,* "but in one form or another they are probably here to stay. While we seek ways to make them more useful and humane for all children, television perhaps can help to prepare poor children to take advantage of the education that exists."

The Children's Television Workshop, then, roughly thirty years after the inauguration of television broadcasting in this country, has produced two graceful and directly useful children's programs, where certainly nothing comparable had existed before. It has not devised anything organically new—a new way of seeing the world. But it has helped young children and poor children to learn to read and to count. It has provided children of American cities (who are the majority of American children) with an imagery of city life which is admittedly somewhat tidied up but which is neither defined mainly by detectives and car chases nor entirely ignored and deprecated in favor of some sweet, ancestral never-countryside or those totemic, speechless, perpetually galloping African animals. And—in spite of some of the deeper questions involved—it has provided, especially through *Sesame Street,* on a daily basis a view of ordinary human life and relationships which is consistently humane and reasonably truthful, and which in our culture has generally been available to a mass audience only through the occasional (and expensive) happenstance of art or literature.

Both the merit and the demerit of these Workshop productions is that they are designed for specific sections of the children's audience: *Sesame Street* for very young children who need instruction in elementary literacy (as well as, perhaps, in elementary life and behavior); *The Electric Company* for school-age children who need special assistance in reading. But the point really is not what these programs do or don't do—for, clearly, within a well-defined area they do a great deal. The point is: What has the commercial-television establishment been doing to take advantage of the Workshop's discoveries of *what can be done?* In dealing with this question, money is often mentioned—or, rather, the lack of it—for the Workshop's expenses (which have been paid by large foundations, such as Ford and the Carnegie Corporation, and also by H.E.W.) have been considerable. Nearly eight million dollars was spent on devising and producing *Sesame Street* through its first year, and that rose to twelve million dollars in 1971 as *The Electric Company* was added. It would be foolish to ignore the money problem here, but it's hard to see that the major obstacle to better children's television is a simple lack of funds. Besides, large sums of money exist (albeit breathing nervously) within our gross national product, as, indeed, they exist within the various industries—both broadcasting and advertising—that feast off our television machines. The difficulty, such as it is, usually lies in what different citizens and institutions choose to do with the money.

Thus far, the record of how the great commercial broadcasters have responded to the possibilities of children's programming has not been very inspiring. It's true that Bozoism has largely declined, and that most of the funny men have put away their funny hats. It's true also that the voice of the Television Consumer has finally begun to be dimly heard in protest—and about something other than the cancellation of last night's *Space Bunny* to make way for *The Miracle of the Fishes*. There have been complaints about too many commercials on children's programs, and too much violence. An organization called Action for Children's Television, originating in Massachusetts, has lobbied for better programs. Lately, indeed, there has been a slight movement—or, anyway, a shuffle—of network executives to the barricades. Educational consultants have been hired. Executive pronouncements have been made proclaiming executive abhorrence of violence and sudden executive enthusiasm for themes of "social responsibility."

The result of the convergence of these various forces on the most profitable, and viewable, territories of children's programming—or "kidvid," as *Variety* calls it—has been a modest improvement here and there, but hardly anything to warrant a great deal of self-congratulation from the networks or thanks from the set-owners. What is chiefly annoying about this phase of the new era is the many evidences of insincerity and commercial manipulation at work. The snake-oil pitchman has been removed, but he has been supplanted by a cleaned-up, modern smoothness which blandly alternates with the still endless advertisements for—now "natural"—breakfast cereals, and is apparently sanctified by the presence of a couple of quickly hired educational advisers in the background.

Thus, instead of taking advantage of the gradual rise in sophistication of the young audience by finally getting rid of that tacky and antiquated array of early U.S. Superpower cartoon heroes (those Wonder People of our dreamlike 1940's, who wafted about the skies expressing the worst of our sexual, political, and military fantasies), the networks today have in several cases merely given them a new coat of paint and tossed in a fillip of modish social consciousness and dropped them back into the key kiddie arena of Saturday morning. Thus, Saturdays on ABC there is an hour-long program called *Super Friends:* a cartoon show that features Superman, Batman, Wonder Woman, and Aquaman, all together in a kind of body-stockinged, Nietzschean street gang—zooming and zipping about the world, solving all manner of global problems as an announcer periodically intones, "Their mission is to fight injustice, to right that which is wrong, and to save all mankind!" Presumably, while our real leaders vainly and confusedly try to cope with the pressing chaos of world problems, children can observe how ideal grownups handle events that matter—for example, how Superman and Aquaman deal with "a break in the Great Coral Reef." Observed Superman quite sternly, before dropping an enormous tanker into the break in the G.C.R., "A break in the chain of life can have drastic consequences, you know." Two cartoon human beings—Wendy and Marvin—and Wonder Dog hovered fitfully in the background of the adventures, doubtless introduced by an educational consultant to add a human touch. Likewise, an avuncular cartoon military officer, Colonel Wilcox, perhaps provided by a military consultant. "The people in the world are counting on you," said Colonel Wilcox before Superman dropped the ship.

Generally more interesting than the reworked cartoon programs are two new Saturday-morning shows on CBS: *The Harlem Globetrotters Popcorn Machine* and *The Hudson Brothers Razzle Dazzle Comedy Show*. Both are a definite improvement on the classic Saturday-morning TV tradition of ancient cartoons and listless games, but that's not saying very much; and although each of the new programs has a certain charm and at least the look of money having been spent on it, what is disheartening in the end is that CBS hasn't really tried very hard to do anything genuinely inventive with the money. In fact, it's been content to *seem* inventive while exploiting the surface effects and approach of *Sesame Street*, with perhaps a certain amount of *Laugh-In* thrown in on the side.

I don't suppose there's anything really wrong in borrowing from other models, but, especially in the case of the *Globetrotters* show and *Sesame Street*, the CBS people seem to have missed the point. The *Globetrotters* show features nine Harlem Globetrotter basketball players as well as a few other regular performers. The show has a children's audience, and also a child actor who plays off on the tall athletes. There is much trendy music. Much quick cutting. There are halfhearted attempts at teaching the alphabet, along with periodic references to physical fitness. Six Globetrotters stand amid the bemused audience, holding up white placards: H-E-A-L-T-H. "That's right, *health!*" they cry. The trumpets blare. Everybody laughs.

It's a pleasant enough show, and the Globetrotters come across as nice, jokey men. But it's all so inextricably show-business. *Sesame Street* deliberately used show-business idiom in some of its educational skits, since its young audience was already well versed in the language, but *Sesame Street's* spirit is larger and more humane, and its purpose has been more carefully thought out. At times, some of the *Globetrotter* skits sound almost like parodies of the Workshop's educational style. Thus, in a recent show a Globetrotter dressed up as a robber was giving another man a lesson in "etiquette." First Gt: "Give me your money." Second Gt: "Say 'please.' " First: "All right, *please*." (Gets the money.) Second: "You didn't say 'thank you.' " First: "*Thank you!*" (Much hooting and laughter from the studio audience as the Globetrotters mug the key words.) Now, surely the real lesson there—which was picked up by the TV-wise children in the studio—was that "please" and "thank you" are jokes, or, at any rate, are pointless additions tacked on to speech by adults who themselves don't believe in them. As if to emphasize this ambivalence, a moment later one of the Globetrotters remarked in mock seriousness, "This whole show is dopey, but it proves that it pays to be polite." At which point the camera cut to another Trotter, who said, "Yeah, but *how much* does it pay?" CBS's other big children's show, *The Hudson Brothers, etc.*, which follows *Globetrotters* on Saturday mornings, seems to be even more snarled up in the spirit of show business. Quick cutting and speeded-up action are flung about the way an amateur chef tosses around spices. There is some soft-rock singing by the Hudson Brothers, which looks dubbed, although CBS insists that it isn't—at any rate, the Brothers manage to sing on camera without discernibly moving their larynxes. There are frantic skits, and the kind of silly bad jokes ("As they say in Helsinki, let's *finish* this song!") which used to come off better in vaudeville, where there was more of an honest rapport between the audience and the performers. Here, again, the principals—in this case, three young Oregonians—seem pleasant, although a bit on the slick side, and without quite the style or presence of the lanky Globetrotters. But what's missing is something *behind* all that strenuous entertainment. In fact, the trouble with so much of today's children's programming isn't that the networks are throwing songs and comedy acts and cartoons at the kids instead of trying to teach them algebra. The trouble is with the shoddiness and insincerity of the entertainment. Children respond avidly to stories and poetry and film and music and dance; to greatness and ordinariness—and to real voices. What they get most of the time is unfelt music, badly drawn cartoons, self-serving educational messages, synthetic adult "personalities," and mediocrity—not the middlingness of ordinary lives, which artists have often reworked into literature or film, but the traces and sounds of careless and distracted grownups who follow the easy road and try for the surefire laugh, and perhaps don't know any better.

To be fair, not everything on children's TV these days is mired in second-rateness. On ABC I saw a fine children's drama called *The Bridge of Adam Rush*. This story about a young boy in the early nineteenth century who suddenly has to adjust to the hardships of rural life—as well as to a new stepfather—was simply and affectingly told, with intelligence, and without mawkishness or false emotion. On Saturdays, CBS still shows its CBS Children's Film Festival, which is mainly foreign children's movies with dubbed English dialogue. The variety here runs from good to indifferent, but most of these movies are interesting, and seem to appeal to kids, and usually possess a texture and singleness of vision that is found in few TV productions. There is also a nice small series called *Other People—Other Places*, produced by Time-Life Films, which WABC shows under the title *Strange Places*. One episode I watched recently was about primitive tribesmen in the Kalahari, and contained the inevitable tribal dances and poisoned-arrow-making sequences; but there was precious little mooning about animals, or even about tribesmen, and the show clearly made an attempt to tell children intelligently about these strangers who were trying to make the hazardous journey into our world and time.

Probably the most interesting current programs for children are public television's *Zoom* and ABC's *Rainbow Sundae*. *Zoom* came first, originating four years ago on Boston's public-television station, WGBH, and is now aired on a weekly basis over most of the PBS network. *Zoom* is performed entirely by children and put together partly by children, and the production ideas are all sent in by children—and it's generally very well done. *Rainbow Sundae* was new last year and clearly derives from *Zoom*, at least in the most interesting and appealing portions of the program, which involve children taking a meaningful role in the show: talking, interviewing, discussing their lives with other children. It's slicker and more fancied-up than *Zoom*, but it's also good. Both programs, in fact, are fine, and, together with the Children's Television Workshop productions and a few others—a *very* few others—represent the first, foot-dragging steps on the part of the television establishment toward finally asserting some sort of felt responsibility toward its younger clients.

Indeed, perhaps the lesson of *Zoom*, and similar programs, is that when children are at least allowed to commune with each other across the airwaves, instead of having to watch middle-aged men hit each other with plates of pizza (as occurred midway through *Bozo's Circus* the other day), they find all kinds of things they want to say to one another—as they always have. Our TV system could probably permit children to speak more often to other children without the foundations of the Republic crumbling. And when it's necessary for adults to speak to children—whether to tell stories or to make jokes or to instruct or to pass the time of day—at least let them speak in a language they believe in, and not in kidvid.

A Crack in the Greasepaint

THIS IS PROBABLY AS GOOD A TIME AS ANY TO SAY A few words about an appealing new comedy program called *Saturday Night*, which is broadcast at eleven-thirty each Saturday night by NBC and is definitely not to be confused with *Saturday Night Live with Howard Cosell*, which comes on earlier in the evening on ABC. The Cosell show and NBC's *Saturday Night* are both mainly live, but there is a crucial difference between the two programs. Cosell's show (as is the case with nearly all entertainment on commercial television), for all its "liveness," is based on and defined by the standard vocabulary of American show business. Some of the acts are well done, others are not so well done. The essential texture of the show, however, depends on that strange fantasy language of celebrity public relations which has been concocted for the public by mass-entertainment producers and stars and in recent years has become almost formalized as a kind of national version of a modern courtier style. It is the language of kisses blown, of "God bless you"s, of "this wonderful human being," of "a sensational performer and my very dear personal friend," and of "You're just a beautiful audience!"—in short, the language of celebrity "hype" or, alternatively (though it amounts to the same thing), of celebrity "roast." It is the language of not daring to let anything alone to stand by itself, the language of bored artifice—perhaps a contemporary equivalent of dandyism and powdered wigs.

Much of the appeal of *Saturday Night* lies in its contrast with this ubiquitous show-business language. Its format, like that of most comedy programs, consists of a familiar assembly of skits, songs, and monologues, but the spirit of the material is in opposition to conventional show business—especially to the rituals of mass-entertainment television. To begin with, the physical presentation of the program is deliberately untidy and informal. The shows are broadcast from a cavernous, undecorated NBC working studio that has been filled largely with young people. In contrast to most studio-audience programs, in which the audience setup is rigid and theaterlike, the effect here is that of a huge, darkened, lively TV cabaret. Each Saturday night, the program has a different host (though neither "host" nor "M.C." seems quite the right word for the part)—for instance, George Carlin, the comedian, or Paul Simon (formerly of Simon and Garfunkel), or Candice Bergen. The hosts don't do very much in the way of "hosting"—in the conventional TV manner of promoting themselves or the guests—but are content mainly to sit around, providing a periodic focus for the loosely tied together skits and sometimes telling a story or two or, as in Paul

Simon's case, singing a few songs. As you might guess, the feel of the show is decidedly loose—loose but with generally able performances.

Skit humor usually defies cold description, so I won't try much of it here. On the recent Saturday with Candice Bergen as host, the show began with a takeoff of a Presidential news conference, which showed the actor impersonating President Ford bumping his head on the lectern, spilling his drinking water, and repeatedly falling down. Then there was a crisply done parody of a TV news program, with the President once again featured ("President Ford has just asked for the resignation of his son Jack"), concluding with a lunatic "News for the Hard of Hearing," which consisted of a newsman yelling items of news very loud. There was also a funny takeoff of one of the local-TV-station counter-editorials. Also a takeoff of a *Black Perspective* program, with the black host attempting to interview a harebrained suburban white girl on the subject of a book she had just written about black ghetto life. Also an amiable but fairly juvenile parody of *Jaws.* Also some funny parodies of TV commercials, and some filmed parodies of TV serials: *Medical Season,* about a heartless, incompetent old doctor; and *The Three of Us,* about an ineptly arranged girl-boy-girl modern living arrangement. Also a freewheeling talk-show interview with a couple of demented kiwi trappers. Also a skit by a fine young comedian, Andy Kaufman, about a TV "guest" who couldn't manage to perform properly, or at all. And so forth.

As I said, you can't convey much of anything about comedy skits by describing them. The truth is that it's a funny show and has enough comic spirit behind it so that even an actress of no notable comic expertise, such as Candice Bergen, can work along easily with the program. Still, it's not really the gross tonnage of jokes in the skits which makes *Saturday Night* worth looking at. What is attractive and unusual about the program is that it is an attempt, finally, to provide entertainment on television in a recognizable, human, non-celebrity voice—and in a voice, too, that tries to deal with the morass of media-induced show-business culture that increasingly pervades American life.

I was going to add that the show is topical, but "topical" has become another of those contemporary vogue words, and, as an automatic value-enhancing adjective, it no longer means what it used to mean. In mass entertainment nowadays, just about everyone is topical. Hardly anyone tells mother-in-law jokes any more. Mary Tyler Moore is topical. Howard Cosell is topical. Even Dean Martin is topical. Any comedian within twelve feet of a microphone makes jokes about government, politicians, even Presidents. Last year, when President Ford dispensed WIN buttons, the airwaves crackled with professional show-business jokes on the subject. Bob Hope, for one, has consistently made jokes on events drawn from the news pages of the newspapers—many of them funny jokes. But Bob Hope (as is true of most of his colleagues) is primarily a joke machine. Jokes are rattled off almost promiscuously: some are about the C.I.A., others about golf—or the energy crisis or football or the White House swimming pool or Bing Crosby. These jokes are topical in the contemporary sense of being about everyday, or "relevant," topics, but they have no center. What does the person telling the joke really think? Bob Hope, for one, rigorously plays the part of a man who doesn't think. He is the conventional professional entertainer. From the audience's vantage point, he has no political sensibility and no personal life. In a way, there is a certain purity to the Hope approach. Everything in the world becomes a potential joke, which can be fashioned crisply, neatly, with detached expertise, and then told *purely*, unmarred by the kind of synthetic personality ("My wife is the kind of woman who . . .") that lesser comedians attempt to inject into their routines. The Hope style (like that of his professional heirs, such as Rowan and Martin, and even Johnny Carson) is basically a triumph of technological comedy. There is a laugh in anything, but the comedian is not necessarily connected to, or disconnected from, the source of laughter. He is a processor of jokes. He stands apart.

This technological approach to humor is difficult to carry off, because each of the isolated, impersonal jokes has to work right. Most conventional mass-entertainment comedians have neither the established presence nor the timing nor the joke writers of a Bob Hope, and so they are usually compelled to create half-realized and synthetic dramatic personalities for themselves: Red Skelton's punch-drunk prizefighter, or Jackie Gleason's roguish fat man, or Lucille Ball's zany housewife, or Milton Berle's life of the party, or Carol Burnett's hysterical wallflower, and so on. Indeed, for years most television comedy has been frozen in these ancient and synthetic molds: of a play-acted dramatic "personality" (where part of the fun, supposedly, lies in knowing that Carroll O'Connor isn't really a bigot, or that Carol Burnett isn't really demented) or else of the detached, technical precision of mass-entertainment topical joke-telling (where the comedian appears to be talking about a topic of current interest but a personally felt texture of concern is rarely acknowledged). This isn't to say that a number of conventional mass-entertainment comedy routines aren't funny, or that there won't always be a place, or a need, for a clown simply to play a clown. But during all the years that commercial television (with a few exceptions, notably Sid Caesar and Imogene Coca) has remained stuck in its conventional postures of synthetic comedy, several wholly new approaches to popular humor have been evolving, which network television (ever the guardian of the Public Weal) has resolutely ignored.

In a sense, there have been two key modern developments in comedy. One originated in America in the postwar period, and on the small, peripheral stages of Chicago and San Francisco: Nichols and May with Chicago's Compass Players (some of whose members evolved into the Second City troupe), Mort Sahl, Shelley Berman, and Lenny Bruce at the "hungry i" in San Francisco. These performers were first acclaimed by the young, and for their qualities of "topicality" and "relevance." Their style was loose, conversational, personal. That was a period when middle-class America was beginning a nearly mass communion with psychiatry, or, certainly, with the forms or language of the psychiatric experience, and it was the personal gropings of the psychiatric patient—the stumbling, sensibility-prone, identity-obsessed assertions—that formed both the underpinning of the new humor and the material to play off on. Many Americans were attempting to find their "real selves." The new entertainers, in addition to playing off on these searches after identity, attempted to gain the good will and regard of their audiences by revealing—or anyway, acknowledging—*their* "real selves." One could almost say that the basis for the new comedy routines was an absence of detachment, an absence of conventional professionalism—an absence of the traditional notions of compartmentalization. Much of the American public was trying to deal with new concepts of "wholeness" and "relatedness" in private life and public life: public officials and ordinary men and women were to be accountable for their whole and interconnected lives—not just for one visible corner of them. The new American comedians seemed to be saying that they would now be accountable for their jokes. For instance, an old-style comedian might make a joke about the C.I.A.: "The C.I.A. is in plenty of hot water lately. Why, things are so bad down there they sent a self-destructing letter to one of their agents and it came back 'Opened by Mistake.' " Superficially, this might be termed a topical joke, but its topicality is virtually meaningless, being buried in traditional show-business paraphernalia. The comedian *uses* the C.I.A. as a fashionable topic, but he doesn't touch it or connect to it. And the audience (which nonetheless thinks for itself) is left out in the cold except for the automatic ha-haing at the punch line. Nor is it true to say that the old-style comedian would spoil the simple clownlike purity of his position if he were to take a personal point of view—by admitting to his own reality.

For the fact is that by claiming to view the "topic" of the C.I.A. only as the detached subject of a disconnected wisecrack he is already being "political." A new-style comedian—for example, Mort Sahl—not only would connect a topic such as the C.I.A. to his own point of view but, by cumulatively and publicly uncovering his various points of view on various topics, would unfold his own "real self" and present *that* to the audience. Whatever else it might feel in the grip of the new humorous self-consciousness, the growing audience for the new comedians was not being left out in the cold.

The other key trend or tributary which fed into modern comedy developed mainly in England, also in the postwar period—first in the radio *Goon Show* routines of Peter Sellers and Spike Milligan, then with such educated lunacies as *Beyond the Fringe*, and more recently with *Monty Python's Flying Circus*. Superficially, the humor of these English actor-comedians seemed to be based largely, and restrictively, on English concepts and English culture. But their considerable success in America has shown that what was actually being exported was two other ingredients. The first was a fairly ancient English comic standby: the eccentric, and the concept of eccentricity. For some time, American Anglophiles had been fond of remarking affectionately, and perhaps a trifle condescendingly, on "the English eccentric." Since Dickens, eccentricity had been regarded as an approved, even a unique, feature of English life and literature. American eccentricity was not thought to properly exist as such. Except for a handful of absentminded college professors and an occasional inventor, American literature had a rather scant record of American eccentricity. Important or established Americans were thought to be too busy, or too important or established, to serve as suitable vessels for eccentricity. Times changed, however, and, with them, national assertions and national self-knowledge. As a result, in recent years American films and literature have fairly teemed with examples of American eccentricity, and what was once thought of as a uniquely English habit of detecting lunacy in seemingly stable Englishmen has turned out to be an extremely successful export item—applicable equally to Foreign Office and State Department, to addled noble lords and demented Pentagon generals. Indeed, it was one of the original Goons, Peter Sellers, who played that quintessential Cold War warrior, Dr. Strangelove. The other ingredient originally exported by the new English comedians can perhaps best be described as a comedy of surplus education. In England, for generations (such being the dutifulness of the English school systems), a major part of the population has consistently been taught vast quantities of useless knowledge. In America, the mass acquisition of useless knowledge didn't really come into its own until the great surge in "humanist" college studies after the Second World War, but since then it has been proceeding apace. When Nichols and May used to do improvised parodies of Pirandello they were connecting to this subterranean pool of expensively acquired surplus information, in the same way that *Monty Python* has appealed to a randomly overinformed audience with its film about the Holy Grail.

What all this has to do with NBC's *Saturday Night* is

simply this. For the most part, in the past twenty years commercial television has largely ignored the important new trends in modern comedy—which are important not as trends but as basic ways of trying to view and organize experience. To deny the public a consistent view of modern art, say, would be to deny people an important way of looking at and identifying with their world. The same is true (perhaps on a different plane) with comedy—the so-called "comic vision." Whether as a result of the caution of advertisers or of the personal prejudices of network bosses, mass-entertainment television comedy has been firmly rooted in the past—a synthetic, Hollywood-style, show-business past—despite the fact that the new forms of comedy have demonstrated a considerable popular appeal. It is not a matter of wishing to replace Bob Hope with an "elitist," in-group kind of humor. The popular audience continues to adore Bob Hope, but it is also true that for years substantial segments of this same popular audience have been sneaking away in droves from its Hoopla Show Business Comedy Hours in order to commune with the rising number of lesser-known, more personal, more political, more sexual, more connectively humorous comedians who for the most part have existed outside the carefully patrolled guard fence of network-television entertainment.

Thus, what is noteworthy about *Saturday Night*, and why I commend it, is not the result of any spectacular, star-studded brilliance on its part; indeed, it has no real stars, though I imagine that the ensemble of actor-comics who perform most of the skits will make individual names for themselves. It is, as the saying goes, an *uneven* program, with ups and downs and too many commercial breaks. But it is a direct and funny show, which seems to speak out of the real, non-show-business world that most people inhabit—and it exists. One wonders (without expecting an answer) what took it so long. One wonders, too, what simple human pleasures the simple, human TV viewer might someday conceivably experience if network television—that grinning, gun-toting, wisecracking ("You're just a *beautiful* audience!"), still youthful courtesan—should ever start peeling off the rest of the cosmetics.

Waltz-Time and the Public Interest

THE INDOMITABLE LIT & CULTURE BRIGADE OF BRITISH television, having galloped over John Galsworthy (*The Forsyte Saga*), skirmished with Thomas Hardy (*Jude the Obscure*), ambushed Feodor Dostoevsky (*The Possessed*), held its own against Émile Zola (*Nana*), and fought Count Tolstoy to a standstill (*War and Peace*), has lately—in the manner of the Turks in 1529—reached the gates of Vienna. *Vienna 1900* is the title of the BBC's latest literary dramatic series to be presented on American public television under the heading of Masterpiece Theatre. There are six installments in the series, based on stories by the Austrian writer Arthur Schnitzler, whose minor but interesting career was about at midpoint in 1900. (He is perhaps best known outside Austria for *Reigen*, his play of sexual games, which later became the film *La Ronde*.) The British producers—perhaps lest anyone should think the tales mere trivialities—have subtitled the series "Games with Love and Death." The American distributors have provided Alistair Cooke as host.

The first episode was introduced by Mr. Cooke in the somewhat distracted but genial manner of the debonair captain of an ocean liner chatting up the skits at the ship's variety show. Mr. Cooke described Arthur Schnitzler rather cheerily as a "literary radical" and "anti-naturalistic," and then—with sudden donnish joviality—declared that "in doing my homework for this series, I have read more pedantic rubbish about a writer whose principal preoccupation can be said to have been 'Boy meets girl.' " With the Works of Schnitzler thereby connected to the soul of the American public-television audience, the opening episode—titled "Mother and Son"—unfolded.

The scene showed an elegant café in what was presumably Vienna in 1900, as was indicated subtly by a portrait of Emperor Franz Josef on a wall, and not so subtly by the elegiac playing of a Strauss waltz (as it happens, the *Waldmeister* Overture) by an offscreen orchestra (as it happens, the Vienna Philharmonic). A gentleman enters—already introduced to us as Dr. Graesler, the "observer," and bearing an uncanny resemblance to the Encyclopædia Britannica photograph of Arthur Schnitzler. He takes a table in the back. Across the café he glimpses a handsome woman in her late thirties. A young man—he is perhaps seventeen or thereabouts—rushes in, greets her with much show of filial affection, and rushes out. Dr. Graesler takes out a notebook and, in a stylish hand, inscribes "Mother and Son." Shortly afterward, the woman returns to her apartment. On her way up, she runs into some friends. There is a reference to her being a widow; also to her son, whose name is Hugo, and his friendship with a woman described as "the Baroness." The widow, whose name is Beate, goes off to see the Baroness—an affected and decadent society lady, who reclines on a chaise longue. Beate begs the Baroness not to ensnare Hugo with amorous advances. Tea is served. The Baroness is very brisk and upper-class. "The idea had up to this moment not even occurred to me," she says. "*Lemon?*" Beate is adamant and solemn. Finally, the Baroness promises that she will leave Hugo alone, though her promise is of a chicness that doesn't seem to warrant much confidence, and Beate strides off. She attends an outdoor lunch; among those present are a dignified old bank director and his wife and two dashing young men. The young men periodically direct roguish glances at Beate. Later, Beate takes a walk with the director, who is clearly fond of her also, though in a dignified and respectful way. Back home again, she finds Hugo—who is again rushing off. Beate is worried and distressed. Later, the younger of the two young men turns up, and he and Beate make love. A few days pass. Beate and Hugo and everyone else in the cast attend a ball given by the decadent Baroness. Beate dances with the dignified bank director. Many elegiac waltzes are played by the Vienna Philharmonic. The young men, including Hugo, gather around the Baroness, and all engage in chic, upper-class gossip—out of which, with many society giggles, emerges the fact that Beate and one of the young men have been lovers. Hugo is undone. Over breakfast, he and Beate have a confrontation. "I'm going to move . . . We'd both be happier alone," he says sullenly. Beate asks why. "Don't ask. It's too awful," says Hugo. Beate is now in tears. Hugo is in tears. "They laughed and made jokes . . . about you!" says Hugo. And "Since I can't bear to look at you, it would be more convenient for you to live by yourself." Beate wails, "No, no, no, no!" Hugo walks out, slamming the door. The final scene takes place in the original café. Dr. Graesler is seated at his table in the back. Beate comes in, sits in the front, and orders coffee and cakes. Then the old bank director comes in. Apparently, Beate has now become a fallen woman. He takes one look at her and walks to the opposite side of the room, where he sits down and begins reading a newspaper. The *Waldmeister* Overture wafts elegiacally through the café. The End.

I have taken up this much space with the details of "Mother and Son" because, as it happens, I had acquired a volume of Arthur Schnitzler tales and thought it might be interesting to compare the BBC's Lit & Culture version with the original. In the first place, the original story (at least, in its first English translation) was called "Beatrice," and not "Mother and Son"—with those stirring intimations of Viennese psychiatry. There was no Dr. Graesler or other "observer." The setting was not Vienna in 1900 but a mountain resort in the Tyrol just before the First World War. It is true that many of the minor incidents in the television production corresponded fairly closely to Schnitzler's story—for instance, Hugo's comings and goings, Beate's visit to the Baroness, her friendship with the bank director, and her love affair with the young man. But the essence of Schnitzler's story lay in its *tone*, and this depended largely on lengthy interior monologues by Beatrice (Beate), which revealed, in an interesting, sinuous fashion, the ambiguities of a woman's sexual involvement with her son as well as the powerful, secret currents of eroticism within herself. Indeed, the texture of the story was that of a personal, unacknowledged sexual reverie. Here, for example, is how Schnitzler presents Beatrice in her room, on the evening when she will be surprised by the desirous young man:

> She leaned on the sill of her open window, and looked into the garden and far away to the dark mountain peaks on the other side of the lake . . . How did it happen that [Hugo] was not there at the hotel? If he had guessed that she might return, he would surely have been there. Was it not strange that they should still desire her, who was the mother of a boy who already spent his nights with a mistress? Why strange? She was as young, perhaps younger than [the Baroness]. And all at once, she felt the outlines of her body under her light garment, with agonizing distinctness, and even a sort of painful pleasure . . . And suddenly she remembered such a sultry summer night a long time ago, when her husband had forced her against her will to go with him from the soft privacy of their chamber into the garden, and there, in the dark black shadows of the trees, to exchange wild and tender caresses.

The television production contained no sense of the resonances of this moment—which, after all, was the "story" that Schnitzler was writing. Instead, one had a glimpse of Beate stirring restlessly in bed, getting up, hearing a noise—and finding the young man, who soon embraced her. Boy meets girl in Old Vienna. Some other differences: Schnitzler's Baroness wasn't an English upper-class cliché, complete with English stage-business affectations ("*Lemon?*"). She was a human, not unsympathetic figure: a former actress, quite brave and lonely, married to an elderly rich man. There was no ball, and thus no Strauss waltzes or finely uniformed dancers; no society smart talk or youthful sniggers. It's true that the young men got drunk and informed Hugo of the affair with his mother; but what happened then was no routine confrontation scene in television's current pop-tragedy manner—with its shrieks and tears and door slammings, and ending with that so English final chord, the bank director's snub. Instead, Schnitzler's Beatrice, tipped into a kind of madness by her "betrayal" of her son, which had resulted from her recently acknowledged eroticism, takes Hugo for a rowboat ride on a lake.

> "You must not be afraid that you can wound me, or offend my modesty [she says]. I have experienced much these past days. I am still not an—old woman. I understand everything . . ."
>
> And the answer came: "I know, Mother."
>
> Beatrice trembled. Yet she felt no shame, only a relieved consciousness of being nearer to him and belonging to him.

At the end, holding Hugo's hand, she turns the boat over and they drown.

I realize that this is an excessive analysis of what to many people must be a pleasing and decorative production, based on a story by a now largely unread writer. Also, someone might well ask, isn't it possible to transfer stories from a distant time to the present, and from one medium to another, without absolute literal fidelity to the original text? The answer to that is obviously yes; and right now on the New York stage there are two examples of adaptation and translation—Ibsen's *A Doll's House* and Molière's *The Misanthrope*—both of which have been staged for contemporary audiences with occasional changes in idiom but without any sacrifice or diminution of the spirit of the original work. The trouble with the BBC/public-television production of *Vienna 1900*, I think, lies in the claims it makes on the audience's seriousness, and in the careless and genteel way it has gone about justifying them.

It is not a question, after all, of whether a good story may not still be a good story even if the precise setting and the precise costumes have been abandoned. In fact, in *Vienna 1900* something of the reverse has taken place, for while solemnly addressing the cultural sensibilities of their audience with many fine-sounding remarks about naturalism and anti-naturalism, Vienna, Freud, psychological themes, and so forth, the Masterpiece Theatre producers have concentrated on the charmingness of the sets, costumes, and waltzes, and have left out the Schnitzler. After all, a tragic, erotic, psychological story of ambiguous love and morality at an Austrian summer resort is not the same thing as a quality-mounted soap opera of English tea-party manners and social snubs. Schnitzler was perhaps not a great writer, but he was a good writer, and he had a voice of his own. It is discouraging to see television—especially public television, which shouldn't be so keen to get a large audience at any price—amenable to trading on the reputation and seriousness of an artist, and then, except for the gauzy tastefulness of the art direction, behaving no more responsibly toward his work than the Hollywood moguls of thirty years ago did with their biographies of Tchaikovsky, Chopin, and Franz ("Franz, finish that symphony!") Schubert.

In order to make sure that I wasn't unfairly judging *Vienna 1900* by an aberrant episode, I watched the second one, which had been published as "The Murderer" and was now retitled "The Man of Honour." It was a slimmer story than the first, so the television bowdlerization was less noticeable. A man, Alfred, has a mistress, Elise, whom he is tiring of, and a new fiancée. He takes the mistress on a farewell holiday. As it happens, she has congenital heart trouble. He gives her an overdose of drugs. She dies. The fiancée then jilts him for a rival. The Masterpiece Theatre troupe simply overwhelmed this very European—not particularly Austrian or Viennese—story with Anglicisms and with those musical riffs of English actors' stage business (sometimes called "character acting") whereby, with harrumphs and "My dear sir"s and wiggles of the finger and clearings of the throat, just about any *mise-en-scène* this side of Dante's Eighth Circle can be transformed into the Whist Room of the Reform Club. Then, too, in the Schnitzler story this is how the mistress died:

> Suddenly he felt a violent shudder pass through Elise's body. Her two hands clutched at his neck, her

fingers seemed to be trying to pierce his skin, and then, with a long groan, she opened her eyes. Alfred freed himself from her embrace, sprang out of bed, watched her try to raise herself, fling her arms into the air, stare into the half-light with wild fluttering eyes, and then suddenly collapse.

In *Vienna 1900* the young lady died quietly and tactfully in her sleep, with her murderer gazing at her soulfully as he sat beside her—perhaps suspecting that when death occurs in Old Vienna the *Waldmeister* Overture and the Vienna Philharmonic can never be far behind.

I mentioned earlier that I was aware of a certain excess in my criticism of these not remarkably significant programs. After all, I realize that many people in this country have come to be fond of the Masterpiece Theatre productions—finding in the rhythms of the British actors and in the literary quality of the scripts a welcome relief from the strident, cops-and-robbers-oriented dramas of commercial television. No critic should be such a spoilsport as to try to cajole people away from having a good time, even at the expense of a dead and bowdlerized Austrian author. But what has bothered me, and implicitly motivated these comments, is that in the same week that I watched the first episode of *Vienna 1900* I read a seemingly unconnected report in *The New York Times* of a petition recently brought before the F.C.C. in Washington by a group called the Puerto Rican Media Action and Educational Council. The plaintiffs were asking for the revocation of the broadcast license of New York's public-television station, WNET, on the ground of discrimination against New York's Hispanic population, partly in matters of employment but mainly in a failure to provide "relevant programming." The F.C.C. had rejected the petition, with only one dissenting vote, stating, significantly:

> . . . the petitioners are not alleging that WNET has failed to provide *any* programming of interest to the Hispanic community, or in response to its needs, but that it has provided insufficient programming in response to the needs and interests of the Hispanic community. As we have previously noted, programming which is responsive to the needs of the licensee's community need not be especially responsive to the particular needs of each ethnic group within that community.

I later read the Puerto Rican petition, and in most of its particulars it seemed strongly political, and contentiously quixotic in its willingness to find anti-Hispanic discrimination throughout WNET's program schedule. For example, *Bill Moyers' Journal*, *An American Family*, *Who's Afraid of Opera?*, *Report to the Nation*, Opera Theatre, NET Playhouse, and *State of the Union* were all listed by the Puerto Rican group as being irrelevant to the interests of the Hispanic community, and thereby discriminatory. But in reading the F.C.C.'s reply and WNET's defense I had the distinct impression that they were chiefly statements against impertinence, though it was the F.C.C. and WNET—not the Puerto Rican group—who apparently felt themselves to be at the barricades. Indeed, this theme of the communications establishment as Horatius at the bridge had been anticipated in a speech that F.C.C. commissioner James H. Quello made to the Oklahoma Broadcasters Association a few weeks earlier. Said Mr. Quello:

> I am concerned with possible abuse of the license-challenge procedure by a small group or groups imposing their will or their program tastes on stations under threat of petitions to deny. The licensee cannot delegate or abrogate responsibility for programming in the public interest . . .
>
> My personal feeling is that all representative community groups should be consulted . . . [that] programming and management decisions should be based on that over-all ascertainment, and not on the basis of demands of one or two groups that may represent only a small fraction of total population served.

Three things seemed clear from this little dispute tucked away in the files of the F.C.C. and the back pages of the *Times:* first, that—despite the establishment's new barricades rhetoric—the Hamilton-Jefferson polarity of the American ideal has persisted as strongly as ever into the broadcast era; second, that the revolutionary tic that appeared only briefly in America in the 1960's but has since been widely exploited by politicians of both parties continues to express itself, albeit inadequately, usually without the benefit of either coherent language or coherent politics but somehow asking at least to be listened to; third, that the one article of faith seemingly held by all political establishments is the *political* significance of communications. Or, to put it another way, it is too often asserted that people on the outside of a communications establishment wish only to play politics with it, while people on the inside of the establishment are merely doing their job.

In short, what is disturbing about the F.C.C.-WNET-Puerto Rican controversy is not so much the merits of the Puerto Rican position—for theirs was something of a dodgy case, full of oversimplification and excess demands—as the complacent reasonableness of the government's and public television's reply. The Puerto Rican group claimed a broadcast audience of roughly two million Hispanics in WNET's area, and found most of the station's key programs discriminatory against the Hispanic community, partly in WNET's English-only programming, mainly in its avoidance of programming that took into account "the richness and uniqueness of Puerto Rican culture." The F.C.C. majority opinion, taking into account a smaller broadcast area than had the Puerto Rican group, pointed out that the Hispanic population was under the one million mark. Earlier, WNET, in its reply to the petition, had said that it was unwilling to accept the implication that "the Puerto Rican community has no interest in classics, music, drama, anthropology, literature, art, cinema, or history"; the F.C.C. found that the Hispanic group had "provided no statistical evidence in support of its assertion that most Spanish-speaking people residing within the WNET coverage area cannot understand the English language." The F.C.C. also said that "a broadcast licensee need not take into consideration the uniqueness and richness of the

Puerto Rican culture to provide effective programming in response to Latinos' housing problems or their educational and economic concerns. [The Puerto Rican group] has neither alleged nor shown that WNET has ignored these problems."

The conclusion one seemed to be asked to draw from this exchange was that once again the children had misbehaved, though for the time being they had been straightened out. After all, does it make sense for the F.C.C., in its majesty, to revoke WNET's license because *Bill Moyers' Journal* is not conducted in Spanish? Because there is too much opera? Could anyone be unaware that WNET is an enlightened broadcaster? On an "attachment" appended to the F.C.C.'s opinion, the WNET management listed twenty-six instances of Hispanic-oriented programming that had been broadcast between November 1973 and January 1974. On the question of alleged employment discrimination, the F.C.C. found that the Puerto Rican group had "failed to make a *prima facie* showing" and that their facts "lacked the required specificity." Management figures were provided to show that 4³⁄₁₀ percent of the station's employees are Hispanic. And, almost as if to underline the sweet reasonableness of the F.C.C. reply, a dissenting statement issued by Commissioner Benjamin L. Hooks was full of the stupefying flora of 1960's media-leftist jargon. "WNET, the radiant jewel in the public television's crown," Commissioner Hooks's statement began, "is unquestionably a media symbol of sophistication and urbanity . . . Its current pattern of establishmentarian predomination must cease; the time has come for a showdown . . . By styling itself . . . as an electronic Harvard liberal arts course, public broadcasting has . . . overlooked the intellectual needs and sensitivities of that core of the population which . . . is just emerging from the chains of the eighteenth and nineteenth centuries." And so forth.

I wrote "And so forth" because the temper of established America at this time inclines many people to think that way. But in truth I believe there is something of importance hovering behind the windy politics of Mr. Hooks's dissenting statement. The fact is that public television was not intended to be a fourth entertainment network, broadcasting to some fourth, ascertainable, homogenized entertainment audience. Part of the explicit intent of Congress when it approved the statute setting up the Corporation for Public Broadcasting, in 1967, was "to assist in establishing innovative educational programs, to facilitate educational program availability." At the time of the signing of the Public Broadcasting Act, these educational limits were plausibly interpreted by President Lyndon Johnson to include "the best in broadcasting good music . . . exciting plays . . . the whole fascinating range of human activity." Even so, the implicit intent for public broadcasting in America—which is dependent largely on public funds—has surely been that it become a communications channel, unswayed by considerations of profit and market salesmanship; that it serve the mass and variety of its clientele.

Ideals, of course, are difficult, and sometimes hazardous to live by. Public television in this country does not serve its clientele very badly. On the other hand, it does not seem to serve it very well. And what strikes me as the most notable aspect of this situation is not so much that men and women striving after a certain achievement have succeeded or failed, as that the ideal of achievement has become gradually tidy, confining, and exclusive. *Vienna 1900* is only an incidental example of meretricious, elite programming—a superficial, falsely conceived series based on the same glossy production values that it is supposed to provide alternatives to. The point is that it represents an increasingly *market* approach to public broadcasting—in a period, moreover, when public broadcasting is receiving more public money than ever before.

As it happens, in the same period in which the *Times* published its report of the F.C.C.'s sturdy defense against the proposed Hispanic takeover of WNET, and a fine Burkean editorial on the subject as well ("The Federal Communications Commission has defended the city's public television station against improper interference bordering on censorship"), I noticed the following item in its business section:

> William T. Gladmon, director of development of television station WETA in Washington, recently returned to public television after a six-year absence. The big change he's noticed is that now when he makes a pitch to a corporation he no longer needs to explain what public television is. "They are much more responsive than in 1962," he recalls of his early days. "Then they didn't even understand it." . . .
>
> He and four other men put on presentations last year

for 60 corporations, presentations that stressed the high quality of the station's supporters and viewers and the public-relations benefits of underwriting.

The title of the flip-chart presentation that they use is "Public Television—A Viable Alternative." . . . An underwriter, the presentation pointed out, gets identification with quality programming, merchandisability, and uncluttered environment, and a quality audience of opinion makers.

And the brief corporate identification at the end of the program ("brought to you—or made possible by—a grant from") is, in the words of Mr. Depew [director of corporate underwriting for WNET], "just the tip of the iceberg."

Perhaps it is only a matter of technics once again triumphing in our national life, which is to say that the men and women whom we have asked to establish public broadcasting have doubtless become so involved in the maintenance and expansion of this establishment that there has been little significant opportunity for reexamining the type or orientation of the structure. At any rate, it might be a good idea to somehow contrive a public conversation in the nation soon on the subject of what the public would like to have broadcast on its stations—keeping in mind that there have been innumerable self-serving interpretations of what this "public" consists of, and there will probably be more in the future, but that none have been so abusive of the best spirit of this country as those which have tried to impose, however reasonably, a homogeneity when there is none. As matters stand, the suggestion that, after all the patience and effort that have gone into the development of a public-television system, its broadcasts should be directed primarily at a "quality audience of opinion makers" is an irony that Arthur Schnitzler might well have appreciated.

White Man Still Speaks with Forked Tongue

A NUMBER OF PEOPLE HAVE SPOKEN TO ME APPROVingly about a two-hour special program called *I Will Fight No More Forever*, concerning the Nez Percé Indians and their stirring, ill-fated campaign against the government in 1877. Though I didn't see the program when it was first broadcast, a few weeks ago, by ABC, I was told that it would be shown again in the future, and so I recently arranged to watch it, partly out of interest in the subject and partly because—the levels of ordinary television programming being what they are—it seemed that a special production such as this (which was accompanied by press information stating that the director, Richard Heffron, had amassed "more than 1,000 pounds" of written material during his research) doubtless represented the higher achievement levels of the craft. In fact, I found it a commendable production in many ways. I also found myself thinking that if this was one of the more ambitious exercises of contemporary television, then perhaps it was worth repaying the compliment, so to speak, and treating it with comparable seriousness, or, at least, with something beyond the usual commentary one hears or reads about the better type of program: "Fine show . . . sensitive . . . carefully researched . . ." What follows, then, is a brief attempt to consider one of the few serious ventures of current commercial television on the terms that I believe it has set for itself: the historical re-creation of the significant events of one of this country's last notable Indian wars.

The television account, which describes itself as accurate ("This story is true"), opens in June 1877 with a scene of two Nez Percé men hunting an eagle on a ridge above the Wallowa Valley, in northeastern Oregon. The Indians are soon surprised by two surly white settlers and (unjustly, it appears) are accused of horse-stealing. One of the settlers, called Grant, shoots the older Indian, Eagle Robe, in a particularly cowardly and sadistic fashion. When the surviving Nez Percé, Eagle Robe's son, returns to his camp, many of the younger warriors are eager for revenge, but Chief Joseph, the thirty-seven-year-old Nez Percé chief (played with earnest dignity by Ned Romero), restrains them. This sequence of events sets the tone for a meeting that then takes place between Joseph and his Nez Percés and Major General Oliver Otis Howard, the commander of the Department of the Columbia, and an Indian agent,

John Monteith. General Howard (played in a grizzled, gruff-but-kindly manner by James Whitmore) is a forty-six-year-old veteran of the Civil War, in which he lost an arm and gained a reputation for soldierly decency in his treatment of freed slaves. Here he is depicted as clearly an apolitical soldier who is personally sympathetic to the Nez Percé position and is a friend of Chief Joseph's. At the beginning of the meeting, Howard and Joseph chat about Joseph's wife and expected child. Howard presents Joseph with a handmade doll as a present for the infant from Mrs. Howard. Then Monteith, the Indian agent, says curtly, "We have all received orders from our government." General Howard adds, compassionately, "I'm sorry it's not favorable to your cause, Joseph." Monteith reads aloud an order from the Secretary of the Interior which, by authority of President Grant, commands the Nez Percés to "give up their land and settle on the reservation within thirty days of this notice."

This far, the story has broadly corresponded with the historical record—at least, in the general sense of showing the hostility between the new Oregon settlers and the Nez Percés, and in pointing out the equally general theme of the government's decision, in 1877, to move the Nez Percés from the Wallowa Valley to a reservation farther north. Still, there are noticeable discrepancies in the television account. Some are minor, and are of what might be called a technical or pedantic nature. For instance, the murder of Eagle Robe by the settler Grant just before the parley with General Howard appears to be at least a partial fabrication, based on the actual but not notably sadistic shooting of Eagle Robe by a settler called Larry Ott, which had taken place two years earlier, in 1875. A more complicated divergence lies in the depiction of General Howard and of his role in the reservation matter. The television account generally presents Howard as a stouthearted military man who has been put in a difficult situation vis-à-vis the Nez Percés by President Grant and Washington bureaucrats. However, the facts seem to show that—though there were undeniably strong pressures on Washington from the Oregon settlers to move the Nez Percés out of the Wallowa Valley—it was actually Howard who forced the issue, at the Indians' expense. Thus, Alvin M. Josephy, Jr., wrote in his excellent history *The Nez Percé Indians and the Opening of the Northwest:*

> Soon afterward [in 1876], Howard's thinking had become settled on the matter. Taking the position . . . that the whites could no longer be ousted, he had decided that the government should end the conflict . . . by extinguishing the Indians' rights to all off-reservation lands through a fair and just purchase of those claims from every band that had not signed the 1863 treaty. . . . Howard, in his future actions, showed that he had totally abandoned his position of 1875, at which time he had said that it had been a mistake to take the Wallowa from the Indians. Now he would take it, by negotiation and payment if possible, but by force if necessary. Moreover, by having the government accept and promptly execute his policy, he would make inevitable an injustice that might have been avoided.

As for the heartwarming scene in which General Howard engages in familial small talk with the Nez Percé chief, this is not totally inconceivable, but it is unlikely to have happened at that time. In fact, at the parley with the Nez Percés which historically preceded this final meeting, Howard had been so alienated from the Indians that he later characterized one of their great war chiefs, old Toohoolhoolzote, as a "large, thick-necked, ugly, obstinate savage of the worst type," and, in a fit of temper, arrested him. The June meeting shown on television (which actually took place on May 14) had thus begun not with gifts of handmade dolls but with the reluctant release by Howard of the furious old chief.

About a month afterward, the Nez Percé war began. In the television account, the Nez Percés return to their camp after the meeting with Howard, and some of the warriors rail angrily at the white men while Joseph counsels that they proceed peacefully to the reservation. That night, three young Nez Percés ride into a nearby settlement, where they find Grant—the killer of Eagle Robe—in a saloon. Grant backs off, reaches for his gun, but a Nez Percé kills him. The three Nez Percés graciously leave the other settlers in the saloon unharmed ("Woman, your white man is not worth killing") and ride back to camp. Joseph is aghast at what they have done. "You have had your revenge," he says. "Now the whites will have theirs!" However, he remains conciliatory. "But if Howard will listen I will speak to him," he says.

Again, this is not significantly untrue to the spirit of the historical record, but certain details have been altered or omitted. For instance, after the meeting with Howard the Nez Percés (counseled by Joseph and his brother Ollokot) had promptly accepted the government's summons to the reservation, and had ridden nineteen days north and were camped within a few miles of their destination when two incidents took place. First–taunted by members of his own tribe for cowardice–the son of Eagle Robe, with two reluctant companions, rode into a settlement near Mount Idaho looking for Larry Ott, to avenge the murder of his father, which had taken place two years previously. Ott had since left the territory, but the Nez Percé trio came upon various other settlers, and killed four men and wounded another. Then, in the next few days, other Nez Percés joined the three warriors, and–fueled by alcohol and past resentments–massacred roughly fifteen white settlers in the area of White Bird Canyon. One evening, Joseph and Ollokot and the remaining Nez Percés were briefly counterattacked by a small band of settlers, and Joseph decided that he would have to join with the raiders. From his headquarters, General Howard notified Washington that another Indian war had broken out in the West.

Thus commenced the great saga of the Nez Percé ride of more than sixteen hundred miles–pursued at various times by ten different detachments of the United States Army–from Oregon through the Idaho Territory, across the Bitterroot Mountains, into the Montana Territory, across the Continental Divide, through Yellowstone Park, and eventually, north across the Absaroka range of the

Wyoming Territory toward Canada. In most respects, the television account appears faithful to the broad outline of the Nez Percé odyssey, but there are certain changes in detail, some of which merely reflect a perhaps human penchant for casual inaccuracy (which might have been less noticeable if it were not for the repeated assertions of historical truth in the narration), though there are others where the inaccuracies, however casual, contribute to a quite different overall effect. An example of a lesser, technical detail may be a scene of the devastating employment by army troops of a howitzer against the Nez Percé encampment at the Big Hole. The facts seem to be that Colonel John Gibbon's command possessed a howitzer but the gun did not reach the battle until the principal day's fighting was over, and then it was rapidly captured by the Indians and overturned.

A more significant alteration of historical fact or likelihood, however, occurs in the dramatization of the battle of White Bird Canyon. At the beginning (in the television account), Joseph and the Nez Percés are pictured as unsure whether or not they are yet in a state of war with the government. "There will be no attack unless the soldiers shoot," says Joseph. Shortly after that, two companies of cavalry appear, accompanied by several armed settlers. The Indians send out three men carrying a truce flag, presumably to parley with the officer in charge, Captain David Perry, and one of the truce Indians is deliberately shot by a trigger-happy settler, who maliciously remarks, "Boys, I got my Indian. You better get yours." The Nez Percés then return fire, and quickly mount a charge against the soldiers, who are routed. However, according to Merrill D. Beal, another scholarly authority on the Nez Percé war, the Nez Percés were clearly set for battle when Perry's troops arrived—perhaps because in actuality they had lately massacred nearly twenty settlers, not merely a fictitious Grant. Then, though there appears to have been an informal truce team, which was mistakenly fired at by an army scout, Arthur Chapman (Perry, however, makes no mention of the truce team in his dispatch), the truce-team Indians were unharmed and backed away, returning to their lines. What followed next was an exchange of rifle fire between the well-protected Nez Percés and the soldiers, with the result that Perry's command was driven off.

There is one further divergence of fact and tone toward the end of the drama, which is worth mentioning not because the particular scene, as played by Whitmore, Romero, etc., was aesthetically displeasing (on the contrary, it seemed an effective dramatic moment) but as a kind of aside, or footnote, for it seems to me that the actual personalities and events of the Nez Percé war were decidedly more interesting—in the context of their own untidy reality—than were their trimly scripted counterparts (by screenwriters Jeb Rosebrook and Theodore Strauss) as recreated for us today. What happened in history was that when Chief Joseph and roughly 550 remaining Nez Percés escaped a trap set by General Howard on the Clark Fork River and headed north toward Canada, Howard desperately sent couriers to Colonel Nelson Miles, whose command lay more than two hundred miles to the northeast, and asked him to hasten across Montana and intercept the

Nez Percés. The television account, while noting Howard's dilemma, implies that the general was still in control of the situation and was thus perpetrating a ruse. ("But we've got to slow the Indians down. There's only one way to do that. Slow down ourselves.") However, the facts seem to show that by then Howard was already embarrassed militarily and in the national press, and was virtually out of the fight. Indeed, it was Miles—a bellicose and ambitious officer, who had once been Howard's aide-de-camp—who actually caught Joseph and ended the war, and who thereafter took the credit for both deeds. In the television version, doubtless in deference to Whitmore's top-billing portrayal of Howard, Miles has little more than a walk-on role: on the cold, bleak terrain of the Bear Paw Mountains, below the Canadian border, the Second Cavalry makes a surprise attack on the Nez Percés and apparently scores a decisive victory. The next day, General Howard and his troops appear, and, flanked by his aide and Colonel Miles, he receives the Nez Percé surrender from Chief Joseph, who drops his rifle on the ground and delivers his famous speech, which ends with the words "I will fight no more forever." Again, the truth is not completely different, but neither is it quite the same. To begin with, though Colonel Miles took over active pursuit of the Nez Percés, Miles and his command (which included at least two cavalry units and one infantry unit) did not really surprise the Indians, and the battle at the Bear Paws was extremely close, with the army taking many casualties and Miles having to order his men to dig in for a siege. The weather was freezing. Snow had begun to fall. Miles was further worried about the presence of Sitting Bull and about two thousand Sioux some forty miles north, across the Canadian border, and asked to have a conference with Chief Joseph. Joseph came to the army camp to discuss surrender (which Miles seems to have been pressing for), and the colonel ignominiously arrested the Nez Percé chief and held him hostage. Fortunately, the Nez Percés had simultaneously held one of Miles's aides hostage in their camp, and the next day the Indian and the cavalryman were exchanged. Some scattered fighting continued. Nearly six inches of snow lay on the ground. General Howard finally showed up five days later. As Miles wrote in his memoirs, *Personal Recollections of General Nelson A. Miles*, published in 1897: "On the evening of the 4th of October, General Howard came up with an escort of twelve men, and, remaining in our camp over night, was present next morning at the surrender of Chief Joseph and the entire Indian camp." About two o'clock of a bitter-cold afternoon, Joseph and five of his surviving warriors approached the army camp. He handed his rifle to Colonel Miles, who took it. The war was over.

Though this "true" film account of the Nez Percé war, then, is generally faithful to the situation as a whole, and achieves a commendable accuracy in matters of costume and war paint and the like, its value to the audience is, all the same, more likely to be that of entertainment (as in a good historical novel) than that of a filmed historical record—or truth. Some of the film's inaccuracies or discrepancies are incidental in terms of telling a dramatic story; for instance, there are several cozy family scenes between Chief Joseph and his "wife, Toma," but the fact is that he had two wives. On television, it probably makes for a more coherent or a more acceptable narrative if he has one. Other askew details are a result of the unscriptability of nature; for instance, a key element in the Nez Percé escape from General Howard after White Bird Canyon was the flood conditions in June on the Salmon River—whose televised counterpart (in Mexico) is shown to be a gently flowing stream.

But, overall, the most important alterations in detail and texture are in the film account's simplification of the two key roles: General Howard and Chief Joseph. James Whitmore's Howard is a dramatic portrait that has been painted with some praiseworthy realism, but in the end it remains that of a conventional actor-hero, and takes into account neither that Howard had a considerable role in provoking the Nez Percé war through his own reservation policies nor that by the end of the campaign he was not the nobly authoritative figure depicted as receiving Joseph's surrender. Ned Romero's portrayal of Joseph, for its part, seems superficially faithful to the dignity and common sense of this notable Indian, but here, too, the television version created distortions in its simplifications—in this case, of Chief Joseph's actual position among the Nez Percés and in the Nez Percé war. Principally, the television account reinforces a kind of popular myth of the time that Joseph was *the* Nez Percé chief and that he was a great military strategist—beliefs that doubtless derived from the fact that in military dispatches from the Nez Percé war American commanders found it convenient to refer to Joseph's relatively accessible name (his father, Tuekakas, had been baptized Joseph by a Presbyterian missionary and had passed the name on to his son), and also from a certain self-serving ignorance in various memoirists. Thus, Colonel Miles (who, as we saw, arrived late to the war) referred to Joseph in his memoirs, twenty years later, as "the Indian Napoleon." Similarly, in the television version General Howard (who had fought against General Robert E. Lee in the Civil War) remarks, "I've never fought a better general." The facts seem to be that though Joseph's sagacity and diplomacy eventually came to carry dominant influence in Nez Percé councils—especially after the Nez Percés had lost the war and were taken to the reservation—during most of the fighting on the long march Joseph had been but one of several chiefs (such as White Bird, Looking Glass, and old Toohoolhoolzote) and by no means the most militarily adept among them. As the historian L. V. McWhorter wrote in *Hear Me, My Chiefs!*, "Joseph, the war chief, is a creature of legend; Joseph, the Indian Napoleon, does not emerge from the Nez Percé chronicles of their great fight for freedom." In a more even-handed approach, Alvin Josephy, Jr., has written:

> The fact that neither Joseph nor any other individual chief had been responsible for the outstanding strategy and masterful success of the campaign is irrelevant. The surrender speech, taken down by Howard's adjutant and published soon afterwards, confirmed Joseph in the public's mind as the symbol of the Nez Percés' heroic, fighting retreat.

Perhaps it is a fine point that would have mattered only to the Nez Percés—though, being uncommonly democratic, they would probably not have pushed it.

It would be unfortunate if these comments dissuaded anyone from watching *I Will Fight No More Forever* when it is next shown on television, for it is certainly an entertaining and interesting rendering of an exceptional saga, and it has been translated into telefilm with a greater concern for the Indian position than has been shown by most filmmakers in the past. All the same, it raises questions of accuracy and truth which I suspect may become more common as the public's longing for reality, or at least dramatized reality, becomes more widespread. After watching the television film, I mentioned my doubts about some of the film's depictions—notably of General Howard—and about the "political" highlighting of white brutality and avoidance of Indian brutality to a television producer, who replied: "The point is that the public gets to see a relatively honest film on a subject that it otherwise mightn't have looked at." I am sure that this is true, and it is an argument based on apparent benefit to the general audience, but I think the questions remain. For instance, what is "relative honesty" when it comes to portraying actual lives and events? Admittedly, our notion of history may be an arrogant impossibility, since each move a person makes is precisely *that* move, so that even the common events of a lifetime become an almost mathematical complex of "moves": a vast molecular network of precise, interlocking factors of event and personality which we peer at from a distance, usually with only the most inadequate equipment for examining the whole structure. All the same, despite what we do with it and to it, there remains something noble and important about truth, and maybe especially about the so-called simple truths of a man's or a woman's life. And possibly this is one of the reasons that until recently imaginative artists have shied away from putting actual people into their fabrications—those tales and novels that are invariably fabricated from the events and personalities of actual people. Lately, the line that separates our ways of looking at life has become more and more blurred—with history, journalism, and storytelling seemingly mixed together as in a stewpot. The tendency derives, one is told, from our less compartmentalized times. "This story is true," asserts the prologue to the television film about the Nez Percé war. Alas, it is not quite true; it is somewhat true; it is nearly true. Much of the genial haziness of our historical perceptions certainly lies in our restless, modern tampering with reality in the guise of providing attractive "information," or even of righting past wrongs: thus, if Indians were once mis-shown as savages, we will now presumably assist the Indian by mis-showing the settlers as brutes. At any rate, the entertainment public appears to be the gainer, and there is merit in that. Moreover, if it happens that there are imperfections in this historical entertainment, with details of fact or character not fully portrayed, or else distorted, perhaps it will also happen that *I Will Fight No More Forever* may encourage some in its audience to pursue the story further, into history and the considerable literature on the subject—and that itself would be no small achievement. But as for larger questions of truth and accuracy, it is surely worth making a distinction between the relativity of truth and the relative care or seriousness with which many nowadays try to approach it. Absolute truth may be as elusive or as distant as the boundaries of the universe, but a commitment to sighting it is what counts; else the alternative is to slide sideways into the propagandizing and counter-propagandizing tendencies of our times. In the end, those surviving primitive peoples who even today direct their quaintly naïve gestures at photographers for fear of losing their souls may be closer to a conception of truth than we are, who ceaselessly dabble with it. After all, how better, finally, to steal someone's soul than by re-creating him on paper or canvas, or stone, bronze, wood or film, with good will and fine intentions and a certain regard for technical accuracy—but *not quite right?*

Three Views of Women

I. "Ring Around the Collar!"

This half-minute commercial for a laundry detergent called Wisk appears fairly frequently on daytime and evening television. In a recent version, a young woman and a young man are shown being led down the corridor of a hotel by a bellman who is carrying suitcases. The hotel seems to be an attractive one—not very elegant but definitely not an ordinary motel. Similarly, the young man and woman are attractive, but with nothing either glamorous or working-class about their appearance. Perhaps he is a junior executive. And she is probably his wife, though there is nothing so far that says that the two people are married. Since the framework of the drama is a commercial, the assumption is that they *are* married. On the other hand, against the familiar framework of similar modern movie scenes, there is no such assumption; possibly it is the beginning of an adventure. Then, suddenly, the bellman drops one of the suitcases in the corridor; some of the contents of the suitcase spill out; the bellman crouches down on the corridor carpet to put the items back in. He notices one of the man's shirts and holds it up. "Ring around the collar!" he says accusingly; these words are then taken up in the kind of singsong chant that has become a feature of these ads. The man looks puzzled and let down. The woman examines the offending shirt and looks mortified and aghast. By now, whatever slight elegance or intimations of adventure may have existed at the beginning of the scene have totally disintegrated, and, indeed, have quickly re-formed themselves into the classic hubby-and-housewife focus of most television commercials. The wife admits her mistake—to the bellman and her husband—of having used an inadequate detergent, and the scene changes to what is apparently the laundry area of her house, where the wife (now back in her regular "wifely" clothes) discusses the merits of using Wisk when doing the family wash.

In a number of ways, this is the most noticeably irritating of the housewife commercials. There is a nagging, whiny quality to the "Ring around the collar!" chant which is almost a caricature of the nagging, whiny voices of earlier Hollywood and TV-commercial housewives but which deliberately stops before the point of caricature is reached. In the manner of certain other ads—especially those for aspirin and "cold remedies"—it is a commercial that expressly announces its own irritatingness. We are going to repeat and repeat and repeat, these commercials say, and we are going to grate on your nerves—and you are going to remember us. At times, this sales approach has been given various fine-sounding methodological names by advertisers, but essentially it is the voice of the small boy who wants something: I want, I want, I want, I want—and finally you give it to him. In this case, the small boy wants you to buy his detergent, and who is to tell him no?

On the level of anti-female condescension, the "Ring around the collar!" ad seems to go even beyond irritation. In most housewife commercials, the housewife is portrayed as little more than a simpering, brainless jelly, almost pathologically obsessed with the world of kitchen floors or laundry, or of the celebrated "bathroom bowl." But in the Wisk commercials the standard trivializing portrait is accompanied by quite unusual brutality. As if in a reverse Cinderella process, the young prince and his companion not only are stopped in their tracks by the hazard of the Dirty Shirt (and the curse cry of "Ring around the collar!") but, instantly, as if under a magic spell, are snatched from the hotel-palace and returned to their previous existence—she to profess folk-happiness among the laundry tubs, and he, presumably, to his northern New England sales route. Sex is back to what it used to be: the identityless woman in the traveling suit is replaced by the beaming housewife in housewifely attire. And it is all the result of *her* failure in not having properly attended to her husband's needs—in having exposed him to the scorn of the bellman who guarded the erotic corridor. The fable does not end in tragedy—for though Cinderella is back among the laundry tubs, she now has good magic on her side. But it has been a sobering experience.

II. Phyllis Doesn't Quite Save Alcatraz

Two recent comedy series, *Phyllis* and *Rhoda*, make much of their portrayals of "new women." Rhoda, who originated as an independent working-girl type on *The Mary Tyler Moore Show*, began her existence as a modern heroine by moving to New York, where she eventually sets herself up as a professional window decorator. Phyllis was also a character part on *The Mary Tyler Moore Show;* after the death of her husband, she moved to San Francisco, where she lives with her late husband's mother and stepfather and works as an assistant in a photography studio. Both heroines are played by capable comic actresses, though Valerie Harper, who plays Rhoda, has a more limited range than Cloris Leachman, who plays Phyllis. The tone of the two programs is assertively "modern," emphasizing what is intended to appear as the humorous, or perhaps practical, side of women's current ambivalence toward feminism. Thus, each episode displays the heroine beneath a gloss of sprightly female independence, as in Rhoda's amused or sometimes impatient (but still playful) put-downs of her comical, old-fashioned mother. But, time after time, this independence turns out to be illusory and not even especially desired; and female self-respect is nearly always revealed as ultimately deriving from benign family relations.

In a film-montage which accompanies each show, Rhoda is fetchingly portrayed as an urban young woman, braving the hazards of New York life and mastering them:

she is the career girl who works hard at her job and marriage and still manages to have a good time. This ideal, at any rate, is what the program claims to be showing. What it does show, however, is something much more familiar: the standard entertainment-comedy heroine who periodically goes through the motions of being liberated. With Rhoda, the ambiguities of modern feminism are less the property of character than they are of the scriptwriters. For instance, shortly after she arrived in New York (with much talk of furthering her career), she began going out with a man, and quickly was married to him. Accordingly, most episodes of *Rhoda* reveal a fairly routine, husband-and-wife domestic comedy which might well be retitled *Rhoda and Joe*, except for those more recent episodes where even Joe is shunted to the background and where Rhoda and her homely, marriage-minded younger sister continue the same comical soap-opera routines that Rhoda once played with Mary Tyler Moore, and which presumably derive from *My Sister Eileen*. Rhoda's career still exists in a remote, technical sense (as does the "city" it takes place in), but it rarely exists on camera, where most of the comedy and the plot action consist of Rhoda playing off on her mother, or sister, or on the genial and masculine Joe—whose masculinity even extends to his profession, which is owning a small demolition company. Rhoda's feminism, in fact, is almost entirely limited to verbal repartee and wisecracks. The content of the jokes, of course, is topically weighted: that is, it is based on the assumed tensions and mishaps that might result from the pairing of good-natured, semi-hardhat Joe and sassy, career-girl Rhoda. But the actuality of the humor remains standard husband-and-wife byplay. A recent episode, for instance, portrayed Rhoda attempting to cajole Joe into hiring a good-for-nothing boyfriend of her sister's. In keeping with standard folklore language, Joe was patient and "strong," Rhoda was sharp-tongued and "smart." Indeed, Rhoda's principal career consists of manipulating Joe.

In the other "new-woman" comedy, *Phyllis*, the heroine's role has been blandly subverted in another familiar show-business way. Where Rhoda has been gradually transformed into a retooled version of the sassy, oh-so-vaguely sexually knowing side of Lucy, in *I Love Lucy*, Cloris Leachman's Phyllis has become the madcap, muddled, meddlesome aspect of the same old vaudeville prototype. In a recent episode, the slight story was set in motion by the device of Phyllis, the *engagée* woman, trying to get signatures for a petition to restore the prison on Alcatraz Island and turn it into a museum. Not only was this device so mechanical and halfhearted that it was never referred to again, but even when Phyllis was shown trying to get the signatures the whole idea of her working on the petition was turned into a joke—another madcap antic. Thus having touched base on Phyllis's social involvement, and also having scored a couple of laughs off this same involvement, the program could pursue its accustomed course, which on this occasion had to do with madcap Phyllis meddling in the romantic affairs of her boss. True to the up-to-date spirit of these "new-woman" comedies, the boss was predictably a woman—and the photographer whom Phyllis here and there "assists" has decided overtones of gayness.

But none of this matters. It is all fuel for show-business comedy routines that existed long before most of the participants were born. "Jerry was *supposed* to be *going* with Julie, but now *he* turns up *here* with *that!*" says Phyllis at one point, getting the harebrained, breathless scansion of the line just right. Thus speaks TV comedy's "new woman."

III. George Sand Sets an Example

Public television has imported from England a number of series programs that deal either historically or obliquely (or both) with the women's movement. *Shoulder to Shoulder* has offered an examination of the woman-suffrage movement in England. *Jennie* has provided a historical and reasonably accurate portrait of a remarkable and ambitious Edwardian figure—Jennie Jerome, who became Lady Randolph Churchill. Recently, *Notorious Woman* has been giving the American public-television audience a glimpse of an even more historically distant woman of unusual qualities—George Sand. These programs are historical in that they refer to historical moments, and thus afford the British stage designers an opportunity to provide the kind of ample, expensive effects that the American public rarely finds in domestic programs save through the budgets of commercial TV; but their main dramatic purpose seems to consist in tuning in to the relatively advanced feminist sympathies (and fantasies) of the more educated, and often more well-to-do, audience.

In *Notorious Woman*, for example, a tacit bond is assumed to exist between the sensibility of the audience and the intent of the program. Anti-feminist dialogue here is spoken with a certain relish and without apparent irony, because there is an assumption that the minority audience will not only perceive the implicit irony of the position but find some satisfaction in feeling superior to it. "A woman is equal to a man in all ways," says George Sand's grandmother, "and superior in many. But never say so—to a man." And "Child, you have very few physical attributes, but thank God you have a good figure." And "A woman needs stability: a home, children." And "When love ceases in a marriage, all that is left is sacrifice." And so on. Much of the point of *Notorious Woman* lies in the inherent satire of such remarks—and in its being played to a modern audience that can automatically detect the correct weight of a line such as "A woman needs stability . . ."

In the second episode of the series, when George Sand has come to Paris, leaving behind her children and a strangely understanding provincial husband, the separation between the drama of events and the drama of the program's sexual politics becomes even sharper. For George Sand was clearly intelligent, ambitious, and one of the great pains in the neck of nineteenth-century Europe. But as she is played by Rosemary Harris and defined by the dialogue, she is to be glimpsed mainly as an embattled feminist. The import of the drama, in fact, is virtually confined to what the producers think might be attractive to a modern feminist sensibility. Men are rascally or brutish or weak—except, of course, for Honoré de Balzac, who is a good fellow. And George Sand is a kind of latter-day Joan of Arc, decked out in stylish gowns (except when she now and then wears men's clothes as a stunt) and trampling resolutely over the various people she has somehow hauled into her path, on her way to "live her own life." It is a handsomely mounted production that begs as many questions as it disposes of.

On the surface, these different views of women seem to have little in common—except, possibly, that they each to some degree represent the general ambiguity toward the shifting of male-female relations.

The least ambiguous approach is that of the "Ring around the collar!" commercial, which seems to speak with relatively little self-doubt to the sizable audience of American women whose lives are still confined to the house and whose anxieties (though unquestionably changing) are still determined largely by feelings of home-oriented inadequacy. Also fairly free of self-doubt are the British-made, public-television productions, such as *Notorious Woman,* which speak to the smaller, growing audience of men and women (though, one imagines, mostly women) who are attempting to rethink and refashion society along more feminist lines. And somewhere between the two, as might perhaps be expected—displaying the least conviction, and the most evasion, confusion, and fast footwork—are *Rhoda* and *Phyllis,* the products of the West Coast entertainment factories.

What the housewife commercials as a whole appear to say, in fact, is not only that the majority of women are still in the kitchen but that they are desperately unsure of where they want to be instead. *Business Week*, for example, displays a woman executive on its cover, accompanied by the headline THE CORPORATE WOMAN: UP THE LADDER, FINALLY, and *Newsweek* publishes a story about the special difficulties of a modern marriage in which both husband and wife are not merely employed but successfully and ambitiously employed—two corporate lawyers, say, or Carla and Roderick Hills. But, at the same time, one of the best-selling paperback books in the nation is a strange little tract called *The Total Woman* ("How to Make Your Marriage Come Alive!"), by Marabel Morgan. The one subject that Mrs. Morgan doesn't address in her book is the total woman, whoever she may be, for the treatise is a curiously chaste (though there is some rather giggly advice for "comforting" your man) self-help manual for those seemingly myriad women who find the actuality of work difficult and unpleasant, and who find the anxieties of their husbands sometimes even more difficult and unpleasant, and who are thereby advised to duck both sets of difficulties and stay in the kitchen, wearing frilly lingerie under the apron and cooing like a partridge. It is a mighty silly book on most levels, and in some ways it is worse than that, because it exploits modern women's new fears by claiming either that they don't exist or that they can be giggled away. On the evidence of the past several years, modern women are embarked upon an irreversible adventure, with important consequences of gain and loss for all parties, though lately some of the surface consequences (such as loneliness, sexual isolation, and fears of financial independence) have jarred progress toward further equality and a more concrete independence. Mrs. Morgan has apparently stepped in to say, "Let your anxieties be your guide; Daddy was right all along." And thousands of women, for the time being, seem willing to agree.

I mention Mrs. Morgan at this point because the success that her book appears to be enjoying across the nation indicates that in some ways the voice of the Wisk commercial—for all its charmless idiocy—speaks more honestly and directly to the mass of viewers than do the supposedly women-enhancing dramatic programs such as *Rhoda* and *Phyllis*. In both these shows, the heroines play at being "new women": independent and involved in the real world. Not only that, but the game is alleged to be a cheery one played out in pleasant surroundings, with no problems between the sexes so tangled or murky that they cannot be resolved by good humor or a wisecrack. In the real world, though, where the women who buy Wisk and *The Total Woman* reside, there seems to be relatively little playing at independence, and such modest role-changing as now exists amid the general populace seems to be often a source of deep new anxieties. The housewife commercial, in short, catches the mass of women at the point where many of them have stopped short—afraid or simply unable to leap over the wall. It is not, perhaps, a noble or romantic position, but it is a human one, and it appears to be a true one. High-minded programs such as *Notorious Woman*, on the other hand, show an elite of remarkable, historic female personages in the act of making the leap (always a romantic, historic leap) and landing safely on the other side. In these programs, sentiments of the kind propounded by Marabel Morgan in the present ("Admire your husband every day . . . Say something nice about his body today . . . Be touchable and kissable . . . God planned for woman to be under her husband's rule") are set back in time a century or so and played for comic or satiric effect. "Surely there are greater accomplishments for a woman than merely being the object of a man's lust?" asks young George Sand. Replies her grandmother, "My dear, I shouldn't ridicule an ambition you may never achieve." And so on. The emancipation of George Sand is real in that it is shown to have taken place, but at the same time it is a dream-world of costume and fine-sounding rhetoric. Also, in as many of these programs as I have seen, there remains a notable absence of sex and of the actuality of sexual problems—an absence that surely plays to one of the crucial fantasies of men and women alike in their imaginings of a new society. George Sand makes much of her wish to have the same sexual freedom as men—or, at least, as gentlemen—but what the reality of her sexual life and disposition was is largely hidden behind the mask of pageant and curiously recycled speech: "Am I nothing more than a sexual receptacle?" this nineteenth-century lady says at one point. Sex is presumed to exist as an important human activity, but what it *is* or *means*—a subject that men and women are now ceaselessly exploring in their private and semi-private lives—apparently must never be explored on television. Public television's "new woman" may not be the addle-pated Kewpie doll of *The Total Woman*, but, for all the rhetoric of emancipation, she is still fairly squeaky-clean: a romantic figure, untouched by sexual nightmares—another fantasy.

In fact, what a cursory examination of the portrayal of women on television reveals is only incidentally the trivialization of women's roles and the ambiguities inherent in most of the portraits. What mainly stands out is the absence of anything resembling true sexual feeling or relationships—except, strangely, in some of the commercials. The Wisk commercial, after all, is chiefly about sex—as was the folklore from which it derives. The inadequacies are sexual inadequacies. The fears are sexual fears. The "drama" of the ad is a sexual drama: a search for erotic fulfillment gone awry through an act of infidelity—with the young couple sent back to acquire sufficient virtue for another attempt. Nothing like such a story seems to exist in television's supposed storytelling sector, where (unlike the world of the poor, simpering housewife) erotic fulfillment never seems to greatly interest any of the fictional characters. Sex for Rhoda, or Phyllis, or Mary Tyler Moore, or Archie Bunker, or Kojak, or Columbo, etc., either doesn't exist or is a joke or a "plot development" out of pulp fiction. Sometimes a tough-guy TV detective, such as Matt Helm, will engage in "sexy" byplay with a "sexy" woman, but this is hardly ever more than childishly unconvincing posturing—a different kind of joke. Perhaps, in a nation that, in its genial madness, insists (at least linguistically) on lumping together physical love and murder in a social concept called "sex and violence," one can't really expect much greater sanity of its popular culture. And, given the remarkable absence of sex from television entertainment (in contrast to its increased presence in virtually every other aspect of American life), there is probably bound to be a certain heightened desire for depictions of violence, even of violent sport: the boarding-school or prison effect. Still, it is a strangely sexless electronic desert that Americans stare into every evening, and much of the day; and one where, as a consequence, it is virtually impossible (even if anyone should wish to try) to portray women with any truth and depth in their present changing situation. Giving sex its human place in television entertainment would not automatically create a roster of brilliant female (or male) characters, but it would be a help, and, at least, it would make it difficult to produce so many false ones.

Blood Marks in the Sylvan Glade

EACH WEEK, THE PARADE OF NATIONAL VIOLENCE continues (and seems even to grow louder), with assassination attempts on public figures, random murder of ordinary citizens, shootings, stabbings, crime in the streets—and inside our houses the accompanying sounds of police sirens, screams, high explosives, and pistol, rifle, and machine-gun fire coming from the television sets. Are Americans generally an unusually violent people—as if marked with some genetic flaw? Or is it that, in the Communications Era, we simply are more aware of violence than before? Do unregulated handguns produce crime? Or do broken homes? Or unemployment? Or do the "mass media" in fact produce much of the violence that they claim to reflect?

For some time now, a kind of perplexed and hazy debate on such questions has been taking place, both in the minds of citizens and through the shriller, more articulate, and usually self-serving voices of various interested parties, such as politicians, rifle-club spokesmen, and broadcasting executives. Nor is it the first time that voices in America have been raised to denounce (or try to justify) what has periodically appeared to be excessive violence in the land. In the 1830's and 1840's, for instance, newspaper editorials continually decried murder and criminality in the big cities, where crime rates were already often growing ten times as fast as in Europe. And in our own century there have been at least two previous occasions of public protest against violence—in each case, as it happens, focused on "media-related" violence. In the 1930's, there was a considerable outcry against gangster movies (such as *Scarface* and *Little Caesar*), which contributed to the creation of the moralistic Motion Picture Production Code, and for a while caused the phrase "Crime Does Not Pay" to be flashed on the screen at the beginning and end of such films; and in the 1950's there was a further agitation, against horror comics—much of it articulated by an impassioned and humorless psychiatrist named Dr. Fredric Wertham—which temporarily put a stop to the genre, and even produced a comics-industry "code."

On the surface, then, there might seem to be a certain cyclical nature to these protests as well as to society's temporary and moralizing ways of resolving the dilemma. But at present television violence seems to demand special attention, partly because of the widespread concern about it, and also because television itself is so much in our lives and so new, and there is so much uncertainty and disagreement about what it actually can do or can't do. As a result, perhaps, there has been a nervous increase in partisan commentary on all sides of the question—with the broadcasting establishment so far appearing to hold the opposition at bay mainly with a bombardment of public-relations jargon. Thus (according to Frederick S. Pierce, president of ABC Television): "Violence on television continues to be a subject of major concern to all broadcasters. But it is more than merely a concern . . ." Or (according to Robert T. Howard, president of NBC Television): "While television violence may be an inflated issue, it is still something that every broadcaster who believes in social responsibility must take seriously . . ." In the meantime—doubtless just in case a new Dr. Wertham should arise to focus public attention on violent television—the networks have lately instituted a self-regulating policy of their own, called "family viewing time," which is supposed to keep programming from 7 to 9 p.m. fairly free of violence. Even *Variety*—a journal not noted for its tender sensibilities—has described the new policy as the "Gore Curtain," adding, "The segment of U.S. society that epitomizes seaminess and violence . . . comes alive at 9 p.m. Criminals may be in a minority in society, but they own 9–11 every night."

The other side of the violence issue—represented by the usual disorganized regiment of educators and politicians, plus a lately formed cadre of "violence researchers" —has hardly been silent, nor are many of its arguments without a good deal of merit. In fact, given the propensities of the public for imposing moralistic judgments on offending industries, probably the chief reason for the broadcasting industry's having remained relatively unfettered—at least to the extent of not having to flash "Crime Does Not Pay" at the beginning and end of most programs—has been the failure of the anti-violence group to better articulate the findings that were so confusedly excavated in 1972 for the United States Surgeon General's Scientific Advisory Committee. The reports (titled *Television and Social Behavior*) took nearly three years to complete and were published in five volumes. Predictably, the findings were expressed in nearly impenetrable social-science jargon, but, equally predictably, beneath the qualifications and scientese the reports contained such relatively important ideas as:

> At least under some circumstances, exposure to televised aggression can lead children to accept what they have seen as a partial guide for their own actions.

And:

> A significant positive correlation has been found much more often than not [between viewing television violence and "aggressive behavior in adolescents"] and there is no negative correlational evidence.

And:

> More overt aggressive behavior follows exposure to violent content than to nonviolent content.

For reasons of politics (as well as of intelligibility), it was decided to release a sixth volume—which, in fact, would be published first—in order to summarize and clarify the significance of the research. This noble task was to be the work of the Advisory Committee, consisting of twelve men—ten from universities and one each from CBS and NBC—and the cloudy ambiguities and discretions of their summary were not only what the world first heard of the reports but for the most part *all* it heard. Thus:

> We have noted in the studies at hand a modest association between viewing of violence and aggression among at least some children, and we have noted some data which are consonant with the interpretation that violence viewing produces the aggression; this evidence is not conclusive, however.

The headline on the *New York Times* account of the committee's findings read TV VIOLENCE HELD UNHARMFUL TO YOUTH, and the opening paragraph went on to say, "The office of the United States Surgeon General has found that violence in television programming does not have an adverse effect on the majority of the nation's youth." The public's knowledge of, or interest in, the six volumes seems pretty much to have stopped there.

In fairness to the overall subject, however (as well as, perhaps, to the public), part of the problem with the Surgeon General's reports was not so much in their social-science prose or their certainly benign intentions as in their dogged attempts to measure the immeasurable—to somehow extract complex and subterranean emotions from narrowly observed behavior; to trap, as it were, a nation's psychic subconscious in butterfly nets of graphs and electrical impulses. Research on violence can obviously be useful and meaningful, especially in finite situations, but studies that allege to define or measure human responses to violence—based, for example, on "units of violence"—are probably in the end going to be overspecialized and misleading. Indeed, the one area of the violence issue where even partisans of the opposing camps seem to agree is on this need to discriminate between what are alleged to be the two significantly different types of violence. "Gratuitous" violence (by which is meant the mechanistic shootouts and killings so frequently seen in popular TV adventure dramas) is generally held to be bad—even, one feels, by broadcast executives, who sanction it in programs for obvious profit reasons but give the impression of actually regarding it as something rather unfortunate and lower-class, to be winked at and eventually dispensed with. On the other hand, "artistic," or "thematic," or "integrated" violence is nearly everywhere held to be good—reminding politicians, broadcasters, and the fiercest anti-violence critics alike of its traditional role in Great Literature (Shakespeare and the Greek dramatists are often mentioned in this connection), and thus serving as a model of higher realism for young and old.

I have been giving this last matter some thought lately, as a result of reading a remarkably interesting and scholarly book called *Regeneration Through Violence: The Mythology of the American Frontier, 1600–1860*, by Richard Slotkin, a professor of American literature at Wesleyan University. The importance of Slotkin's study lies, I think, in its emphasizing the uniquely American character not only of our violence but of our literary or mythic response to that violence, and in its charting of the strange, and also unique, way in which our myth of violence split into two channels: one high, one low.

Other people (notably Vernon Parrington and Henry Nash Smith) have written amply on the presence of violence in American myth and experience, tracing it to a conjunction of frontier life and the Puritan mind. Slotkin's study begins in the wilderness of the first American experience—that New World wilderness conceived of traditionally by Old World poets either as "Arcadia" or as "the kingdom of death and dreams." It was here, at the beginning, that violence first appeared in the American experience—and, says Slotkin, it appeared and began even then to be dealt with in a special fashion. Previously, other European voyagers to America had also struggled against the wilderness and used violence against the Indians, but, as with the Spanish conquistadores, most previous European attempts at settlement in the New World had foundered because the Colonists themselves had been held together by little more than greed or military force. It was the Puritans' genius, however, to have invented a strategy—call it a psychic strategy—for conquering the Indians, surviving in the wilderness, and preventing their settlements from fragmenting. Slotkin calls it "the re-mythologization of the West": the formally imposed group belief that the Puritans' presence in the difficult and terrifying land was decreed by God with definite ends in view, including the "redemption" both of the land and of its original inhabitants, and that any deviation from those ends was equivalent to mortal sin.

Thus, violence entered the Colonial landscape in its earliest days—and not really as the traditional violence of combat and military aggression (though there was that, too) but as a strange, new, half-hidden violence of "redemption" and "God's will." Yet there was more to it than that, for the Puritans had brought not only muskets but printing presses—those machines for teaching, exhorting, and making myths—and therefore out of the violence of the first American settlements soon came the first major Colonial literary art: the so-called captivity myth, which dominated American prose for at least forty years.

Certainly, real-life sources existed for the myth (among the best known of which was the *Narrative of the Captivity and Restauration of Mrs. Mary Rowlandson*), for, at various times, several hundred Colonists had been carried off into the wilderness by Indians; some of them were eventually ransomed and returned, while the remainder either perished or, worse still, became "savages." It was this latter specter of the white settler's "going native" which especially haunted the Puritan mind—and doubtless helped to provoke the early Puritan visions of Indian "cannibalism" and "monstrousness." At any rate, the necessary and redeeming conquest of the Indians proceeded; and so, to disguise the actual direction that Puritan violence was taking, the captivity stories were turned into literature and into myth. In these parables, it was the white settlers who were cast as helpless victims, everywhere beleaguered and on the defensive. In short, as the first Americans were actively pushing their way farther into the continent, and discovering (as Profesor Slotkin writes) that "in the tangled and isolated wilderness, white troops often behaved precisely like their Indian enemies—burning the villages of their enemies; slaughtering not only the warriors, but also the wounded, the women, and the children; and selling their captives into slavery," a complex literature was meanwhile being evolved wherein the Puritans were portrayed as helpless prisoners in the grip of the violent and ungodly Indians. From victim it was then an easy step to the role of avenger, for the captivity myth allowed only two basic responses: either "passive submission or violent retribution."

It is eerie now to read passages from these murky, cumbersome tales of "captivity," with their coarse, paranoid scenes of torment—and with the dreamlike screams of white-skinned virgins drowning out the actual sounds of trees falling and muskets firing—and perhaps it is eerier still to realize the extraordinary persistence of these Colonial literary myths down to our own time; for surely the captivity myth remained the basis for much "antebellum" Southern literature, and even shows up today on television, as it did the other evening in a story of the terrified wife of a suburban banker (that "passive" majority again!) kidnapped and held prisoner by a small band of primitive, demonic toughs.

Myths of transmuted violence, growing in the early American soil! Even so, as the wilderness and the Indians continued to be "redeemed"—indeed, as the eastern Indians were gradually killed off or pushed toward the Plains states—a new American myth made its appearance. In

1784, a schoolmaster-turned-surveyor named John Filson published a bizarre narrative titled *The Discovery, Settlement, and Present State of Kentucke*, which was originally designed to promote real estate in the Kentucky farmlands to Easterners and Europeans, and whose second section was subtitled "The Adventures of Col. Daniel Boon." Filson's story of Boone was an instant success; the long section was soon removed from the original work and widely reprinted, and Daniel Boone (as re-created by Filson) became a national hero.

With Boone, the active "wilderness-tamer" had replaced the passive "captive." But the wilderness still contained Indians, who, though no longer a serious threat, needed to be exterminated; and still contained its own natural wildness, which needed to be reduced or destroyed. Thus, in the figure of the hunter—especially that of the mystic hunter devised by Filson—the Puritan mind had once again organized a mythic strategy for concealing the real direction of its physical and violent energies. For, though Boone's life was filled with the evidence of violence, and though his actions were clearly those of a nomad—an American Odysseus—rather than of a settler, the deliberate language of the Filson narrative remains philosophic, agrarian, and decidedly ambivalent. Boone at one point begins a passage with the phrase "My footsteps have often been marked with blood," only to conclude it a few moments later in the dreamy present: "Peace crowns the sylvan glade."

A great deal has been written in the past twenty years

on the myth of the hunter in American literature, and with inevitable references to Daniel Boone. But what Slotkin's book points out is that there were several Boones—perhaps two particularly significant ones—and that each of them has differently concealed the same theme of violence. Schoolmaster Filson's Boone was the hunter as dreamer—the man who, for example, gave Dreaming Creek its name, because he had once had a "peculiarly impressive" dream beside it. About fifty years later, another version of the Boone story was published, this one by a Cincinnati journalist called Timothy Flint and titled *Biographical Memoir of Daniel Boone*. In Flint's Boone, the American hero appeared with nearly all the ambiguities and philosophy—nearly all the "art"—left out. If anything, this new and equally popular Boone was closest to the model of Davy Crockett—a contemporary popular hero (*A Narrative of the Life of Col. David Crockett*, 1834) who appeared to relish killing for its own sake, always making it a point to number the animals he had gratuitously killed, as later did one of his mythic successors, Buffalo Bill. On one celebrated hunting spree, Crockett attested to killing "105 bears," a glorious statistic he frequently returned to in the narrative. Flint's Boone was slightly less of a bloodthirsty roughneck than Crockett, but he was certainly a killer—of Indians as well as of animals. Hunting itself had long since stopped being the necessity it had been; indeed, the new Boone admitted that it was now a "luxury" and an "indulgence." It was also, as Flint wrote, a "profession"—a discipline in which Boone could display his "tact and superiority." As Richard Slotkin puts it, Flint's Boone had become "a professional killer."

What to make of these two Boones, or, perhaps, why try to make anything at all? There is little "constructive" that can be said on the subject of original American violence—little that is likely to find its way into new regulations or a new code. Call it part of a conversation, if you will. Even so, it seems remarkable to me to realize not just the extent to which American myths have been dominated by the subject of violence but, more importantly, the dimensions and success of the effort to conceal and transmute the actual energies of this violence. The paranoid inversion of the captivity myth was one such way. Another way was by turning the killer of Indians into the hunter of animals, and then turning that figure into "art." Since John Filson's early Boone, a dreamy, ambiguous, supposedly complex and philosophic killer has hovered over much of American myth—making and remaking that myth in his own image. Deerslayer was such a figure, and so was Hawthorne's guilt-ridden hunter, Reuben Bourne. On a grander level, there was Ahab, the alternatively murderous and redemptive sea hunter, questing aboard a ship decorated with "the chased bones" of his enemies. On a lesser level—though still "artistic"—there have been such philosophic and destructive American heroes as Owen Wister's Virginian, Jack Schaefer's Shane, and even Hemingway's Robert Jordan, in *For Whom the Bell Tolls*.

When critics speak of our excessive celebration of violence, it seems to me they rarely speak of such literarily conceived American heroes. The concern is with the sounds of gunfire, the big-city or Western shootout, the inartistic murder. These inheritors of the other Boone—of Timothy Flint's "professional" and Davy Crockett's roughneck desperado—are nowadays easier to spot, and seem somehow more noticeable in our cool, less physical times: from Deadwood Dick through Jesse James, Billy the Kid, and Wild Bill Hickok, through all the Cagney-type maverick gangsters, through all the Mike Hammer-type private-eye killers, and down, certainly, to the standard television cops-and-robbers hero of the present time (for instance, Lieutenant McGarrett, in *Hawaii Five-O,* Hondo, in *S.W.A.T.*, or Cannon). On an aesthetic level, it is hard to feel much adult regard for these confident, assertive tough guys, with their predictable adventures, mechanical entrapments, and casual blam-blam-blam of gunfire. And despite the fact that most of the gratuitous violence is also "thematic"—in the sense of having been deliberately placed there, chiefly to conclude the episodes on a note of proper seriousness—there is something abrasive in this relentlessly childish and aggressive, comic-book approach to life; for surely that is what it is. But surely, too, these heirs of the "unliterary" Boone and Crockett are also no more or no less than what they appear to be: rough, violent, often populist (the renegade backwoodsman that the Puritans so worried about), and with only the barest and crudest traces of a redemptive purpose to their killing.

Thus, though one can find in the Crockett hero, with his mindless enumeration of those recklessly slaughtered bears, an antecedent for our later reckless and mindless "body counts" in Vietnam, this "body counting" itself was but part of a larger and vastly more destructive quest or hunt—a hunt that has been dignified and orchestrated for generations of Americans by the literary-mythic figure of the nobly ambivalent, philosophizing, redemptive hunter. There have been some inroads made on this myth in the past few years. As the writer Michael Novak has suggested, ethnic assimilation has finally begun to infuse a few de-rigidifying strains into popular culture, as is evident in the Southern European temperament of Kojak, or in the skepticism and unassertiveness of Columbo. Even so, the strength and rigors of the old Puritan myths seem far from gone—as if they had been literally welded to the American soul at its time of greatest hardship and violence. Murder as redemption! Aggression as passivity! Not just violence but a falsity to violence fused into American myth. As Professor Slotkin points out, even President Lyndon Johnson (in his Johns Hopkins address of 1965, calling for an escalation of the Vietnam war) found himself unknowingly drawn into the symbolic imagery of the captivity myth, with his anthropomorphizing of South Vietnam as a "member of the Free World family" that was passively beset by "brutality . . . assassination and kidnapping. Women and children are strangled in the night . . . And helpless villages are ravaged by sneak attacks."

In short, if we are worried about cultural sources for our violence, and are devising ways of making choices between "permissible" and "impermissible" mythic models, I am not sure that the best solution lies at the expense of roughneck Davy Crockett, or Mike Hammer, or Clyde Barrow, or even Lieutenant McGarrett—leaving us with the artistic, murderous ambiguities of Deerslayer, or of John Filson's Boone, whose transposed view of early American aggressions ("The innocent husbandman was shot down, while busily cultivating the soil for his family's supply") has underlain so much of our later, larger national violence.

American sensibilities, especially in the modern era, seem to have a propensity for imposing cosmetic, moralistic solutions—"codes" and "prohibitions"—on the problems arising from our deeper natures. Such, anyway, has been the focus of the recent concern with television violence. This violence is obviously inseparable from violence elsewhere in the country; yet most of it, as many people have pointed out, comes down to the psychic energies and concealments "organized" by the American literary myths. For some reason, these myths—notably the myth of hunting—live with us still, in a powerful, eerie, irrelevant half-life, glowing behind the puzzled, manly frowns, the articulate doubts, the deep thinking, the carefully fashioned guilts of so many of our literarily conceived heroes. Art—another of our redeemers, with those fascinating glimpses of artistic violence! Assuredly, it has not been false to what we think we are, but what if what we *think* is false? Or dangerous?

In the end, it looks as if we are stuck for the time being—complaining of our comic-book savageries, worrying about crime rates, fearing for the lives of Presidents—while we await the eventual disintegration of our myths;

and not just of the myths themselves, these clever, artistic organizations of experience, but of the guilt that produced these myths. People have a need to be "doing something" about a problem such as violence, and perhaps it fills part of this need to try, at least, to measure violence—units of violence—and electronically gauge responses, elements of aggression, inclinations to murder. Our popular culture, imitative of—but often healthier than—our higher culture, spews forth themes of manhood and hunting on television each evening, and, naturally, among the restless or disaffected young there has been a tendency to imitate: to embark on other hunts down side streets or in alleys.

But if anyone truly wishes to lessen violence in this country, it is hard to believe that more than a cosmetic alteration will be produced by censoring gunfights in television entertainments; or even, or especially, by relying on the "higher realism" of the classic American literary imagination. Indeed, at present there are new literatures, or attempts at new literatures, waiting in the wings. But as long as the guilt persists which locks our central culture to the theme of hunting—those murderous Boones—as if to abandon hunting were to admit the dimensions of that dreadful guilt, then it seems that our newer quests (whatever the art of language or of film) will only produce more hunters, employing more bullets, redeeming more wilderness and Indians.

It is a transient time—the hardest place. The wilderness of the mind was never cleared as much as we thought.